TWO DISSERTATIONS

TWO DISSERTATIONS

I ON ΜΟΝΟΓΕΝΗΣ ΘΕΟΣ
IN SCRIPTURE AND TRADITION

II ON THE 'CONSTANTINOPOLITAN' CREED
AND OTHER EASTERN CREEDS OF THE
FOURTH CENTURY

BY

FENTON JOHN ANTHONY HORT D.D.
FELLOW AND DIVINITY LECTURER OF EMMANUEL COLLEGE
FORMERLY FELLOW OF TRINITY COLLEGE
CAMBRIDGE

Wipf and Stock Publishers
EUGENE, OREGON

Wipf and Stock Publishers
199 West 8th Avenue, Suite 3
Eugene, Oregon 97401

Two Dissertations In Scripture and Tradition
On The 'Constantinopolitan' Creed & Other Eastern Creeds of the 4th Century
By Hort, F.J.A.
ISBN: 1-57910-653-6
Publication date: May, 2001
Previously published by Macmillan and Co., 1876.

PREFACE

THE former of these Dissertations is an attempt to examine in some detail a single point of textual criticism, the true reading of a phrase occurring in a cardinal verse of the New Testament. Once only has the evidence been discussed with anything like adequate care and precision, namely in a valuable article contributed by Professor Ezra Abbot to the American *Bibliotheca Sacra* of October 1861. After having long had occasion to study the matter pretty closely, I am unable to accept the conclusions drawn by this eminent biblical scholar; and accordingly it seemed worth while to place on record the results of an independent investigation. My own opinion has not been formed hastily. Some years passed before increasing knowledge and clearness of view respecting the sources of the Greek text of the New Testament convinced me of the incorrectness of the received reading in John i 18. This conviction did not however remove the sense of a certain strangeness in the alternative phrase transmitted by the best authorities; and for a considerable time I saw no better solution of the difficulty than a conjecture that both readings alike were amplifications of a simpler original. It was a more careful study of the whole context that finally took away all lingering doubt as to the intrinsic probability of the less familiar reading.

In all cases where the text of a single passage is dealt with separately, a deceptive disadvantage lies on those who have learned the insecurity of trying to interpret complex textual evidence without reference to previously ascertained relationships, either between the documents or between earlier lines of transmission attested by the documents. Their method presupposes a wide induction, the evidence for which cannot be set out within reasonable limits. Thus, so far as they are able to go beyond that naked weighing of 'authorities' against each other which commonly passes as textual criticism in the case of the New Testament, they are in danger of seeming to follow an arbitrary theory, when they are in fact using the only safeguard against the consecration of arbitrary predilection under the specious name of internal evidence.

The exhibition of the documentary evidence itself needs hardly any further preface. It will, I trust, be found more completely and more exactly given than elsewhere: but the additions and rectifications, though not perhaps without interest, make no extensive change in the elementary data which have to be interpreted, unless it be in some of the patristic quotations. The decisiveness of the external evidence would not be materially less if it were taken as it is presented in any good recent apparatus: in other words, the legitimacy of an appeal to internal evidence on less than the clearest and strongest grounds would hardly be increased.

It is however in internal evidence that the supposed strength of the case against the less familiar reading undoubtedly consists: and throughout this part of the discussion I have had to break fresh ground. What is said about the relation of the eighteenth verse of St John's Prologue to preceding verses is intended to meet the more serious of the two apparent difficulties, that arising from supposed incongruity with the context and supposed want of harmony with the language of Scripture elsewhere, and is addressed equally to upholders of the received reading and to those who distrust the originality of either reading. The question of relative probabilities of change in transmission, less pertinent in itself, finds, I have tried to shew, in the actual phenomena of the biblical and patristic texts an opposite answer to the answer assumed by anticipation when the manner in which ancient transcribers would be affected by dogmatic proclivities is inferred from the crudities of modern controversy. Here Professor Abbot's original argument is supplemented by an ingenious article in the *Theological Review* for October 1871, written by Professor James Drummond, and also by a short paper in the *Unitarian Review* of June 1875 by Professor Abbot himself, for a separate impression of which I have to thank the author's courtesy. Had Professor Drummond's article come into my hands sooner, I might have been tempted to follow his speculations point by point. As it was, it seemed best to refrain from rewriting an exposition of facts which, if true, was fatal to his very premisses. It was obviously desirable that the comments on the evidence itself should be encumbered as little as possible with controversial digressions, though I have tried to do justice, in argument as well as in mind, to every tangible suggestion adverse to my own conclusions, whether offered in the articles already mentioned or elsewhere. On the other hand against the verdicts of oracular instinct I confess myself helpless: they must be left to work their legitimate effect on such readers as find them impressive.

Since this Dissertation was set up in type as an academic exercise some months ago, in which form it was seen by a few friends, it has been revised and slightly enlarged under the sanction required by the University Ordinances. The last three of the appended Notes are likewise now first added. The two longer of these supply illustrations of incidental statements in the Dissertation rather than contributions to its argument. Indeed I should be specially unwilling to seem to make the principal issue in any way dependent on the theory propounded in the last Note. At the same time the history of the detached phrase taken from the verse of St John cannot safely be neglected in any thorough investigation of the text. Wetstein's pardonable but misleading confusion between the text and the phrase was unfortunately overlooked by Dr Tregelles, to whom belongs the credit of recalling attention to the passage, and pointing out the inferiority of the external evidence for the received reading. But Professor Abbot's warning against this confusion carries us only a little way. The traditional use of the phrase remains itself a part, though a subordinate part, of the evidence; and the remarkable inverseness of its currency with that of the parent reading invited, if it did not necessitate, an enquiry into the true construction of the corresponding clauses in the Nicene Creed.

The latter Dissertation grew out of the last Note accompanying the former. The 'Constantinopolitan' modification of the Nicene language needed explanation: and while the recent researches of friends had disproved the direct responsibility of the Council of Constantinople for the Creed which bears the same name, it was unsatisfactory to rest without investigating whatever evidence might lead to a positive conclusion respecting the origin of this Creed and the motives of its authors. But the results actually obtained were wholly unexpected, and it was only by degrees that they presented themselves. The main outlines are, I trust, established: but it will be surprising if no fresh data are brought to light by those whose knowledge of early Christian literature and history is wider and surer than mine. Continental criticism is unfortunately silent, with a single exception, on most of the questions which I have had to raise: and it has been disappointing to find how little help was to be obtained, even on conspicuous points, from the studies in the history of doctrine which have been carried on for the last two or three generations. The exception is furnished by Professor C. P. Caspari of Christiania, whose book on *Ungedruckte, unbeachtete, und wenig beachtete Quellen zur Geschichte des Taufsymbols und der Glaubensregel* is a mine of new texts and original illustrations. Although the separate obligations are all, I hope, acknowledged in the proper places, it is a duty to say here how much the latter pages of the Dissertation owe to his patient and conscientious labours; and the more since I have been often obliged to dissent from his conclusions. Perhaps it may be found a corroboration of the view here taken that it serves to link together his scattered researches, so far as they relate to Eastern Creeds. The publication of the *Dictionary of Christian Antiquities* has given me the advantage of seeing Mr Ffoulkes's articles on the Councils of Constantinople and Antioch while the last sheets were passing through the press. I have thus been led to add in a note the Greek text of the fifth canon of Constantinople; but have not found reason to make any other change.

Both Dissertations are of a critical nature, and directed solely towards discovering the true facts of history respecting certain ancient writings. On the other hand I should hardly have cared to spend so much time on the enquiry, had the subject matter itself been distasteful, or had I been able to regard it as unimportant. To any Christian of consistent belief it cannot be indifferent what language St John employed on a fundamental theme; and no one who feels how much larger the exhibition of truth perpetuated in Scripture is than any propositions that have ever been deduced from it can be a party to refusing it the right of speaking words inconvenient, if so it be, to the various traditional schools which claim to be adequate representatives of its teaching. Nor again is it of small moment to understand rightly the still living and ruling doctrinal enunciations of the ancient Church, which cannot be rightly understood while their original purpose is misapprehended. Even the best theological literature of that age, as of every age, contains much which cannot possibly be true: and it is difficult to imagine how the study of Councils has been found compatible with the theory which requires us to find Conciliar utterances Divine. But the great Greek Creeds of the fourth century, and the 'Constantinopolitan' Creed most, will bear severe testing with all available resources of judgement after these many ages of change. Assuredly they do not contain all truth, even within the limits of subject by which they were happily confined. But their guidance never fails to be found trustworthy, and for us at least it is necessary. Like other gifts of God's Providence, they can be turned to deadly use: but to those who employ them rightly they are the safeguard of a large and a progressive faith.

CONTENTS

		PAGE
I	ON ΜΟΝΟΓΕΝΗϹ ΘΕΟϹ *IN SCRIPTURE AND TRADITION* .	1
	NOTE A The details of early Greek Patristic Evidence . .	30
	NOTE B The details of Latin Evidence	43
	NOTE C Some details of Æthiopic Evidence	46
	NOTE D Unicus *and* unigenitus *among the Latins* . . .	48
	NOTE E On ΜΟΝΟΓΕΝΗϹ ΘΕΟϹ *in the Nicene Creed* . .	54
II	ON THE 'CONSTANTINOPOLITAN' CREED AND OTHER EASTERN CREEDS OF THE FOURTH CENTURY .	73
	The Creed of Cæsarea	138
	The Nicene Creed	139, 140
	The Revised Creed of Jerusalem or 'Constantinopolitan' Creed	141, 143, 144
	The Earlier Creed of Jerusalem	142
	The Interpolated Nicene Creed	145
	The Creed of Cappadocia	146
	The Revised Creed of Antioch	148
	The Creed of Mesopotamia	149
	The Creed of Philadelphia	150

Ἐκ τούτων καὶ τῶν τοιούτων μανθάνομεν ὅτι τοσοῦτον μὲν οἶδεν ἡ θεόπνευστος γραφὴ τῆς ἐπιγνώσεως τὸ ἀπέραντον, τοσοῦτον δὲ τῆς ἀνθρωπίνης φύσεως τὸ τῶν θείων μυστηρίων ἐν τῷ παρόντι ἀνέφικτον, ἀεὶ μὲν κατὰ προκοπὴν ἑκάστῳ προστιθεμένου τοῦ πλείονος, ἀεὶ δὲ τοῦ πρὸς ἀξίαν ἀπολιμπανομένου ἁπάντων, ἄχρις ἂν ἔλθῃ τὸ τέλειον ὅτε τὸ ἐκ μέρους καταργηθήσεται· οὐκοῦν οὔτε ἑνὸς ὀνόματος ἀρκοῦντος πάσας ὁμοῦ δηλῶσαι τὰς τοῦ θεοῦ δόξας, οὔτε ἑκάστου ἐξ ὁλοκλήρου ἀκινδύνως παραλαμβανομένου.

     BASILIUS

ON THE WORDS

ΜΟΝΟΓΕΝΗC ΘΕΟC

IN SCRIPTURE AND TRADITION

THE purpose of this Dissertation is to investigate the true reading of the last verse in the Prologue to St John's Gospel (i 18). The result, I think it will be found, is to shew that μονογενὴς θεός should be accepted in place of the received reading ὁ μονογενὴς υἱός, alike on grounds of documentary evidence, of probabilities of transcription, and of intrinsic fitness. The reading of three primary Greek MSS. has been known only within the last half-century; so that naturally this verse has not shared with other disputed texts of high doctrinal interest either the advantages or the disadvantages of repeated controversial discussion; and thus it offers a rare opportunity for dispassionate study. The history of the phrase μονογενὴς θεός in early Greek theology, of which I have attempted to give a rude outline, has also an interest of its own.

The verse stands as follows in the better MSS.:
θεὸν οὐδεὶς ἑώρακεν πώποτε· μονογενὴς θεὸς ὁ ὢν εἰς τὸν κόλπον τοῦ πατρὸς ἐκεῖνος ἐξηγήσατο.

The *Documentary Evidence* for μονογενὴς θεός consists of

Manuscripts: ℵBC*L 33 (ℵ* omits the following ὁ ὤν; ℵᶜ and 33 prefix ὁ).

Versions: the Vulgate ('Peshito') or Revised Syriac; the margin of the Harclean Syriac; the Memphitic; and one of the two Æthiopic editions (the Roman, reprinted in Walton's Polyglott), in accordance with one of the two earlier British Museum MSS., a third of the MSS. yet examined having both readings[1]. The article is prefixed in the Memphitic rendering. The Thebaic and the Gothic versions are not extant here.

ὁ μονογενὴς υἱός is found in

Manuscripts: AC°EFGHKMSUVXΓΔΛΠ and all known cursives except 33.

Versions: the Old Latin (q has *u. filius Dei*); the Vulgate Latin; the Old Syriac; the text of the Harclean Syriac; the Jerusalem Syriac Lectionary; the Armenian; and Mr Pell Platt's Æthiopic edition, in accordance with many MSS.

The *Patristic* evidence, though remarkable on any possible view, admits of various interpretation on some points. The grounds for the chief conclusions here stated will be found in a note at the end: it must suffice here to mark the limits of doubtfulness as clearly as the circumstances permit.

The reading μονογενὴς θεός, with or without ὁ, in direct quotations from St John or clear allusions to his text, is attested as follows. Two independent reports of VALENTINIAN doctrine furnished by Clement of Alexandria (*Exc. ex Theodoto*, p. 968 Pott.: a paraphrastic allusion a little later has υἱός by a natural combination, see p. 32), and Irenæus (p. 40 Mass.: corrupted in the inferior MSS. of both Epiphanius, who supplies the Greek, and the old translation, which in this *allusion* is faithfully literal). IRENÆUS himself at least once (256), and I strongly suspect two other times (255, 189): in all three places the original Greek is lost. CLEMENT himself twice (695, 956: in the second place, where the language is paraphrastic,

---

[1] It is impossible to convey a true impression of the Æthiopic evidence in few words. Some particulars will be found in Note C.

Clement has ὁ μ. υἱὸς θεός, as in a still looser paraphrase at p. 102 he has ὁ μ. ...λόγος τῆς πίστεως). ORIGEN at least three times (on John i 7 [the commentary on i 18 itself is lost], iv. p. 89 Ru.; [on John i 19, p. 102, the reading of two MSS. only is recorded, and they vary suspiciously between ὁ μ. υἱὸς θεός and ὁ μ. υἱὸς τοῦ θεοῦ; in an indirect reference shortly afterwards τὸν μ. stands without a substantive;] on John xiii 23, p. 439; *c. Cels.* ii 71, p. 440, certainly in two MSS., apparently in all except two closely allied MSS., from which De la Rue introduced υἱός). Eusebius twice, once as an alternative not preferred by himself (*De Eccl. Theol.* p. 67, ὁ μονογενὴς υἱός, ἡ μονογενὴς θεός), and in one other exceptional but seemingly unsuspicious place, p. 174. EPIPHANIUS three or four times (*Ancor.* p. 8 [the clear statement here confessedly leaves no doubt as to the quotation at p. 7, hopelessly mangled in the printed text]; *Panar.* 612, 817). BASIL at least twice (*De Sp. Sanct.* 15, 17, pp. 12, 14 Garn., quotation and statement confirming each other, as the Benedictine editor notes, adding that earlier editions, unsupported by any of his six MSS., read υἱός; the quotation with υἱός at p. 23, which has no note, may therefore be only an unwary reprint). GREGORY OF NYSSA ten times, always somewhat allusively, as is his usual manner in citing Scripture, (*c. Eunom.* ii p. 432 [469 Migne]; 447 [493]; 478 [540]; iii 506 [581]; vi 605 [729]; viii 633 [772]; ix 653 [801]; x 681 [841]; *De vit. Mos.* 192 [i 336]; *Hom. xiii in Cant.* 663 [i 1045]: on the other hand υἱός is printed twice, *c. Eun.* ii 466 [521]; *Ep. ad Flav.* 648 [iii 1004]). The (Homœousian) Synod of Ancyra in 358 (in Epiph. *Pan.* 851 c: the allusion here is reasonably certain[1]). DIDYMUS three times (*De Trin.* i 26 p. 76; ii 5, p. 140 [cf. i 15, p. 27]; on Ps. lxxvi 14, p. 597 Cord. [with absolute certainty by the context, though υἱός is printed]: an allusion on Ps. cix 3, p. 249 Cord. or 284 Mai, drops the substantive). CYRIL OF ALEXANDRIA (*ad l.*

---

[1] The laxity of a reference to Prov. viii 25 (υἱόν for γεννᾷ με) in the same sentence was unavoidable, and it was guarded by ample previous exposition (852 BC, 853 B—D): here it would have been gratuitous and misleading.

p. 103 [without ὁ] by Mr Pusey's best MS. and repeated references in the following comment), and in at least three other places (*Thes.* 137, [without ὁ] 237; *Dial. quod Unus*, 768 : twice (*Thes.* 365 ; *Adv. Nest.* 90[1]) Aubert's text has υἱός, which will probably have to give way, as it has had to do in the commentary[2]. To these might perhaps be added the emperor JULIAN (p. 333 Spanh.), for though the full quotation and one subsequent reference have υἱός, another has θεός, which the argument seems on the whole to require.

The patristic evidence for [ὁ] μονογενὴς υἱός has next to be given. Irenæus twice, but only in the Latin translation (see above), and exactly in the Old Latin form, with *nisi* inserted before *unigenitus*, and once with *Dei* added to *Filius*, so that we seem to have the reading of the translator, as often, not of Irenæus. HIPPOLYTUS (*c. Noetum* 5) without ὁ: all depends on Fabricius's editing of a modern copy of a single Vatican MS., and the context is neutral. An EPISTLE from certain bishops at ANTIOCH (260—270 A.D.) to Paul of Samosata (Routh, *R. S.* iii 297), again dependent on a single MS., unexamined for some generations, and with the detached phrase τὸν μονογενῆ υἱὸν τοῦ θεοῦ θεόν occurring not long before. The Latin version of the "ACTS" of the disputation between ARCHELAUS and Mani, c. 32, where again the inserted *nisi* shews the impossibility of deciding whether author or translator is responsible. EUSEBIUS OF CÆSAREA six times, *De Eccl. Theol.* p. 67 (with θεός as an alternative, see above), 86, 92, 142; in Ps. lxxiv. p. 440 Mont.; in Es. vi. p. 374. EU-

---

[1] In this case the text is also Pusey's (p. 170); but it rests on a single MS. of the fifteenth century: it is followed in a few lines by ὅ γε μὴν ἐν κόλπῳ τοῦ θεοῦ καὶ πατρὸς μονογενὴς θεὸς λόγος.

[2] In the 'Dialogues' of an unknown CÆSARIUS (*Inter.* 4, post Greg. Naz. iv 864 Migne), probably of the fifth if not a later century, the context implies θεός, though υἱός is printed. The apparent conflict of text and context has been lately pointed out by Prof. Abbot, who still regards the reading as only doubtful. The possibility of reconciling with the actual language an inferential argument from John i 18 containing υἱός seems to me infinitesimal : but I am content to leave Cæsarius in a note.

STATHIUS, *De Engastr.* p. 387 All. ALEXANDER of Alexandria, *Ep. ad Alex.* in Theodoret, *H. E.* i 3; but with the detached phrase τοῦ μονογενοῦς θεοῦ on the next page. ATHANASIUS seven times (*Ep. de Decr. Nic.* 13, 21; *Or. c. Ar.* ii 62; iv 16, 19, 20, 26). GREGORY OF NAZIANZUS, *Orat.* xxix 17. Basil of Cæsarea, *Ep.* 234, p. 358, besides one of the three places in the *De Spiritu Sancto* already mentioned, where at least one Moscow MS. has θεός: but the evidence adduced above casts doubt on both places. Gregory of Nyssa twice (see p. 3); but the reading is most suspicious. TITUS OF BOSTRA (*adv. Man.* p. 85 Lag.: but p. 93 ὁ μ. υἱὸς θεός). THEODORE OF MOPSUESTIA (*ad l. bis* in Mai, *N. P. B.* vii 397 f.). CHRYSOSTOM *ad l.*, and later writers generally. On Julian see p. 4.

It is unsatisfactory that so much of the patristic testimony remains uncertain in the present state of knowledge; but such is the fact. Much of the uncertainty, though not all, will doubtless disappear when the Fathers have been carefully edited. In familiar passages scribes, editors, and translators vie with each other in assimilating biblical quotations to the texts current among themselves; and from the nature of the case the process is always unfavourable to ancient readings, whether true or false, which went out of use comparatively early. It would therefore be absurd to treat the uncertainty as equally favourable to both readings. Where we have a Greek original, without various reading noted, and without contradictory context, υἱός has a right to claim the authority provisionally, in spite of private suspicions: but it would be unreasonable to concede to υἱός any appreciable part in Origen, Gregory of Nyssa, Didymus, or Cyril—I ought to add, in Irenæus or Basil—notwithstanding the variations already mentioned. Serious doubt must also rest on an isolated υἱός in a neutral context, when, as in the case of the Epistles of the Antioch bishops and of Alexander, μονογενὴς θεός is found at no great distance, though without any obvious reference to John i 18: the doubt is not removed by the fact that one or two Latin Fathers[1] have *unigenitus Filius* in their quotation, and *unigenitus Deus* often elsewhere.

To gather up the documentary evidence with the usual abbreviations, we have

θεός ℵBC*L 33
  Memph. Syr.vulg. Syr.hcl.mg. [?Aeth.]
  *VALENTINIANI. Iren. *CLEM. *ORIG. [Euseb.]
  †Syn.Anc. *EPIPH. *DID. *BAS. *GREG.NYSS. *CYR.AL.
  Cf. Caes.

υἱός AX &c. &c. [?D]
  Latt.omn. Syr.vet. Syr.hcl. Syr.hier. Arm. [Aeth.codd.]
  [?? Iren.(lat.)] ? †Ep.Ant. ? †Act.Arch.(lat.) *EUSEB.
  *ATH. †Eust. ? †Alex.Al. [??Bas.] Greg.Naz. [?? Greg.
  Nyss.] †Tit.Bost. *THEOD.MOPS. *CHRYS., &c.

Testimonies marked with * prefixed are clear and sufficient: those marked with † depend on a single quotation, with a neutral context. The Latin Fathers, as almost always, attest only what was read in the Latin versions: all Latin authorities have *unicus Filius* or *unigenitus Filius*, q adding *Dei*.

Against the four best uncials υἱός has no tolerable uncial authority to set except A and X, of which even A is in the Gospels very inferior to any one of the four, much more to their combination, and it is here deserted even by Syr.vulg., its usual companion, while 33 is approached by no other cursive. Manifestly wrong readings of AX and their associates abound hereabouts as everywhere: see i 16, 21, 26 bis, 27 quater, 30, 31, 39, 42, &c.: when D is added, wrong readings still recur, as iii 34; iv 2, 21, 25, 36, 37, 39, 42, 52, &c. The solitary position of 33 among cursives here arises from the peculiarity of its position generally, and not merely from its comparative excellence, great as that is. The good readings supported by the

---

[1] Hilary and Fulgentius. The latter twice quotes the text with *unigenitus Deus*, but doubtless not from a Latin copy of the Gospels.

other good cursives of the Gospels are, with rare exceptions, found likewise in the authorities called 'Western', such as D and the early Latins; that is, their ancient element is almost wholly 'Western', for good and for evil: the ancient element in 33 on the other hand can be only in part 'Western', for it abounds in true ancient readings which, as here, have little or no 'Western' authority. That the Old Syriac has υἱός is quite natural, when it has so many early 'Western' readings: what is really singular is the introduction of θεός at the revision, when few changes came in at variance with the late Antiochian text (Theodore, Chrysostom, &c.); and as θεός is not an Antiochian reading, its support by the Syriac Vulgate acquires especial weight. Among early versions this and the invaluable Memphitic more than balance the Old Latin and Old Syriac, which so often concur against BCL Memph. in wrong readings of high antiquity, as i 4, 24, 26, 38, 42; iii 8, 25; iv 9. In the later versions υἱός has no doubt the advantage.

The Ante-nicene Fathers follow the analogy of the versions. With the exception of the Antioch epistle, υἱός occurs in writers with a predominantly Western type of text, Hippolytus and Eusebius (compare the gloss in iii 6 at p. 72 of the *De Ecc. Th.*); while Irenæus leaves their company to join Clement and Origen in behalf of θεός. After Eusebius the two readings are ranged in singular conformity with the general character of the respective texts generally. Cyril of Alexandria, Didymus, Epiphanius, are almost the only Post-nicene writers in whom we find any considerable proportion of the true ancient readings of passages corrupted in the common late text, while Basil and Gregory of Nyssa have also a sprinkling of similar readings, a larger sprinkling probably than Athanasius or Gregory of Nazianzus, certainly than Theodore, Chrysostom, or their successors. Thus it comes out with perfect clearness that υἱός is one of the numerous Ante-nicene readings of a 'Western' type (in the technical not the strictly geographical sense of the word) which were adopted into the eclectic fourth century text that forms the basis of later texts generally. As far as external testimony goes, θεός and υἱός are of equal antiquity: both can be traced far back into the second century. But if we examine together any considerable number of readings having the same pedigree as υἱός, certain peculiar omissions always excepted, we find none that on careful consideration approve themselves as original in comparison with the alternative readings, many that are evident corrections. No like suspiciousness attaches to the combination of authorities which read θεός. Analysis of their texts completely dissipates the conjecture, for it is nothing more, that they proceed from an imagined Egyptian recension. The wrong readings which they singly or in groups attest can be traced to various distant origins, and their concordance marks a primitive transmission uncorrupted by local alterations. Such being the case, θεός is commended to us as the true reading, alike by the higher character of the authorities which support it, taken separately, and by the analogy of readings having a similar history in ancient times.

External evidence is equally decisive against the insertion of ὁ, omitted by the four uncials, one passage of Origen probably (*c. Cels.* ii 71), and two of Cyril (*ad l.* and *Thes.* 257). On such a point the evidence of versions and quotations is evidently precarious.

Probabilities of Transcription will doubtless be easily recognised as favourable to θεός. Μονογενὴς θεός is an unique phrase, unlikely to be suggested to a scribe by anything lying on the surface of the context, or by any other passage of Scripture. Μονογενὴς υἱός (the reading of Hippolytus and of Eusebius once, *in Ps.*), and still more ὁ μονογενὴς υἱός, is a familiar and obvious phrase, suggested by the familiar sense of μονογενής in all literature, by the contrast to τοῦ πατρός in the same verse (and παρὰ πατρός in 14), by two other early passages of this Gospel (iii 16, ὥστε τὸν υἱὸν τὸν μονογενῆ ἔδωκεν, and iii 18, ὅτι μὴ πεπίστευκεν εἰς τὸ ὄνομα τοῦ μονογενοῦς υἱοῦ τοῦ θεοῦ), and by a passage of St John's first Epistle (iv 9, ὅτι τὸν υἱὸν αὐτοῦ τὸν μονογενῆ ἀπέσταλκεν ὁ θεὸς εἰς τὸν κόσμον). The always questionable suggestion of dogmatic alteration is peculiarly out of place here. To the *Monogenes* in the Ogdoad of the Valentinians, among whom by a mere accident we first meet with this and other important verses of St John, θεός could be only an awkward appendage: the Valentinians of Clement take it up for a moment, make a kind of use of it as a transitional step explaining how St John came to give the predicate θεός (in i 1) to *Logos*, whom they anxiously distinguish from *Monogenes* (= *Arche*), and then pass on to their own proper view, in which Sonship alone appears as the characteristic mark of *Monogenes*; while the Valentinians of Irenæus content themselves with reciting the bare phrase (Ἰωάννης...Ἀρχήν τινα ὑποτίθεται τὸ πρῶτον γεννηθὲν [sic] ὑπὸ τοῦ θεοῦ, ὃ δὴ καί Υἱόν καί Μονογενῆ θεόν κέκληκεν, ἐν ᾧ τὰ πάντα ὁ Πατὴρ προέβαλε σπερματικῶς) and leaving it, justifying i 1 by the general remark τὸ γὰρ ἐκ θεοῦ γεννηθὲν θεός ἐστιν, but not otherwise referring again to any θεός except Him whom St John, they say, distinguishes in i 1 from *Arche* (= *Son*) and *Logos*. Neither in the Valentinian nor in any other known Gnostical system could there have been any temptation to invent such a combination as μονογενὴς θεός. Nor is it easy to divine what controversial impulse within the Church could have generated it in the second century; for the various doctrinal currents of that period are sufficiently represented in later controversies of which we possess records, and yet there is, I believe, no extant writer of any age, except that very peculiar person Epiphanius[1], who makes emphatic controversial appeal either to θεός *per se*, or to θεός as coupled with μονογενής, or (with a different purpose) to μονογενής as coupled with θεός, whether in this verse or in the derivative detached phrase mentioned hereafter. The whole verse, with either

---

[1] Also Cæsarius, if the printed υἱός is wrong. The emperor Julian may be added, as finding matter of accusation against St John in this verse, if I am right in surmising that μονογενὴς θεός was the reading before him.

reading, soars above the whole extant theology of the second century antecedent to the great Catholic writers at its close: but I could almost as easily believe that that age invented St John's Gospel, as some learned persons say it did, as that it invented μονογενὴς θεός. Once more, assuming μονογενὴς θεός to have obtained a footing in MSS., we cannot suppose that it would gain ground from ὁ μονογενὴς υἱός in transcription, unless we trust modern analogies more than actual evidence. The single fact that μονογενὴς θεός was put to polemical use by hardly any of those writers of the fourth century who possessed it, either as a reading or as a phrase, shews how unlikely it is that the writers of our earliest extant MSS. were mastered by any such dogmatic impulse in its favour as would overpower the standing habits of their craft.

The only other possible explanation is pure accident. The similarity of $\overline{\text{YC}}$ to $\overline{\text{ΘC}}$, though doubtless greater than that of the words at full length, is hardly strong enough to support a word forming a new and startling combination, though it might be able to cooperate in a transition *to* so trite a term as μονογενὴς υἱός. But a still more serious objection to this suggestion is the absence of the article in what we must consider the primitive form of the reading, μονογενὴς θεός. Supposing for the sake of argument that $\overline{\text{YC}}$ might pass into $\overline{\text{ΘC}}$, the change would still have left ὁ standing ten letters back, and there would have been as little temptation to drop ὁ before θεός as before υἱός, as is shown by the profuseness with which the Fathers (and their scribes) supplied it subsequently. On the other hand the known boldness of 'Western' paraphrase would have had little scruple in yielding to the temptation of inserting ὁ after changing υἱός to θεός, whether immediately or after an interval in which the article remained absent.

Thus, on grounds of documentary evidence and probabilities of transcription alike, we are irresistibly led to conclude that μονογενὴς θεός was the original from which ὁ μονογενὴς υἱός and ὁ μονογενής proceeded. More than this no evidence from without can establish: but in a text so amply attested as that of the New Testament we rightly conclude that the most original of extant readings was likewise that of the author himself, unless on full consideration it appears to involve a kind and degree of difficulty such as analogy forbids us to recognise as morally compatible with the author's intention, or some other peculiar ground of suspicion presents itself.

This is perhaps the best place to mention a third reading to which Griesbach was somewhat inclined (it must be remembered that BC were as yet assumed to agree with most MSS. in reading υἱός, and ℵ was unknown), and which at one time seemed to me probable, namely ὁ μονογενής without either substantive. It is supported however by neither MS. nor version except the Latin St Gatien's MS., but by a few quotations in Greek and Latin Fathers, almost wholly writers who use one or other of the fuller readings elsewhere; the only considerable exception being Cyril of Jerusalem (*Cat.* vii 11). It is doubtless common to find different authorities completing an originally elliptic or condensed expression in different ways. But the stray instances of ὁ μονογενής and *Unigenitus* are sufficiently explained by the extreme frequency of this simple form of phrase in the theological writings of the fourth and fifth centuries. Nor, on an attentive scrutiny, does it commend itself even as a conjecture, these unsubstantial shreds of authority being discarded. To those indeed who justly recognise the conclusiveness of the evidence which shews that μονογενὴς θεός cannot be a corruption of ὁ μονογενὴς υἱός, yet are unable to believe that St John wrote it, ὁ μονογενής affords the best refuge. In sense it suits the immediate context, having in this respect an advantage over ὁ μονογενὴς υἱός; though it seems to me to fail in relation to the larger context formed by the Prologue, and to lack the pregnant and uniting force which I hope to shew to be possessed by μονογενὴς θεός. But serious difficulties as to transcription have to be added to the want of external evidence. It is as inconceivable that θεός should have been supplied to complete ὁ μονογενής in the second century, with the further omission of the article, as that ὁ μονογενὴς υἱός should have been altered to μονογενὴς θεός. Nor is the case improved by supposing accidental errors arising out of similarity of letters, CO becoming CΘ̄C̄O, and O being lost after Є. It would be an extraordinary coincidence either that both slips of the pen should take place at the same transcription, though separated by ΜΟΝΟΓЄΝΗC; or that two corruptions of the same clause should take place at different times, yet both before the earliest attested text of the New Testament. And again to suppose μονογενής without ὁ to be the true reading would only change one difficulty for another: μονογενής without either article or substantive, followed by ὁ ὤν, and caught up by ἐκεῖνος, would be harsh beyond measure. Thus the conjectural omission of the substantive produces no such satisfying results as could for a moment bring it into competition with the best attested reading, except on the assumption that the best attested reading is impossible.

Accordingly the field of criticism is now in strictness narrowed to the alleged impossibility of μονογενὴς θεός. It will however be well for several reasons to examine the readings on their own positive merits, without reference to the strong assertions of private and overpowering instinct by which criticism is sometimes superseded. We have therefore, thirdly, to consider *Intrinsic Fitness*.

St John's Prologue falls clearly and easily into three divisions:

(*a*) 1. The Word in His Divine relations in eternity antecedently to creation.

(β) 2—13. The Word in His relations to creation, and especially to man, chiefly if not altogether antecedently to the Incarnation.

(γ) 14—18. The Word as becoming flesh, and especially as thereby making revelation.

(The two digressions 6—8, 15, in which the Baptist's office of witness is put forth in contrast, do not concern us here.)

The first division ends with the simple affirmation that the Word, who was πρὸς τὸν θεόν, was Himself θεός. In the second division, after the initial οὗτος which reintroduces the second clause of verse 1, His original name is not repeated: He is presented as the universal Life, and as the Light of mankind; coming into the world, and ignored by it; visiting His own special home, and receiving no welcome there, though in a manner accepted elsewhere: so ends the history of the old world. The third division pronounces at once the name unheard since verse 1, but now as part of the single stupendous phrase ὁ λόγος σὰρξ ἐγένετο, and adds the visible sojourning of the Word 'among us', whereby disciples were enabled to behold His glory. This glory of His is further designated, by a single phrase which is a parenthesis within a parenthesis, as being "a glory as of an only-begotten from a father". Neither the Son nor the Father, as such, has as yet been named, and they are not named here: there is but a suggestion by means of a comparison (the particle ὡς and the absence of articles being mutually necessary), because no image but the relation of a μονογενής to a father can express the twofold character of the glory as at once derivative and on a level with its source. Then the interrupted sentence closes in its original form with the description πλήρης χαρίτος καὶ ἀληθείας, followed, after the interposition of the Baptist's testimony, by a notice of this fulness of grace as imparted to Christians, and its contrast with the preceding Law. Finally verse 18 expounds the full height of this new revelation. Now, as truly as under the Law (Ex. xxxiii 20; Deut. ix 12), Deity as such remains invisible, although the voice which commanded has been succeeded by "the Truth" which was "beheld". Yet a self-manifestation has come from the inmost shrine: One of whom Deity is predicable under that highest form of derivative being which belongs to a μονογενής, not one of imperfect Deity or separate and external place but He who in very truth is εἰς τὸν κόλπον τοῦ πατρός,—He, the Word, interpreted Deity to the world of finite beings.

Part of this meaning is undeniably carried by the common reading ὁ μονογενὴς υἱός; but incongruously, and at best only a part. Here as in v. 14 special force lies in μονογενής in contrast to the *share* possessed by one among many brethren; and for this purpose υἱός adds nothing, if indeed it does not weaken by making that secondary which was meant to be primary, for other 'children of God' had just been mentioned (vv. 12, 13). There would also be something strangely abrupt in the introduction of the complete phrase ὁ μονογενὴς υἱός, as a term already known, which ill suits the careful progress of St John: the leap from ὡς μονογενοῦς παρὰ πατρός would be too sudden; the absence of any indication identifying ὁ υἱός with the Word would be dangerously obscure, while the article would mar the integrity of the Prologue by giving its crowning sentence a new subject in place of ὁ λόγος; and in any case a designative name would serve the argument less than a recital of attributes. This last point comes out more clearly as we follow the exquisitely exact language of the whole verse. The ruling note is struck at once in θεόν, set before οὐδείς in emphatic violation of the simple order which St John habitually uses: and further θεόν has no article, and so comes virtually to mean 'One who is God', 'God as being God', and perhaps includes the Word, as well as the Father[1]. In exact correspondence with θεόν in the first sentence is μονογενὴς θεός in the second. The parallelism brings out the emphasis which the necessary nominative case might otherwise disguise, and a predicative force is again won by the absence of the article. St John is not appealing to a recognised name, as an inserted article would have seemed to imply, but setting forth those characteristics of the Revealer, already described (v. 14) as 'the Word', which enabled Him to bring men into converse with 'the Truth' of God, though the beholding of God was for them impossible. It needed but a single step to give the attribute μονογενής to Him whose glory had been already called a glory *as* of a μονογενής from a father. It needed no fresh step at all to give Him the attribute θεός, for He was the Word, and the Word had at the outset been

---

[1] Cf. Greg. Naz. *Ep.* 101 p. 87 A, θεότης γὰρ καθ' ἑαυτὴν ἀόρατος.

declared to be θεός. The two elements of the phrase having thus been prepared, it remained only to bring them together, associating Deity with Him as Son (for that much is directly involved in the single term μονογενής) as expressly as it had been already associated with Him as Word; and then the combination is fixed and elucidated by the further description ὁ ὢν εἰς τὸν κόλπον τοῦ πατρός[1]. It begins with the article, for now that One has been called μονογενὴς θεός,—and in One alone can both attributions meet,—there is no longer need for generality of language; we exchange "One that is—" for "He that is—". In like manner now that He has been set forth as actually μονογενής as well as θεός, it has become right to speak definitely of τοῦ πατρός. The connecting phrase ὢν εἰς τὸν κόλπον is a repetition of ὁ λόγος ἦν πρὸς τὸν θεόν, translated into an image appropriate to the relation of Son to Father.

Thus St John is true to his office of bringing to light hidden foundations. The name 'The Word', in which he condenses so much of the scattered teaching of our Lord and the earlier apostles, leads gradually, as he expounds it, to the more widely current idea of Sonship, which after the Prologue he employs freely; and yet is not lost, for ἐξηγήσατο suggests at once the still present middle term of v. 1 through which μονογενής has become linked to θεός. The three salient verses of the Prologue are 1, 14, 18. These by themselves would suffice to express the absolute primary contents of St John's 'message': the intervening verses are properly a statement of the antecedents of the Gospel, and of its meaning as illustrated by its relation to its antecedents. Verse 1 declares the Word to have been 'in the beginning' θεός; verse 14 states that the Word, when He became flesh, was beheld to have a glory as of a μονογενής; verse 18 shews how His union of both attributes enabled Him to bridge the chasm which kept the Godhead beyond the knowledge of men. Without μονογενὴς θεός the end

---

[1] Cf. Cyr. Al. ad l. p. 107 B, ἐπειδὴ γὰρ ἔφη Μονογενῆ καὶ Θεόν, τίθησιν εὐθὺς ‘Ο ὢν ἐν τοῖς κόλποις τοῦ πατρός, ἵνα νοῆται καὶ υἱὸς ἐξ αὐτοῦ καὶ ἐν αὐτῷ φυσικῶς κ.τ.λ.

of the Prologue brings no clear recollection of the beginning: θεός is the luminous word which recites afresh the first verse within the last, and in its combination with μονογενής crowns and illustrates the intervening steps.

It is therefore vain to urge against the phrase that it is unique in the New Testament. The whole Prologue is unique, and μονογενὴς θεός seems to belong essentially to a single definite step in the Prologue. No writer except St John applies μονογενής to our Lord at all, and he only in the three other closely connected places already cited. In each of them there is a distinctly perceptible reason why υἱός should be introduced; and moreover there were obvious objections to the employment by St John of the definite title ὁ μονογενὴς θεός, that is, with the article. If we examine the combination dispassionately, it is hard to see in it anything inconsistent with the theology of St John, unless the idea of an antecedent Fatherhood and Sonship within the Godhead, as distinguished from the manifested Sonship of the Incarnation, is foreign to him. This idea is nowhere enunciated by him in express words; but it is difficult to attach a meaning to ὁ ὢν εἰς τὸν κόλπον τοῦ πατρός on any other view, and it is surely a natural deduction from the Prologue as a whole (with either reading) except on the quaint Valentinian theory that the subjects of vv. 14 and 18 are different, while it seems impossible to divine how he can have otherwise interpreted numerous sayings of our Lord which he records. The paradox is not greater than in the other startling combination ὁ λόγος σὰρξ ἐγένετο, the genuineness of which no one affects to question, though its force has been evaded in different directions in all ages.

The sense of μονογενής is fixed by its association with υἱός in the other passages, especially v. 14, by the original and always dominant usage in Greek literature, and by the prevailing consent of the Greek Fathers. It is applied properly to an only child or offspring; and a reference to this special kind of unicity is latent in most of the few cases in which it does not lie on the surface, as of the Phœnix in various authors, the μονογενὴς οὐρανός of Plato (*Tim.* 31 B) as made by the 'Father' of all (28 C), and the μονογενὴς κόσμος of writers who follow him. Instances are not entirely wanting in which μονογενής is used of things that are merely alone in their kind (as if from γένος, and in its widest sense); but this rare laxity of popular speech, confined, if I mistake not, to inanimate objects, cannot be rightly accepted here. It finds indeed some support from Gregory of Nazianzus (*Orat.* xxx 20 p. 554 A) and Ammonius (on iii 16 in the catenæ): but Basil's simple rendering (*adv. Eun.* ii 20 p. 256 A) ὁ μόνος γεννηθείς, put forward in opposition to Eunomius's arbitrary invention ὁ παρὰ μόνου γενόμενος, (compare Athanasius's negative definition, *Or. c. Ar.* ii 62 p. 530 A, ὁ γάρ τοι μονογενὴς οὐκ ὄντων ἄλλων ἀδελφῶν μονογενής ἐστιν,) expresses the sense of the greater writers of different ages[1], though they sometimes *add* ἐκ μόνου to μόνος. While however the idea conveyed by the verb itself in the paraphrase μόνος γεννηθείς belongs essentially to the sense, the passive form goes beyond it, as perhaps even in *unigenitus*, and the narrower sense of the English verb in 'only-begotten' departs still further from the Greek. If ὁ μ. υἱός were the true reading, it would on the whole be a gain to adopt 'the only Son' from Tyndale in iii 16, 18, and from the English Apostles' Creed, where 'only' represents the μονογενής of this or the other like passages, as 'only-begotten' represents it in the 'Nicene' Creed of the English Communion Service. But no such expedient is possible with μονογενὴς θεός; and so the choice lies between some unfamiliar word, such as 'sole-born', and the old rendering which certainly exaggerates the peculiarity of the Greek phrase, though it may be defended by imperfect analogies from other passages of the New Testa-

[1] A few out of the many somewhat later patristic illustrations of the true sense are collected, not without confusion in the appended remarks, by Petau *de Trin.* ii 10 10 ff.; vii 11 3 ff. Cyr.Al. *Thes.* 239 f. is specially clear: μονογενὴς...διὰ τὸ μόνον τοῦτον εἶναι καρπὸν πατρικόν: again ὡς μόνος φυσικῶς γεννηθείς: again ὡς μόνος φυσικῶς γεννηθείς: again εἰ δὲ μηδεὶς πώποτε μονογενὲς τὸ μόνον ἔργον κέκληκε, πῶς ὁ υἱὸς ὡς γενόμενος ἀλλ' οὐχ ὡς γεννηθεὶς μονογενὴς νοηθήσεται;

ment. A change of a different kind however seems absolutely required, either the insertion of 'One who is', or the resolved rendering 'An Only-begotten who is God, even He who &c.': without some such arrangement the predicative force of μονογενὴς θεός is lost, and the indispensable omission of the English article becomes perilous.

But these matters of translation do not affect, though they illustrate, the primary question as to St John's own Greek text. I have, I trust, now given sufficient reasons for concluding not only that μονογενὴς θεός presents no such overwhelming difficulty as to forbid its acceptance notwithstanding the weight of evidence in its favour, but that the whole Prologue leads up to it, and, to say the least, suffers in unity if it is taken away.

All these considerations are entirely independent of the truth of any theological doctrines which have been deduced, or may be deduced, from St John's text. When it is urged that certain words are incongruous with the context and with St John's teaching generally, it becomes legitimate and perhaps necessary to discuss their genuineness on grounds of sense; and not the less legitimate where, as in this case, the sense is manifestly theological, the criterion for the present purpose being not doctrinal truth but doctrinal congruity. Since however it is matter of fact that a fear of theological consequences is acting in restraint of dispassionate judgement, and that in opposite quarters, I feel justified in appending to the critical discussion a few remarks on the treatment of μονογενὴς θεός in ancient times, which may at least suggest some diffidence in relying on the infallibility of modern instincts.

The list already given of Fathers who read [ὁ] μονογενὴς θεός in their text of John i 18 takes no account of the much more widely diffused use of the phrase [ὁ] μονογενὴς θεός without a biblical context. Professor Ezra Abbot justly points out that the phrase in itself affords no sufficient evidence as to the reading of St John followed by those who employ it, since it is a favourite with one or two who undeniably read ὁ μονογενὴς υἱός when they quote the Gospel[1]. Yet it is equally true that this widely spread usage bears an indirect testimony which may be fitly noticed here, partly by its mere existence, partly by its probable connexion with public formularies.

Origen's voluminous remains contain the detached phrase μονογενὴς θεός eight or ten times, usually softened by the addition of λόγος or in some other way. It lurks in one place in the Antioch Epistle against Paul of Samosata (ὃν οὐκ ἄλλον πεπείσμεθα ἢ τὸν μονογενῆ υἱὸν τοῦ θεοῦ θεόν, p. 292), and ought, I suspect, to be restored to another (τοῦτον δὲ τὸν υἱόν, γεννητὸν μονογενῆ †υἱόν†, εἰκόνα τοῦ ἀοράτου θεοῦ τυγχάνοντα,...πρὸ αἰώνων ὄντα οὐ προγνώσει ἀλλ' οὐσίᾳ καὶ ὑποστάσει, θεὸν θεοῦ υἱόν, p. 290), where the second υἱόν cannot be sustained by any punctuation, but must either be omitted or, with better reason, exchanged for θεόν. With these exceptions it is, I believe, absent from the extant Ante-nicene literature, notwithstanding the diffusion of the corresponding biblical text. The absence of this reading from good secondary MSS. and from almost all the later versions shews how rapidly it was superseded in the fourth and fifth centuries; yet we encounter the phrase itself on all sides in this period, and certainly not least abundantly in the latter part of the fourth century. Without attempting an exhaustive list, it may be useful to set down the following names and references, partly taken from Wetstein and other critics, partly from my own notes. Athanasius (c. Gent. 41 p. 40 C, διὸ καὶ ὁ τούτου λόγος ὤν καὶ οὐ σύνθετος, ἀλλ' εἷς καὶ μονογενὴς θεός, ὁ καὶ ἐκ πατρὸς οἷα πηγῆς ἀγαθῆς ἀγαθὸς προελθών; c. Apoll. ii 5 p. 944 A, οὐχὶ ἀνθρώπου πρὸς τὸν θεὸν ὄντος, ὡς ὑμεῖς συκοφαντοῦντες λέγετε, διασύροντες τὸ τῶν Χριστιανῶν μυστήριον, ἀλλὰ θεοῦ τοῦ μονογενοῦς

---

[1] The few Greek writers coming under this description, all of whose quotations with υἱός are either solitary or otherwise doubtful, cannot properly be taken into account.

[i.e. One who is God, even ὁ μονογενὴς θεός] εὐδοκήσαντος τῷ πληρώματι τῆς θεότητος αὐτοῦ τὴν τοῦ ἀρχετύπου πλάσιν ἀνθρώπου καὶ ποίησιν καινὴν ἐκ μήτρας παρθένου ἀναστήσασθαι ἑαυτῷ φυσικῇ γεννήσει καὶ ἀλύτῳ ἑνώσει); Arius (ap. Ath. de Syn. 15 p. 728 E, λοιπὸν ὁ υἱός...μονογενὴς θεός ἐστι; Epiph. Haer. 732 A, ὁ υἱός...θελήματι καὶ βουλῇ ὑπέστη πρὸ χρόνων καὶ πρὸ αἰώνων πλήρης θεὸς μονογενὴς ἀναλλοίωτος[1]); Alexander the bishop of Alexandria with whom Arius came into conflict (l. c. p. 734 Noess. ἡ τοῦ μονογενοῦς θεοῦ ἀνεκδιήγητος ὑπόστασις); Marcellus (ap. Eus. c. Marc. i 4 p. 19 C[2]); Asterius (ap. Ath. Or. c. Ar. ii 37 p. 505 C [v. l.]; de Syn. 18 p. 732 B); Theodorus of Heraclea (on Isaiah in Mai, N. P. B. vi 226); Eusebius [of Emesa, by Thilo's identification] (de fide &c. [Latine] in Sirmondi Opp. i 3 B, 16 D, 22 A); Rufinus of Palestine (Latine in Sirmondi Opp. i 274 ff. cc. 39, 52, 53, and with Verbum often); the Synod of Ancyra (ap. Epiph. Haer. 854 C); Epiphanius (Haer. 755 C, 817 C, 857 A, 912 A, 981 A); Cyril of Jerusalem (xi 3, θεῷ θεοῦ μονογενεῖ); Eunomius (Apolog. 15, 21, 26; Expos. Fidei 2 bis); Basil (Ep. xxxviii 4 p. 117 C; de Sp. S. 19 p. 16 C; 45 p. 38 B; c. Eun. ii 1 p. 238 C; also ὁ μ. υἱὸς καὶ θεός, i 15 p. 228; 26 p. 237 B); the Apostolic Constitutions (iii 17; v 20 § 5; vii 38 § 3; 43 § 1; viii 7 § 1, 35); the interpolator of the Ignatian Epistles (ad Philad. 6); Gregory of Nazianzus (Ep. 202 p. 168 C); Gregory of Nyssa repeatedly and in various writings (Professor Abbot counts 125 examples in the treatise *against*

---

[1] It has been urged that πλήρης invalidates the reference. On the contrary the sense is that before χρόνων and αἰώνων the Son attained that full height, subject to no change, which is expressed by μονογενὴς θεός.

[2] Marcellus seems to be quoting a Creed, but in such a manner as to make its language his own. Γέγραφε γάρ, says Eusebius (c. Marc. 19 c) πιστεύειν εἰς πατέρα θεὸν παντοκράτορα, καὶ εἰς τὸν υἱὸν αὐτοῦ τὸν μονογενῆ θεόν, καὶ εἰς τὸ πνεῦμα τὸ ἅγιον· καὶ φησιν ἐκ τῶν θείων γραφῶν μεμαθηκέναι τοῦτον τὸν τῆς θεοσεβείας τρόπον. Quite different in form is the Creed presented by him to Julius of Rome (Epiph. Haer. 836), the suspiciously Western character of which is well known. In the epistle to Julius (835 D) he uses the phrase εἷς θεὸς καὶ ὁ τούτου μονογενὴς υἱὸς λόγος, where the added λόγος probably implies θεός, itself excluded by τούτου.

IN SCRIPTURE AND TRADITION

Eunomius alone); Didymus (*de Trin.* i 25 p. 68 Ming.; i 26 p. 72; with καὶ υἱός, i 18 p. 53; 26 p. 76; with υἱὸς καί interposed, i 16 p. 40; with λόγος, i 26 p. 75); the 'Macedonian' interlocutor in an anonymous Dialogue on the Trinity (Ath. *Opp.* ii 509 B[1]); Isaac 'ex Judaeo' (Sirmondi *Opp.* i 406 ABC); Cyril of Alexandria repeatedly; Andrew of Samosata (ap. Cyr. Al. *Ap. adv. Or.* p. 290 Pusey [ix 333 Migne]); Theodoret (*Repr. xii Capp. Cyr.* 12 with λόγος[2]; *c. Nest.* iv 1047 Schulze); Theodotus of Ancyra, once with λόγος, once without[3] (post Cyr. Al. x 1336 f. Migne); Basil of Seleucia (*Hom.* i p. 5 A; cf. xxv p. 139 D); Isidore of Pelusium (*Ep.* iii 95); even John of Damascus in compound phrases[4], perhaps following the *Henoticon* of Zeno (see p. 24 n. 1); Hilary in peculiar abundance in different writings (a single typical instance will illustrate his use: "Deus a Deo, ab uno ingenito Deo unus unigenitus Deus, non dii duo sed unus ab uno," *de Trin.* ii 11); the fragments of a Latin Arian commentary on St Luke (in Mai *S. V. N. C.* iii 2 191, 199) and of Latin Arian sermons (ib. 217: cf. *per filium unigenitum Deum* in the Arian *Primus capitulus fidei catholicae*, ib. 233); the Latin *Opus Imperfectum* on St Matthew a few times (e.g. i 20 bis, 25) &c. The chief apparent exceptions are the later Antiochian school of Greek writers, and Ambrose and his disciple Augustine among Latin writers. Yet the subsequent theologians of North Africa by no means eschew the phrase, and it is of frequent occurrence in the

---

[1] The 'Orthodox' interlocutor neither objects to the term nor uses it himself.

[2] So in Pusey's text of Cyril (*Apol. adv. Theodoret.* p. 492) with (apparently all) the Greek MSS. and the Syriac and Latin versions. Prior editions (as Schulze of Theodoret v 66 and Migne of Cyril ix 449 c) substitute τοῦ θεοῦ for θεός, apparently without authority.

[3] In his *Exposition of the Nicene Creed*. But the context leaves it doubtful whether he assumed the combination to be already in the Creed, or only took its elements from the Creed.

[4] Ὁ μονογενὴς υἱὸς καὶ λόγος τοῦ θεοῦ καὶ θεός (*De fid. orth.* i 2 p. 792 c Migne; iii 1 p. 984 A); ὁ μ. υἱὸς τοῦ θεοῦ καὶ θεός (iii 12 p. 1029 B); ὁ μ. υἱὸς καὶ θεός (i 2 p. 793 B). In the third passage θεός might be independent of μονογενής; not so, I think the context shows, in the others.

writings of Fulgentius in particular. Even in the days of Alcuin and Theodulphus it is not extinct.

In the later times the tradition doubtless passed directly from writer to writer: but this explanation will hardly account for the wide and various acceptance found by μονογενὴς θεός in the fourth century, combined with the almost complete absence of attempts to argue from it by any of the contending parties. This remarkable currency arose, I cannot but suspect, from its adoption into Creeds. We look for it of course in vain in Latin Creeds[1], for Latin Christendom from the earliest times known to us did not possess the fundamental reading in the Gospel: Hilary must have learned it, as he learned much else, from his Greek masters. Among the very few Greek Creeds belonging clearly to the second or third century of which we have any knowledge, we can identify μονογενὴς θεός only in that of Antioch, incorporated with the remarkable exposition of Lucianus (Sozom. *H. E.* iii 5 9; vi 12 4), who suffered martyrdom about 311. Here we read καὶ εἰς ἕνα κύριον Ἰησοῦν Χριστόν, τὸν υἱὸν αὐτοῦ τὸν μονογενῆ θεόν, δι' οὗ τὰ πάντα, τὸν γεννηθέντα πρὸ τῶν αἰώνων ἐκ τοῦ πατρὸς θεὸν ἐκ θεοῦ, ὅλον ἐξ ὅλου κ.τ.λ. (*Graece* ap. Ath. *de Syn.* 23 p. 736 A; Socr. *H. E.* ii 10; *Latine* ap. Hil. *de Syn.* 28 p. 478 c: cf. Bull *Def. Fid. Nic.* ii 13 4—7). The word θεόν after μονογενῆ was perhaps not in the earliest forms of this Creed (see pp. 24, 26): but there is no reason to doubt that it stood there in the time of Lucianus, of whose amplifications there is no sign till further on. In the passage of Marcellus of Ancyra referred to by Eusebius (about 336), in which he apparently follows some Creed (see p. 20), we have already found the identical Antiochian phrase τὸν υἱὸν αὐτοῦ τὸν μονογενῆ θεόν. The exposition of Lucianus was one of the four formularies brought forward at Antioch in 341: another, perhaps a modification of the local Creed of Tyana, the see of Theophronius who recited

---

[1] One elaborate private formulary, long attributed to Jerome or Augustine, the Confession of Pelagius (Hieron. *Opp.* xi 202 Vall.), has *verum Deum unigenitum et verum Dei filium.*

it, has in like manner, καὶ εἰς τὸν υἱὸν αὐτοῦ τὸν μονογενῆ θεὸν λόγον, δύναμιν καὶ σοφίαν, τὸν κύριον ἡμῶν Ἰησοῦν Χριστόν, δι' οὗ τὰ πάντα, τὸν γεννηθέντα ἐκ τοῦ πατρὸς πρὸ τῶν αἰώνων θεὸν τέλειον ἐκ θεοῦ τελείου, καὶ ὄντα πρὸς τὸν θεὸν ἐν ὑποστάσει κ.τ.λ. (ap. Ath. *de Syn.* 24 p. 737 B). Once more the formulary of the Synod of Seleucia in Isauria held in 359 declares, πιστεύομεν δὲ καὶ εἰς τὸν κύριον ἡμῶν Ἰησοῦν Χριστὸν τὸν υἱὸν αὐτοῦ, τὸν ἐξ αὐτοῦ γεννηθέντα ἀπαθῶς πρὸ πάντων τῶν αἰώνων, θεὸν λόγον, θεὸν ἐκ θεοῦ μονογενῆ, φῶς, ζωήν, ἀλήθειαν, σοφίαν, δύναμιν, δι' οὗ τὰ πάντα ἐγένετο κ.τ.λ. (ap. Ath. *de Syn.* 29 p. 746 C; Epiph. *Haer.* 873 B, C; Socr. *H. E.* ii 40). The influence of the two latter documents would probably be limited and temporary: but the details of their language, so far as it was not shaped by current controversy, must have been inherited directly or indirectly from formularies now lost, matured before the outbreak of the Arian disputes. Nay the original Nicene Creed itself appears to embody the phrase, though in a form which admits of being interpreted either as a deliberate retention or as a hesitating and imperfect obliteration of an earlier statement of doctrine (see Note D). Indeed it occurs once without any ambiguity, as a friend points out, in what purports to be a copy of the Nicene Creed included in a memorial from Eustathius of Sebastia and other representatives of the Asiatic Homœousians proffering their communion to Liberius of Rome, and expressly accepted by him as the Nicene Creed, shortly before his death in 366. This copy differs in nothing but two or three trivial particles from the usual ancient form except in the words καὶ εἰς ἕνα μονογενῆ θεὸν κύριον Ἰησοῦν Χριστόν, τὸν υἱὸν τοῦ θεοῦ, and the omission of μονογενῆ from its accustomed place in the next clause (ap. Socr. *H. E.* iv 12). In the familiar Creed usually regarded as the Constantinopolitan recension of the Nicene Creed μονογενὴς θεός was undoubtedly wanting, for reasons explained in Dissertation II. But finally in 451 it stands included, though with the old Alexandrine addition λόγον, in the carefully chosen last words of the Definition of Chalcedon: οὐκ εἰς δύο πρόσωπα μεριζόμενον ἢ διαιρούμενον, ἀλλ' ἕνα καὶ τὸν αὐτόν, υἱὸν καὶ μονογενῆ θεὸν λόγον, κύριον Ἰησοῦν Χριστόν ("sed unum eundemque Filium et unigenitum Deum Verbum Dominum Jesum Christum," in Mansi's primary old version), καθάπερ ἄνωθεν οἱ προφῆται περὶ αὐτοῦ καὶ αὐτὸς ἡμᾶς ὁ κύριος Ἰησοῦς Χριστὸς ἐξεπαίδευσε, καὶ τὸ τῶν πατέρων ἡμῶν παραδέδωκε σύμβολον. It is true that Evagrius (*H. E.* ii 4), Agatho (in Mansi *Conc.* xi 256), and the third Council of Constantinople in 680 omit καί so as to bring υἱόν and μονογενῆ into combination, as also most Latin versions omit *et*, some further making transpositions: but the reading of the best authorities is sustained not only by its less obvious character but by the unquestionable separation of υἱόν from μονογενῆ a few lines above, in the sentence πρὸ αἰώνων μὲν ἐκ τοῦ πατρὸς γεννηθέντα κατὰ τὴν θεότητα, ἐπ' ἐσχάτων δὲ τῶν ἡμερῶν τὸν αὐτὸν δι' ἡμᾶς καὶ διὰ τὴν ἡμετέραν σωτηρίαν ἐκ Μαρίας τῆς παρθένου τῆς θεοτόκου κατὰ τὴν ἀνθρωπότητα, ἕνα καὶ τὸν αὐτὸν Χριστόν, υἱόν, κύριον, μονογενῆ[1].

At this point a possible suspicion requires notice, whether μονογενὴς θεός may not owe its origin to Creeds, and have passed from them into the text of St John. The authority of a Creed might doubtless succeed in importing a difficult and peculiar reading, the introduction of which in any other way would be inconceivable. But the facts already stated are as fatal to this as to all other suggested explanations of a change from ὁ μονογενὴς υἱός to μονογενὴς θεός; and the evidence of Creeds does but corroborate the other evidence. I do not press the late date, the close of the third century at Antioch, at which we first find μονογενὴς θεός actually standing in a Creed. The Creed of Antioch in that form might be of earlier date: and the same may be said of any Creeds which may have supplied materials at Nicæa in 325, at Antioch to Theophronius in 341, and at Seleucia in 359, though these might also belong in their corresponding form to Lucianus's or even to the next generation. But

---

[1] The *Henoticon* of the emperor Zeno, promulgated in 482, begins its final confession with the words Ὁμολογοῦμεν δὲ τὸν μονογενῆ τοῦ θεοῦ υἱὸν καὶ θεόν, τὸν κ.τ.λ. (Evagr. *H. E.* iii 14).

conjectures of this kind will not avail unless we are prepared to go so far as to say that μονογενὴς θεός stood in several distant Creeds towards the close of the second century, or that it stood in some one leading Creed near the beginning of the second century, for nothing less would account for its presence in such various biblical texts. Ptolemæus (see p. 30) speaks either from Italy for himself in the third quarter or at most a few years later, or from Alexandria or Rome for his master Valentinus in the second quarter of the century; Irenæus from Asia Minor or (less probably) Gaul; Clement and the Memphitic version from Alexandria; Origen a little later from Alexandria and probably also Palestine. It would not be easy to trace these scattered texts to Alexandria, the only imaginable single centre, at that early period: but if it were, we should find ourselves still confronted by two weighty facts. First, there is not a trace of theological activity at Alexandria, except that of the 'Gnostic' chiefs, till the Catechetical School of the Church (Athenagoras, Pantænus, Clement) arose in the last third of the century, which is too late for our purpose: if such existed, some record of it must have been preserved by Eusebius, who had a special interest in Alexandria, and has given us a tolerable roll of contemporary writers from other parts of the East. Secondly, little as we know of the Creed of Alexandria, it happens that that little suffices to shew that it did not contain μονογενὴς θεός. There is no trace of the words in the rule of faith expounded in Origen's early work *De Principiis* (Preface to Book i § 3 f.), though in various places where he speaks in his own name (as in i 2; ii 6) there are suspicious signs that the translator Rufinus had them before him. But even in the days of Arius μονογενὴς θεός is clearly absent from the Alexandrian Creed as recited by Alexander, notwithstanding his own use of the term; for the evidently ancient words run καὶ εἰς ἕνα κύριον Ἰησοῦν Χριστόν, τὸν υἱὸν τοῦ θεοῦ τὸν μονογενῆ, γεννηθέντα κ.τ.λ. Thus all external evidence fails to sustain a derivation from Creeds in the second century: if we are to consider intrinsic probabilities, it must be repeated that the invention of the phrase in the first half (and more) of the century is at variance with all that we know of any of its theologies: and as for the Creeds of the Church, that in those early days of elementary simplicity they should admit such a combination without direct Scriptural warrant would contradict all that we know of their manner of growth. Whether it could have been so admitted in the third century, with the theology of which it easily associates itself, is highly questionable; but that is not the period with which we have to deal. Yet even in the third century, as has been shown, the usage is cautious and tentative, by no means such as we should expect with words freely pronounced in Creeds. Origen quotes the verse almost half as often as he employs the phrase, and in a majority of cases he adds to the phrase some tempering word. At Antioch, where alone else it appears, it is conceivable that the Creed had an influence, though hardly if unsupported by Greek MSS., in changing the reading of the Syriac version; but the converse is equally possible. It is only in the fourth century that the phrase pervades the greater part of the extant literature: and the cause surely is that, though μονογενὴς θεός as a reading was being swept out of biblical MSS. by the same accidental agencies of transcription which removed hosts of Antenicene readings of no doctrinal moment, as a formula it had at last established itself in widely known Creeds. We cannot look to Creeds as the sources of the reading without inverting history.

The one historical demerit then, if demerit it be, which attaches to the combination μονογενὴς θεός is that each of the great parties in the fundamental and necessary controversies which began in the days of Constantine was willing to pronounce it, and that it has never itself become a watchword of strife. It was not avoided by Arius or his successor in the next generation, Eunomius, though neither of them inserted it in his own shorter Creed (see the letter of Arius and Euzoius to Constantine, in Socr. *H. E.* i 26; Sozom. *H. E.* ii 27, without even μονογενής; and the Confession in Eunomius's *Apologeticus*, c. 5, καὶ εἰς ἕνα μονογενῆ υἱὸν τοῦ θεοῦ, θεὸν λόγον), by the

Latin Arian commentator on St Luke, or by the author of the *Opus Imperfectum*, usually classed as an Arian. It appears sporadically in various quarters in the intermediate movement, commonly called Semi-Arianism, which, however inconsequent in thought, retained much of the letter of Antenicene language; while on the other hand it was not used spontaneously by Eusebius, who habitually followed his MS. or MSS. in reading υἱός in St John. It is uttered but sparingly and guardedly by Athanasius, once in youth and once in old age, probably for a similar reason[1]; for he seems hardly likely to have shrunk from it on grounds of doctrine or feeling, when we remember that he speaks of τὴν τοῦ θεοῦ γέννησιν (*Or. c. Ar.* i 28 p. 432 c) and that the phrase in which he most loves to clothe his characteristic teaching is ἴδιον τῆς τοῦ πατρὸς οὐσίας γέννημα. Once more we find μονογενὴς θεός in Marcellus, the blind violence of whose antagonism to Arius conducted him to a position of his own. Hilary, the wisest as well as the most successful champion of the cause of Athanasius in the West, employs it with startling freedom, evidently as the natural expression of his own inmost thought. Among the greatest of the theologians who continued and developed the same line of tradition in the East are confessedly Basil, Gregory of Nyssa, Didymus, and Cyril of Alexandria; and to none of these, widely as they differ from each other, is μονογενὴς θεός strange, while with two of them its use is habitual. Finally, with an accompaniment which guards but does not neutralise it, it obtains a place in the definition of the last of the 'four' primary Councils.

This great variety of belief among those who have received μονογενὴς θεός into their theological vocabulary suggests at once that its utility is not that of a weapon of offence or defence. Experience has shown that it is possible to affix a con-

---

[1] Sometimes (as *de Decr.* 16 p. 221 E; *Or. c. Ar.* ii 47 p. 515 E; *Ep. ad Afr.* 5 p. 895 A, c) he has the derivative form [ὁ] μονογενὴς λόγος, which occurs in a passage of Origen quoted by him *de Decr.* 27 p. 233 c, and is not rare elsewhere.

siderable range of meaning to words which simply express either Deity or Sonship, and even, as here, to a combination of the two predicates in the same subject. But it is rarely by the literal and apparent cogency of single texts that deliberate convictions have ever been formed: power in producing belief is not to be measured by convenience in argument. Understanding as I do both terms in the highest sense, and holding that the doctrine of perfect and eternal Sonship within the Godhead, for which Origen and Athanasius contended, and which the Nicene and 'Constantinopolitan' Creeds explicitly set forth, is fundamental truth, I cannot affect to regret that a reading of St John's words which suggests it, though it does not prove it, is established as genuine by a concurrence of evidence which I could not disregard without renouncing critical honesty. Perhaps the words may prove in due time instructive, thus much may be said without presumption, both to us who receive the doctrine and to those who as yet stumble at it.

It does not however follow that good results would now arise from a resuscitation of the ancient formula detached from the context of the Gospel. To employ it with the article prefixed would open the way to serious evil; while without the article it requires arrangements of diction which could seldom be contrived in common usage, and which incautious writers would be perpetually tempted to discard. The danger of the article is somewhat less in Greek than in English: nevertheless it must have been a dread of possible misuse that induced the Greek theologians so often to temper the article, as it were, by adding afterwards λόγος, υἱός, or some other term which fixed the denotation of θεός without lowering its sense or suggesting 'division'.

Yet these considerations can have no place in determining the text of St John. Taught by himself to "believe on the name of the Only-begotten Son of God", we do well to adhere to the name thus entrusted to us: but we need not shrink from accepting and trying to interpret his other language in the single instance when he is led—not to put forward another name but—to join two attributes in unwonted union, that he may for a moment open a glimpse into the Divine depths out of which his historical Gospel proceeds.

30 ON THE WORDS ΜΟΝΟΓΕΝΗC ΘΕΟC

Note A

The details of early Greek Patristic Evidence

The earliest known Greek reference to John i 18 occurs in two independent accounts of Valentinian doctrine, furnished by Irenæus and Clement respectively[1]. The Valentinianism sketched by Irenæus in his first book is commonly recognised to be that of Ptolemæus, who apparently belongs to the generation succeeding the middle of the second century. He cannot at all events be later than the episcopate of Eleutherus, about 175—190, under which Irenæus wrote (p. 176 Mass.). "They further teach", Irenæus says (p. 40), "that the First Ogdoad was indicated (μεμηνυκέναι) by John the Lord's disciple, these being their words: 'John, the Lord's disciple', intending to give an account of the genesis of the universe whereby the Father put forth (προέβαλεν) all things[2], supposes a certain Ἀρχή, the first thing gendered by God (τὸ πρῶτον γεννηθὲν ὑπὸ τοῦ θεοῦ), which he has also[3] called (κέκληκεν) Son and μονογενὴς θεός, in

---

[1] The recent criticisms of Heinrici (*Die Valentinianische Gnosis und die heilige Schrift*) and Lipsius (*Protestantische Kirchenzeitung* of Feb. 22 1873, pp. 182 ff.: cf. *Quellen d. ältesten Ketzergeschichte* 90) have not thrown so much light on the mutual relations of these two accounts as might have been hoped for from such otherwise instructive investigations. It seems clear that neither Clement drew from Irenæus nor Irenæus from Clement, nor both from a common *immediate* source. More than this it would be rash to assert at present.

[2] The text followed up to this point is that of the Greek extract preserved in Epiphanius (p. 196 Pet.), which shews no sign of amplification here. The old Latin version has omitted some words, including those which mark the quotation as verbal; while at the end of the quotation it adds "Et Ptolemaeus quidem ita," omitted by Epiphanius. But both texts imply a Valentinian appeal to "John the Lord's disciple" for what follows.

[3] There is no reason to change *quod etiam nunc* (al. *q. e. me*) of the MSS. to *quod etiam Nun* with Erasmus,

whom (or which) the Father seminally put forth all things[1]." The Valentinian writer proceeds to treat St John's Prologue, clause by clause, as a commentary on his theory that Λόγος was derived from Ἀρχή, and Ἀρχή from Θεός, all three being nevertheless intimately united; and endeavours to extract the personages of his Ogdoad from St John's terms. From i 14 he obtains the first Tetrad, Pater and Charis, Monogenes and Aletheia; and there he stops, the second Tetrad having been already found in i 1—4, so that i 18 is not quoted in so much of the passage as Irenæus transcribes. But the simple term Monogenes, required as a masculine synonym of Arche to make a syzygy with Aletheia, is distinctly taken from i 14; so that when the writer parenthetically attributes to St John two other designations of Arche, Son and μονογενὴς θεός, neither of which is convenient for his present purpose, he cannot mean only that they are fair deductions from language used in i 1—14, but must have in view some literal use by St John elsewhere; that is doubtless i 18; iii 16, 18.

The same result presents itself at once in the Valentinian statements of doctrine, partly copied, partly reported by Clement of Alexandria in the Excerpta found at the end of the Florence MS. of the *Stromates*, and now reasonably supposed to belong to his lost *Hypotyposes* (Bunsen, *Anal. Antenic.* i 159 ff.). "The Valentinians", he says, (p. 968 Pott.; p. 210 Buns.) "thus interpret" Jo. i 1: "they say that Arche is the Monogenes, who is likewise called (προσαγορεύεσθαι) θεός, as also in what follows he [John] expressly signifies Him to be

---

whose conjecture is adopted by later editors. *Quod etiamnunc* (or *etiamnum*) is a natural rendering of ὃ δὴ καί: and though Νοῦς occurs in Clement's parallel exposition, and has been noticed already by Irenæus (p. 5), it could have no place among the terms enumerated as taken from St John, and it is absent from the context which follows.

[1] So in the Venice MS. (the best) of Epiphanius ὃ δὴ καὶ υἱὸν καὶ μονογενῆ θεὸν κέκληκεν; the common text inverting καί and μονογενῆ. The true order is retained in the Latin, "et Filium et Unigenitum Deum", though in some of the inferior MSS. and in the editions *Domini* (Dn̄i) has been substituted for *Deum* (Dm̄), as read by others, including the Clermont and Arundel MSS., the two best, and representatives of different families.

θεός (ὡς καὶ ἐν τοῖς ἑξῆς ἄντικρυς θεὸν αὐτὸν δηλοῖ), saying ὁ μονογενὴς θεὸς ὁ ὢν εἰς τὸν κόλπον τοῦ πατρὸς ἐκεῖνος ἐξηγήσατο." The word 'expressly' was doubtless used because the writer considered the Deity of Arche, though not explicitly stated by St John, to be obviously included in the attribution of Deity to Logos (θεὸς ἦν ὁ λόγος), since Logos was derived from θεός not directly but through Arche[1]: but this preliminary inference only throws into clearer relief the coupling of the Monogenes with θεός by the Evangelist himself in i 18[2]. When then in what follows reference is made to the Father's 'putting forth' of the Monogenes, who is further identified with the Son (τοῦτ' ἐστὶν ὁ υἱός, ὅτι δι' υἱοῦ ὁ πατὴρ ἐγνώσθη), we have at once in the combined designations a sufficient explanation of the appearance of υἱός in a succeeding allusion to i 18 (καὶ ὁ μὲν μείνας μονογενὴς υἱὸς εἰς τὸν κόλπον τοῦ πατρὸς τὴν ἐνθύμησιν διὰ τῆς γνώσεως ἐξηγεῖται τοῖς αἰῶσιν, ὡς ἂν ὑπὸ τοῦ κόλπου αὐτοῦ προβληθείς), without supposing υἱός to have stood here in the writer's text of St John. The *Hypotyposes* were probably written in the early years of the third century, certainly not later[3]. If all the Valentinian Excerpts belong to the 'Eastern School' mentioned in the obscure title (cf. Hippol. *Haer.* vi 35), the coincidence with the Valentinianism in Irenæus would bring the evidence as to St John's reading far back, perhaps to the second quarter of the second century; for Ptolemæus is named by Hippolytus (l. c.) as belonging to the

[1] So the writer in Irenæus (p. 41). Ἐν γὰρ τῷ πατρὶ καὶ ἐκ τοῦ πατρὸς ἡ ἀρχή, ἐν δὲ τῇ ἀρχῇ καὶ ἐκ τῆς ἀρχῆς ὁ λόγος. Καλῶς οὖν εἶπεν Ἐν ἀρχῇ ἦν ὁ λόγος, ἦν γὰρ ἐν τῷ υἱῷ· καὶ Ὁ λόγος ἦν πρὸς τὸν θεόν, καὶ γὰρ ἡ ἀρχή· καὶ Θεὸς ἦν ὁ λόγος ἀκολούθως, τὸ γὰρ ἐκ θεοῦ γεννηθὲν θεός ἐστιν. οὗτος ἦν ἐν ἀρχῇ πρὸς τὸν θεόν, ἔδειξε τὴν τῆς προβολῆς τάξιν.

[2] The next sentence appears to contain a retrospective argument justifying the ascription of Deity to the Logos, as in i. 1, by the subsequent ascription of Deity to the Monogenes (=Arche=Noῦs), as in i. 18, which would imply the presence of θεός in each verse. But in other respects the language is obscure, and probably corrupt.

[3] Without referring to the *Hypotyposes*, which must be a late work, Heinrici (l.c. 12 f.) places the Excerpts and the cognate *Eclogae Propheticae* in Clement's youth, about 170—180. His argument is not convincing.

other or 'Italian' School, and thus the coincidence would have to be traced to Valentinus as the common source of both schools. But this assumption cannot be trusted, and we must be content to take Clement's author as probably belonging to the same period as Ptolemæus.

Irenæus himself thrice quotes i 18, "Deus qui fecit terram... hic et benedictionem escae...per Filium suum donat humano generi, incomprehensibilis per comprehensibilem et invisibilis per visibilem, cum extra eum non sit sed in sinu Patris exsistat. *Deum enim*, inquit, *nemo vidit unquam nisi unigenitus Filius Dei qui est in sinu Patris, ipse enarravit*. Patrem enim invisibilem existentem ille quia in sinu ejus est Filius omnibus enarrat" (p. 189). "Deus...qualis et quantus est, invisibilis et inenarrabilis est omnibus quae ab eo facta sunt, incognitus autem nequaquam, omnia enim per Verbum ejus discunt,... quemadmodum in evangelio scriptum est, *Deum nemo vidit unquam nisi unigenitus Filius qui est in sinu Patris, ipse enarravit*. Enarrat ergo ab initio Filius Patris, quippe qui ab initio est cum Patre, &c." (p. 255). "Manifestum est quoniam Pater quidem invisibilis, de quo et Dominus dixit, *Deum nemo vidit unquam*. Verbum autem ejus...claritatem monstrabat Patris... quemadmodum et Dominus dixit, *Unigenitus Deus qui est in sinu Patris, ipse enarravit*" (p. 256). The Greek original being lost, the text may be due either to Irenæus or to his translator, who frequently transcribes an Old Latin version of the New Testament when he comes to a quotation, even in cases where the extant Greek shews that Irenæus had other readings. Now the two former quotations coincide exactly (waiving *Dei*[1]) with most Old Latin authorities[2], even to the insertion of the characteristic *nisi*: the *Deus* of the third quotation is unknown to Latin texts of St John, and therefore doubtless represents the Greek. The only question that can reasonably arise is

---

[1] Itself found in q.

[2] Not it is true the oldest. But this is of no consequence except on Massuet's groundless theory that Irenæus was known to Tertullian through the translation. There is no real evidence, as Dodwell has shown, for an earlier date than the fourth century.

whether Irenæus followed different texts in different places, or *Filius* was introduced by the translator. But the close proximity of the two latter quotations is unfavourable to the supposition of a variation in the original Greek, and the addition of *Dei* after *Filius* in the first passage savours of a corrective combination of a Latin *Filius* with a Greek θεός[1]. In neither case is the context available as evidence; for though it contains references to sonship, they are such as might easily be founded on the single word μονογενής. Irenæus therefore read μονογενὴς θεός at least once, and there is no solid evidence that he ever read otherwise.

Hippolytus the disciple of Irenæus, in the fragment against Noetus now generally recognised to be the close of a larger work, which is almost certainly the lost early *Syntagma* against Heresies[2], has the following sentence: Ὁρῶν δὲ τὸν θεὸν οὐδ' εἰς εἰ μὴ μόνος ὁ παῖς καὶ τέλειος ἄνθρωπος καὶ μόνος διηγησάμενος τὴν βουλὴν τοῦ πατρός· λέγει γὰρ καὶ Ἰωάννης Θεὸν οὐδεὶς ἑώρακεν πώποτε, μονογενὴς υἱὸς ὁ ὢν εἰς τὸν κόλπον τοῦ πατρὸς αὐτὸς διηγήσατο (c. 5 p. 47 Lag.). It is to be regretted that the text depends on Fabricius's editing of a modern copy of a single Vatican MS.; and the context is neutral. There is however no sufficient reason for doubting that Hippolytus read υἱός, but without the preliminary article. The *Syntagma* must have been written in the last decade of the second century[3]: the later Hippolytean remains are barren of evidence.

Clement himself quotes the whole verse once only (*Strom.* v p. 695), and then reads ὁ μονογενὴς θεός. He adds that St John gives the name κόλπος θεοῦ to τὸ ἀόρατον καὶ ἄρρητον, and this remark explains the combination of τὸν κόλπον τοῦ πατρός with

---

[1] Compare the similar case of Origen, pp. 35 f., 38.

[2] See especially Lipsius *Zur Quellenkritik d. Epiphanios*, 37 ff.; *Die Quellen d. ält. Ketzergesch.* 128 ff.

[3] So Lipsius, *Q. Ep.* 33—43, and much better *Q. Ketz.* 137 ff. Harnack (*Zeitschrift f. d. hist. Theol.* 1874 191 ff.) places it in the following decade: but, after Volkmar, he refers the fragment against Noetus to a supposed treatise against all Monarchians, for which, if I understand him rightly (p. 183), he accepts the date assigned by Lipsius to the *Syntagma*.

ἐξηγήσατο[1] in a sentence in his tract *De divite salvando* (p. 956), θεῷ τὰ τῆς ἀγάπης μυστήρια, καὶ τότε ἐποπτεύσεις τὸν κόλπον τοῦ πατρός, ὃν ὁ μονογενὴς υἱὸς θεὸς μόνος ἐξηγήσατο· ἔστι δὲ καὶ αὐτὸς ὁ θεὸς ἀγάπη καὶ δι' ἀγάπην ἡμῖν ἀνεκράθη· καὶ τὸ μὲν ἄρρητον αὐτοῦ πατήρ κ.τ.λ. Here υἱός and θεός stand side by side, and it may be that the two readings are combined: but it is more likely that υἱός was inserted simply to soften the peculiar combination ὁ μονογενὴς θεός; just as elsewhere Clement (*Exc. Theod.* p. 969), in controverting the Valentinian interpretation already cited, inserts λόγος, perhaps from the familiar Alexandrine form θεὸς λόγος founded on John i 1: ἡμεῖς δὲ τὸν ἐν ταυτότητι λόγον θεὸν ἐν θεῷ φαμέν, ὃς καὶ εἰς τὸν κόλπον τοῦ πατρὸς εἶναι λέγεται, ἀδιάστατος, ἀμέριστος, εἷς θεός· πάντα δι' αὐτοῦ ἐγένετο κατὰ τὴν προσεχῆ ἐνέργειαν τοῦ ἐν ταυτότητι λόγου...οὗτος τὸν κόλπον τοῦ πατρὸς ἐξηγήσατο, ὁ σωτήρ. And the process is carried a step further in an allusion which drops θεός but retains λόγος (*Paed.* i p. 102): πῶς γὰρ οὐ φιλεῖται δι' ὃν ὁ μονογενὴς ἐκ κόλπων πατρὸς καταπέμπεται λόγος τῆς πίστεως; It will be observed that there is no trace of υἱός except in the passage from the tract *De divite*, where the subject, ἀγάπη, would have rendered the introduction of λόγος inappropriate.

Origen's extant quotations of the verse are confined to his commentary on St John's Gospel and his treatise against Celsus. Commenting on John i 7, he transcribes the whole passage 15—18 (iv 89 Ru.), reading ὁ μονογενὴς θεός. Unfortunately we do not possess his exposition of the passage itself, his third, fourth, and fifth tomes being lost. The sixth tome begins, after the preface, with i 19, treating the 'witness of John' as a second witness of his, that is, of the Baptist, and arguing against Heracleon who had attributed v. 18 (though strangely not 16, 17) to the Evangelist. He thus sets up a former witness of John, as ἀρξαμένης ἀπὸ τοῦ Οὗτος ἦν ὃν εἶπον Ὁ ὀπίσω μου ἐρχόμενος, καὶ λεγούσης εἰς τό Ὁ μονογενὴς υἱὸς τοῦ

[1] The same combination occurs, as we shall see (pp. 48 f.), in early Latin authorities.

θεοῦ (or υἱὸς θεὸς) ὁ ὢν εἰς τὸν κόλπον τοῦ πατρὸς ἐκεῖνος ἐξηγήσατο (iv 102). The variation of reading is here significant. The Benedictine text adopts υἱὸς τοῦ θεοῦ from the Bodleian MS.[1], while Huet reads υἱὸς θεός[2] with the Paris MS. It is hard to believe that in a *verbal* citation of this kind Origen would have inserted the superfluous τοῦ θεοῦ, and υἱὸς τοῦ θεοῦ is quite like a scribe's correction of υἱὸς θεός; while this phrase is too peculiar to have been substituted for υἱὸς τοῦ θεοῦ, yet might easily be written by Origen, either as a combination of the two alternative readings which certainly existed in his time, or to provide against possible misinterpretation. No inference can be drawn from the loose form of expression a few lines further down, when he pleads for the consistency of supposing τὸ τὸν μονογενῆ εἰς τὸν κόλπον ὄντα τοῦ πατρὸς τὴν ἐξήγησιν αὐτῷ (the Baptist) καὶ πᾶσι τοῖς ἐκ τοῦ πληρώματος εἰληφόσι παραδεδωκέναι. In his 32nd tome the description of St John as reclining ἐν τῷ κόλπῳ τοῦ Ἰησοῦ occasions the remark that he ἀνέκειτο ἐν τοῖς κόλποις τοῦ λόγου, ἀνάλογον τῷ καὶ αὐτὸν εἶναι ἐν τοῖς κόλποις τοῦ πατρός, κατὰ τό Ὁ μονογενὴς θεὸς ὁ ὢν εἰς τὸν κόλπον τοῦ πατρὸς ἐκεῖνος ἐξηγήσατο (iv 438), where the selection of the term λόγος confirms what appears to be the reading of all the MSS. Again in the second of the books against Celsus (c. 71 i 440 Ru.), which are transmitted in a different set of MSS. from those of the commentary on St John, we find: Ἐδίδαξε δὲ ἡμᾶς ὁ Ἰησοῦς καὶ ὅστις ἦν ὁ πέμψας ἐν τῷ Οὐδεὶς ἔγνω τὸν πατέρα εἰ μὴ ὁ υἱός καὶ τῷ Θεὸν οὐδεὶς ἑώρακε πώποτε· ὁ μονογενής γε ὢν θεὸς ὁ ὢν εἰς τὸν κόλπον τοῦ πατρὸς ἐκεῖνος ἐξηγήσατο· ἐκεῖνος θεολογῶν ἀπήγγειλε τὰ περὶ θεοῦ τοῖς γνησίοις αὐτοῦ μαθηταῖς. Such is the reading of one of

[1] *Prima facie* the lost Venice MS. used by Ferrari for his Latin version might appear to have read the same, as Ferrari has *Filius Dei*. But it is morally certain that he would have rendered υἱὸς θεός likewise by *Filius Dei*; since in the two other quotations, where there is no υἱός to help him, he gets rid of θεός by simple omission, adding nothing after *Unigenitus*.

[2] The silence of the collator of the Barberini MS. favours this reading, as he can have had no other standard than Huet's edition. But the collation is evidently too imperfect to be trusted negatively.

Höschel's two MSS., confirmed by Gelenius's Latin version, *Unigenitus quippe Dei Deus;* Höschel's other MS. merely substituting καὶ μονογενής for ὁ μονογενής. The Benedictine text has the received reading ὁ μονογενὴς υἱός, but only on the authority of the Basel and Paris MSS., two closely related representatives of a single archetype, abounding in excellent readings but also in manifest corruptions. The silence of De la Rue as to his other MSS. (about six) implies the absence of at least any recorded difference from Höschel's readings. The combination of θεολογῶν with τὰ περὶ θεοῦ in the closing paraphrase moreover suggests the presence of θεός following on the initial θεόν[1]. To these four quotations may be added the following places,—the list is doubtless not exhaustive,—where the detached phrase is used. Τῶν τετιμημένων ἀπὸ θεοῦ διὰ τοῦ μονογενοῦς θεοῦ λόγου μετοχῇ θεότητος διὰ τοῦτο δὲ καὶ ὀνόματι (*Cels.* iii 37 p. 471 Ru.). Πῶς δεῖ ἀκούειν περὶ μονογενοῦς θεοῦ υἱοῦ τοῦ θεοῦ, τοῦ πρωτοτόκου πάσης κτίσεως (*Cels.* vii 43 p. 725). Τὸ πρωτότυπον πάντων ἀγαλμάτων, τὴν εἰκόνα τοῦ θεοῦ τοῦ ἀοράτου, τὸν μονογενῆ θεόν (*Cels.* viii 17 p. 755). Ὕμνους γὰρ εἰς μόνον τὸν ἐπὶ πᾶσι λέγομεν θεὸν καὶ τὸν μονογενῆ αὐτοῦ λόγον καὶ θεόν· καὶ ὑμνοῦμέν[2] γε θεὸν καὶ τὸν μονογενῆ αὐτοῦ ὡς καὶ ἥλιος καὶ σελήνη καὶ ἄστρα καὶ πᾶσα ἡ οὐρανία στρατία· ὑμνοῦσι γὰρ πάντες οὗτοι, θεῖος ὄντες χορός, μετὰ τῶν ἐν ἀνθρώποις δικαίων τὸν ἐπὶ πᾶσι θεὸν καὶ τὸν μονογενῆ

---

[1] Ὁ...γὲ ὤν singles out μ. or μ. θ.

[2] Origen can hardly be introducing here the language of an actual hymn, as the context shews. Celsus has been rebuking the Christians for their scruples against consenting to join in a pæan to a heavenly body or a goddess, ἐὰν δὲ κελεύῃ τις εὐφημῆσαι τὸν ἥλιον ἢ τὴν Ἀθηνᾶν, προθυμότατα μετὰ καλοῦ παιᾶνος εὐφημεῖν· οὕτω τοι σέβειν μᾶλλον δόξεις τὸν μέγαν θεὸν ἐὰν καὶ τούσδε ὑμνῇς. The reply is Οὐ περιμένομεν εὐφημῆσαι τὸν ἥλιον τὸν κελεύοντα, οἱ μαθόντες οὐ μόνον τοὺς τῇ διατάξει ὑποτεταγμένους εὐφημεῖν, ἀλλὰ καὶ τοὺς ἐχθρούς· εὐφημοῦμεν οὖν ἥλιον ὡς καλὸν θεοῦ δημιούργημα, καὶ τοὺς νόμους φύλασσον θεοῦ, καὶ ἄκουον τοῦ Αἰνεῖτε τὸν κύριον, ἥλιος καὶ σελήνη (Ps. cxlviii 3), καὶ ὅσῃ δύναμις ὑμνοῦν τόν τε (so read for ὑμνεῖτε τὸν and ὑμνοῦντα τὸν of the MSS.) πατέρα καὶ τὸν δημιουργὸν τοῦ παντός· Ἀθηνᾶν μέντοι μετὰ ἡλίου τασσομένην κ.τ.λ....πολλῷ μᾶλλον οὐ χρὴ ὑμνῆσαι καὶ ὡς θεὸν δοξάσαι τὴν Ἀθηνᾶν, εἴγε οὐδὲ τὸν τηλικοῦτον ἥλιον προσκυνεῖν ἡμῖν θέμις, κἂν εὐφημῶμεν αὐτόν. Then follows the passage in the text, as an answer to Celsus's second sentence.

38   ON THE WORDS ΜΟΝΟΓΕΝΗC ΘΕΟC

αὐτοῦ (*Cels.* viii 67 p. 792): for λόγον καὶ θεόν Hoeschel has θεὸν λόγον, probably rightly. "Qui enim &c., et qui in medio etiam nescientium se consistit, Unigenitus Dei est Deus Verbum et sapientia et justitia et veritas &c.: secundum hanc divinitatis suae naturam non peregrinatur &c.": and after a few sentences, "Speciem autem dicimus Verbi et sapientiae et veritatis et justitiae et pacis et omnium quidquid est Unigenitus Deus" (*In Matt. Com. Ser.* 65 iii 883). "Unigenitus ergo Deus[1] Salvator noster, solus a Patre generatus, natura et non adoptione filius est. ... Sed [Deus] ... factus est Verbi pater, quod Verbum in sinum Patris requiescens annuntiat Deum quem nemo vidit unquam, et revelat Patrem quem nemo cognovit nisi ipse solus, his quod ad eum Pater caelestis attraxerit" (quoted from the second book on St John in Pamph. *Apol. pro Orig.* c. 5). Lastly the most plausible instance of a seeming testimony to the reading υἱός in any form of Origen's writings is in Rufinus's version of the commentary on Canticles: "Possumus...etiam hoc addere quod *promurale* (Cant. ii 14) sinus sit Patris, in quo positus unigenitus Filius enarrat omnia et enuntiat ecclesiae suae quaecunque in secretis et in absconditis Patris sinibus continentur: unde et quidam ab eo edoctus dicebat *Deum nemo vidit unquam: Unigenitus Dei Filius qui est in sinu Patris ipse enarravit*" (iii 81). Yet here too the evidence doubly breaks down. Had *Filius* stood alone, the Greek quotations would have suggested that, as in many undoubted cases of doctrinal phraseology, the translator's very free hand introduced the Latin reading. But we have *Dei Filius*, that is, one more instance of a disguised θεός.

[1] Two pages earlier Pamphilus quotes from the *fifth* book on St John the single sentence, "Unigenitus Filius Salvator noster, qui solus ex Patre natus est, solus natura et non adoptione filius est." If, as seems probable (for the manifestly incomplete state of our second book renders superfluous the natural suggestion that II may be a corruption of v), the two passages are distinct, no allusion to John i 18 is perceptible *here*. If they are identical, the words that follow in the longer quotation suggest that *Unigenitus Deus* rather than *Unigenitus Filius* is the true reading, though ὁ μονογενὴς υἱὸς θεός is also possible; in any case their own reference to i 18 contains not *Filius* but *Verbum*, which implies θεός.

The first five books of Origen on St John were written about the second decade of the third century, the sixth not long afterwards, the later books, including the 22nd and therefore doubtless the 32nd, after 235, the treatise against Celsus between 244 and 249. Thus our quotations cover a long period, and proceed alike from Alexandria and from Palestine.

The epistle addressed to Paul of Samosata by certain bishops assembled at Antioch between 260 and 270[1] quotes the verse with υἱός and the article (ap. Routh *R. S.* iii 297). The doubts which have been raised as to the genuineness and age of the epistle appear to be unfounded. Its theology fits well into the third century; while the text of its quotations from the New Testament is mostly good, and entirely free, John i 18 excepted, from early 'Western' readings. As in the case of Hippolytus, the text of the epistle appears to rest on a single Roman MS. Two other passages probably contain the phrase μονογενὴς θεός, as has been already noticed (p. 19): but it has become detached from John i 18; and there is at present no sufficient reason to doubt that ὁ μονογενὴς υἱός was read there.

The Acts of the disputation alleged to have been held in Mesopotamia between Archelaus and Mani should perhaps be noticed here, though it is doubtful whether they belong to the last quarter of the third century or the first quarter of the fourth. The ancient Latin translation has (c. 32) "Dominum nemo vidit unquam nisi unigenitus Filius qui est in sinu Patris"; where once more the presence of the Latin insertion *nisi* throws some doubt on the whole reading: elsewhere the quotations shew clear traces of modification, though not of transcription, from Latin texts of the New Testament. This part of the Acts has been printed only from a Vatican copy of a Monte Cassino MS.

In Eusebius of Cæsarea we have the last virtually Antenicene writer, that is, whose training belongs to the days before

---

[1] It is unnecessary here to attempt greater definiteness, the chronology of the proceedings against Paul being singularly difficult.

Constantine. The clearest evidence for our purpose is furnished by two of his latest treatises, those against Marcellus, written in 336. Both treatises abound in the detached phrase ὁ μονογενὴς υἱός; but there is no reference to John i 18 till a few pages after the beginning of the second and longer work, *De ecclesiastica theologia*, where Eusebius says τοῦ τε εὐαγγελιστοῦ διαρρήδην αὐτὸν υἱὸν μονογενῆ εἶναι διδάσκοντος, δι' ὧν ἔφη Θεὸν οὐδεὶς ἑώρακε πώποτε· ὁ μονογενὴς υἱός, ἢ μονογενὴς θεός, ἐκεῖνος ἐξηγήσατο (p. 67 D). No one can doubt that Eusebius here adopts the reading υἱός: but it is wholly arbitrary to reject the clause ἢ μονογενὴς θεός as a gloss of scribes[1]. It would be difficult to find any similar interpolation of theirs in a scriptural quotation, especially if it introduced for once a reading which elsewhere they persecute. It is more likely that Eusebius, familiar as he must have been with the reading θεός through his Origenian lore, took advantage of this first quotation to indicate in passing that, while he adhered to his own reading, he did not care to rest his case upon it[2]. Accordingly, having thus appealed to "the evangelist", he goes on at once to claim the yet greater authority of "the Saviour Himself" whom he supposes to have spoken John iii 16, which contains τὸν υἱόν αὐτοῦ τὸν μονογενῆ. At p. 86 A he again quotes the verse, with a context which confirms υἱός, and again at p 142 C, with a neutral context; and υἱός recurs for the fourth time in a clear allusion at p. 92 D. On the other hand in a solitary passage the sentence ὁ δὲ ἐπέκεινα τῶν ὅλων θεὸς καὶ πατὴρ τοῦ κυρίου ἡμῶν Ἰησοῦ Χριστοῦ...μόνος εἰκότως ὁ ἐπὶ πάντων

---

[1] It has been urged in favour of this conjecture that in a quotation of 1 Tim. i 15 by Origen (*c. Cels.* i 63 p. 378 Ru.), Hoeschel's text has πιστὸς ὁ λόγος ὅτι Ἰησοῦς Χριστὸς ὁ θεὸς ἦλθεν εἰς τὸν κόσμον ἁμαρτωλοὺς σῶσαι. Such a wild collocation as the supposed "gloss" is evidence of nothing. It can be only a blunder of a scribe or the editor, probably Ο ΘΣ ΗΛΘΕΝ for ΕΙΣΗΛΘΕΝ.

[2] Marcellus (see pp. 20, 22) used the phrase τὸν μονογενῆ θεόν (Eus. c. Marc. p. 19 c); and his theological tendency was to evade the idea of Divine Sonship. On both grounds there would be force in a refusal of Eusebius to haggle about the various reading.

καὶ διὰ κ.τ.λ. θεὸς ἀνείρηται παρὰ τῷ ἀποστόλῳ φάντι (Eph. iv 6) is continued by καὶ μόνος μὲν αὐτὸς εἷς θεὸς καὶ πατὴρ τοῦ κυρίου ἡμῶν Ἰησοῦ Χριστοῦ χρηματίζοι ἄν, ὁ δὲ υἱὸς μονογενὴς θεὸς ὁ ὢν εἰς τὸν κόλπον τοῦ πατρός, τὸ δὲ παράκλητον πνεῦμα οὔτε θεὸς οὔτε υἱός (p. 174 f.). It is vain to urge that χρηματίζοι ἄν is not the same as ἀνείρηται παρὰ τῷ ἀποστόλῳ, where the title maintained for the Son is found verbally in a single verse of Scripture, and where the preceding title is likewise transcribed from Scripture (2 Cor. i 3 &c.) with the exception of the word εἷς used just above[1]. Corruption of text is also unlikely, as υἱός could hardly stand here in both subject and predicate, to say nothing of intrinsic improbability[2]. Doubtless therefore Eusebius did on this occasion for a special purpose avail himself of the reading[3] to which he habitually preferred another. It probably never occurred to him that one of the two must be right, and the other wrong: an inability to part absolutely with either of two respectable traditions is not unusual in his writings. Lastly υἱός stands, with neutral contexts but probably rightly, in two of Eusebius's Commentaries, on Psalm

---

[1] Indeed εἷς has so little force here, as an adjunct, that it becomes suspicious. It may represent ὁ (ΕΙΣΘΣ for ΘΣ); or Eusebius may have written εἷς θεὸς ὁ πατήρ [1 Cor. viii 6, quoted p. 93] καὶ ὁ θεὸς καὶ πατὴρ τοῦ κυρίου κ.τ.λ., the intervening words ὁ πατὴρ καὶ ὁ θεός being lost by homœoteleuton.

[2] The concluding words οὔτε θεὸς οὔτε υἱός are probably all in antithesis to the second clause ὁ δὲ υἱός...πατρός; and, if so, they imply θεός, whether they refer to the alternative readings (as at p. 67 D), or simply take up υἱός from the beginning of the clause. But it is not impossible to take οὔτε θεός as in antithesis to the first clause καὶ μόνος...χρηματίζοι ἄν.

[3] Passages like the following shew that it could not have been a stumbling-block to his own mind on the score of doctrine, though ὁ μονογενὴς υἱός had a sharper edge against Marcellus: indeed the first (on which more hereafter) substantially contains it. Καὶ τῷ πατρὶ ὡς υἱὸν διὰ παντὸς συνόντα, καὶ οὐκ ἀγέννητον ὄντα γεννώμενον δ' ἐξ ἀγεννήτου πατρός, μονογενῆ ὄντα λόγον τε καὶ θεὸν ἐκ θεοῦ (Dem. Ev. IV 3 p. 149 A). Διὸ δὴ εἷς θεὸς τῇ ἐκκλησίᾳ τοῦ θεοῦ κηρύττεται, καὶ οὐκ ἔστιν ἕτερος πλὴν αὐτοῦ· εἷς δὲ καὶ μονογενὴς τοῦ θεοῦ υἱός, εἰκὼν τῆς πατρικῆς θεότητος, καὶ διὰ τοῦτο θεός (Eccl. Th. p. 62 A). Τὸ γὰρ πρόσωπον τοῦ θεοῦ λόγου καὶ ἡ θεότης τοῦ μονογενοῦς υἱοῦ τοῦ θεοῦ θνητῇ φύσει οὐκ ἂν γένοιτο καταληπτή (Com. in Es. 375 D).

lxxiv (lxxiii) 11¹ without the article, and on Isaiah vi 1² with the article.

---

¹ In Montfaucon, *Coll. No. Patr.* I 440. A freely condensed extract in Corder's *Catena*, II 535, has the article.

² In Montfaucon, *ib.* II 374. The comment of Procopius, p. 91, founded here chiefly on Eusebius but perhaps also on Origen, has ὁ μονογενὴς τοῦ θεοῦ λόγος ὁ ὢν κ.τ.λ.

Note B

The details of Latin evidence

The Latin patristic evidence is properly speaking only a branch of the evidence of Latin versions. So far as it refers clearly to St John's own text, it supports υἱός exclusively. Tertullian's citations, all occurring, as is not unnatural, in the single treatise against Praxeas, are in no case quite verbal; but they leave no reasonable doubt. He says (not to quote references to the first clause only), "Apud nos autem solus *Filius Patrem novit*, et *sinum Patris ipse exposuit*, et *omnia apud Patrem audivit et vidit*", &c. (c. 8); "*Deum nemo vidit unquam*: quem Deum? Sermonem? Atquin, *Vidimus et audivimus* [*et contrectavimus*] *de sermone vitae*, praedictum est: sed quem Deum? scilicet Patrem *apud quem Deus erat Sermo, unigenitus Filius* qui *sinum Patris ipse disseruit*" (c. 15, some early editors for *sinum* reading *est in sinu*, and Rigaut [1634, ? on MS. authority] simply *in sinum*); "Hujus *gloria visa est tanquam unici a patre*, non tanquam Patris: hic unius (? *Unicus*[1]) *sinum Patris disseruit*, non sinum suum Pater, praecedit enim, *Deum nemo vidit unquam*" (c. 21). Cyprian does not quote the verse; but had he read *Deus*, he would probably have used it in his *Testimonies* (ii 6) under the head *Quod Deus Christus*, the texts of which from the New Testament are Matt. i 23; Jo. i 1; (x 34—38;) xx 27 ff.; Apoc. xxi 6 f. The same may be said of Novatian (*de Regula Fidei* 11, 13, 14, 18, &c.), and is probably to be inferred from the only pas-

---

[1] Pamèle's reading *unus*, which is probably likewise conjectural, deserves mention, as it might represent εἷς (see next note): but *Unicus* makes as good sense, and was more likely to be altered.

sage in which he alludes to this clause, being part of an argument to shew that Christ is *idem Angelus et Deus:* "Manifeste apparet non Patrem ibi tunc loquutum fuisse ad Agar, sed Christum potius, cum Deus sit; cui etiam angeli competit nomen, quippe cum *magni consilii Angelus* factus sit, angelus autem sit dum *exponit sinum Patris,* sicut Joannes edicit: si enim ipse Joannes hunc eundem, *qui sinum exponit Patris, Verbum* dicit *carnem factum esse,* ut *sinum Patris* possit *exponere,* merito Christus non solum homo est sed et angelus; nec angelus tantum sed et Deus per scripturas ostenditur, et a nobis hoc esse creditur" (c. 18). It will be observed that to both Tertullian and Novatian the last words of the verse must have stood as *sinum Patris [ipse] exposuit* (Tert.[1] Nov.[3]) or *sinum Patris ipse disseruit* (Tert.[2], perhaps his own rendering, as it occurs nowhere else), and we have the same construction with a different Latin verb in *a*, the oldest of existing Old Latin MSS., which reads "Deum nemo vidit umquam nisi unicus Filius solus sinum Patris ipse enarravit[1]." These primitive forms of the Old Latin rendering were smoothed away by degrees. The inserted *nisi*[2], probably derived from vi 46, vanishes only in the Vulgate and one or two other late revisions (f q). *Unicus*[3] is exchanged for *unigenitus,* and *sinum* for *qui est in sinu,* with hardly an exception. *Solus* lingers only in

---

[1] Tischendorf calls attention to the coincidence of this part of the rendering of *a* (he might have added Tertullian and Novatian) with the omission of ὁ ὤν in ℵ*, suggesting that εἰς was read as εἷς: and apparently with good reason, for ℵ* has readings hereabouts in common with what must have been the original of the Old Latin in an early form, and *solus* stands for εἷς in many authorities in Mark ii 7, and several in x 18, both passages having a similar turn. The correction was probably suggested by ἐξηγήσατο, for transitive verbs used absolutely are always a distress to scribes and translators. As we have seen, Clement likewise supplies τὸν κόλπον τοῦ πατρός in interpretation.

[2] There is no Greek authority of any kind, as far as I am aware, for *nisi:* it might of course be introduced from vi 46 in Latin as easily as in Greek.

[3] Retained only, it would seem, by the Manichean Adimantus as cited by Augustine (*c. Adim.* VIII 2 t. viii p. 120 bis). *Sinum Patris* gives place altogether to *in sinu Patris* (*in Patre c*). But negative statements as to the Latin quotations could not be made quite confidently without disproportionate labour.

mm, and probably other revised MSS. of the same group. The final verb is represented pretty constantly[1] by *enarravit*, varying occasionally (after *ipse*, it will be remembered) into *narravit*. The final form, as it stands in the present MSS. of the Vulgate, answers exactly to the prevalent Greek text: "Deum nemo vidit umquam; unigenitus Filius, qui est in sinu Patris, ipse[2] enarravit." This statement includes the Latin Fathers of the fourth and following centuries, and it is needless to give references: various types of Old Latin are represented, as the names of Victorinus, Vigilius, Hilary, Ambrose, and Augustine will sufficiently shew.

[1] Adimantus (l. c.) has *adnuntiavit*: Victorinus once (*adv. Ar.* i 2) *exposuit* with Tertullian and Novatian, elsewhere *enarravit*.

[2] *Ipse* similarly represents ἐκεῖνος in ix 37, and in scattered authorities elsewhere. Like αὐτός, which is to be found in Greek quotations but not MSS., it was evidently suggested by the apparent sense.

NOTE C

Some details of Æthiopic evidence

Dr Wright has most kindly ascertained the texts of the two MSS. at Cambridge, and of the nineteen in the British Museum. They singularly illustrate the truth of Dr Tregelles's account of the Æthiopic version (Horne's *Introduction* iv 319 f.), which has been questioned of late, being all paraphrastic, and exhibiting no less than 12 combinations of readings, owing in part to the addition of pronouns, and the insertion of conjunctions in various places. Nineteen MSS. are of the 17th century or later: of the remaining two, ascribed to the fifteenth, one (B.M. Or. 525) agrees *prima manu* with the Polyglott. The accusative particle is here prefixed to μονογενὴς θεός, doubtless owing to a misinterpretation natural in a language incapable of expressing μονογενής otherwise than by a word like *unicus* (*wahed*), since it was not to be supposed that "the only God" denoted the Son. To μονογενὴς θεός (or -νῆ -όν) six other MSS. add υἱός followed by *wahed*, which in this second place probably stands for μόνος or εἶς; two of them (including the other 15th century copy, B.M. Or. 507) having μονογενὴς θεός, the other four the accusative form. This interpolation supplied another possible construction for the accusative *unicum Deum*: it could be taken either simply in apposition to the previous θεόν (*Deum nemo vidit unquam, unicum Deum:* [*Filius unicus*] *qui* &c.), or as the object of ἐξηγήσατο (*unicum Deum* [*Filius unicus*] *qui est in sinu…enarravit*), or as the object of an intermediate clause (*unicum Deum* [sc. *vidit*] *Filius unicus* (or *unus*): *qui est* &c.): all three constructions seem to be indicated by punctuation and conjunctions in different MSS. An eighth MS.

omits μονογενής, retaining θεὸς υἱὸς *wahed*. The remaining thirteen likewise omit θεός. The probable sequence was as follows, the position of the second *wahed* in all known MSS. being fatal to other interpretations of the facts which might be suggested. The original text (preserved now, as far as the MSS. yet examined shew, only with the accusative modification) had μονογενὴς θεός, the Memphitic reading. With this was next combined the alternative reading υἱός, accompanied by *wahed*, either a relic of the early reading mentioned in Note B or a like but independent interpolation: similar couplets of readings originally alternative are not uncommon in this version[1]. The first *wahed* would then be dropped as a needless superfluity in MSS. which escaped the accusative prefix: and lastly the further omission of θεός would reduce the phrase to a familiar shape. The evidence is not very important; but its history is instructive.

The verse is closed by a gloss from Heb. i 2 in one of the seventeenth century MSS. which omits μονογενὴς θεός (B.M. Or. 521).

---

[1] It is possible, but much less likely, that the Æthiopic had originally the double reading, and that υἱὸς *wahed* was then omitted in some MSS.

Note D

Unicus *and* unigenitus *among the Latins*

The varieties in the Latin rendering of μονογενής in the New Testament are sufficiently interesting to be given in full. Sabatier's references have of course been freely used.

I *Passages referring to our Lord*

John i 14 δόξαν ὡς μονογενοῦς παρὰ πατρός.
- A *unici (a patre)* Tert.$^{\frac{1}{2}}$ (*Prax.* 21) Fr.Arian.(Mai, *S.V.N.C.* iii 2 228) Hil.$^{\frac{1}{2}}$(*Trin.* i 10 in comment.).
  unici (patris sic) e.
  unici filii (a patre) a.
  unici nati (a patre) Oros.[1](*Ap. de arb. lib.* 613 Hav.).
- B *unigeniti (a patre)* b c f vulg. Tert.$^{\frac{1}{2}}$(*Prax.*16) Novat. (*Reg. Fid.* 13) Hil.$^{\frac{1}{2}}$(*Trin.* i 10 text) Amb.[1](i 1204 F) Iren. lat.[2](42, 315) Aug.(*ad l. &c.*) Hieron.[1](Eph. v 33) &c.

John i 18 ὁ μονογενὴς υἱὸς ὁ ὢν εἰς τὸν κόλπον τοῦ πατρός.
- A *unicus (filius)* a Adimant.[1](ap. Aug. viii 120).
  unigenitus (filius) b c e f Tert.[1](*Prax.*15: cf.7) Hil.(*Ps.* 138 § 35 &c.) Victorin. Iren.lat. Amb. Aug. &c.

John iii 16 τὸν υἱὸν αὐτοῦ τὸν μονογενῆ ἔδωκεν.
- A *(filium suum) unicum* a b d e m g¹ gat mm mt Tert.[1](*Prax.* 21) Rebapt.[1](13) Fr.Arian.(226) Lucif.[1](151 Col.) Hil.cod. al.[3]
- B *(filium suum) unigenitum* c f ff vulg. Hil.[1](*Trin.* vi 40 cd.) Amb.(ii 406, 626) Aug. &c.

John iii 18 τὸ ὄνομα τοῦ μονογενοῦς υἱοῦ τοῦ θεοῦ.

IN SCRIPTURE AND TRADITION 49

A *unici* (*filii Dei*) a d Tert.(l.c.) Cyp.(*Test.* i 7; iii 31) (Fr. Arian. 226) Lucif.(l.c.)
B *unigeniti* (*filii Dei*) b c e f ff m vulg. Iren.lat.(325) Amb. (i 762) Aug.(ad l.) Vig.(*Trin.*213 Chif.) &c.

1 John iv 9 τὸν υἱὸν αὐτοῦ τὸν μονογενῆ ἀπέσταλκεν ὁ θεός.
A (*filium suum*) *unicum* m Lucif.(140).
B (*filium suum*) *unigenitum* vulg. Aug.(ad l.)

II *Other passages*

Luke vii 12 μονογενὴς υἱός (or *v. μ.*) τῇ μητρὶ αὐτοῦ.
A (*filius*) *unicus* all, including Amb. (waiving order).
Luke viii 42 θυγάτηρ μονογενὴς ἦν αὐτῷ.
A (*filia*) *unica* all, including Amb. (waiving order).
Luke ix 38 τὸν υἱόν μου, ὅτι μονογενής μοί ἐστιν (or ἐ. μοι).
A *unicus* (*mihi est*) all (waiving order).
Heb. xi 17 τὸν μονογενῆ προσέφερεν ὁ τὰς ἐπαγγελίας ἀναδεξάμενος.
A *unicum* (without *filium* or *suum*) d Ruf.[Orig.](*In Gen. Hom.* i 1, ii 81 Ru.) Aug.(*C.D.* xvi 32).
B *unigenitum* vulg.

In the canonical books of the Old Testament יָחִיד, the only Hebrew original of μονογενής, is uniformly rendered by *unigenitus* in the Vulgate where an only son or daughter is meant (Gen. xxii 2, 12, 16; Jud. xi 34; Prov. iv 3; Jer. vi 26; Am. viii 10; Zech. xii 10). Singularly enough the LXX has ἀγαπητός (ἀγαπώμενος Prov.) in all cases but that of Jephthah's daughter, though μονογενής was used by one or more of the other translators in at least five of the other places (no record being known for Gen. xxii 16; Zech.). But at least some form of the LXX must once have had μονογενής for Isaac[1] (the

[1] Gregory of Nyssa (*De Deit. F. et Sp. S.* iii 568 Migne) has Gen. xxii 2 Λαβέ μοι, φησί, τὸν υἱόν σου τὸν ἀγαπητόν, τὸν μονογενῆ, where μονογενῆ, if only a gloss on ἀγαπητόν, must at least have been found by Gregory in his MS., for he remarks in his comment πῶς ἀνεγείρει τὸ φίλτρον καὶ υἱὸν ἀγαπητόν καὶ μονογενῆ καλῶν, ὡς ἂν διὰ τῶν τοιούτων ὀνομάτων κ.τ.λ. This case

H.   4

Vatican MS is wanting here), for we have clear Old Latin authority accidentally preserved for *unicus* in Gen. xxii. 2, 12 and Judges, though most Old Latin quotations follow ἀγαπητός. *Unicus* is also the Old Latin word in three of the four remaining passages, all peculiar, Ps. xxii (xxi) 21; xxxv (xxxiv) 17 (*solitarius* Hier.); xxv (xxiv) 16 (*solus* Hier.). In the Apocrypha the uniform *unicus* of the Old Latin was not disturbed by Jerome; Tob. iii 15; vi 10 cod.; viii 17 or 19 (*duorum unicorum*, Tobias and Sarah); and even Sap. vii 22.

Thus throughout the Bible *unicus* is the earliest Old Latin representative of μονογενής; and *unigenitus* the Vulgate rendering of יָחִיד, however translated in Greek, except in St Luke and the Apocrypha, where Jerome left *unicus* untouched, and the four peculiar verses from the Psalter (lxviii [lxvii] 7, and the three already mentioned), in which he substituted other words. But *unicus* had been previously supplanted by *unigenitus* in one or more forms of the Old Latin in all the five passages where it has reference to our Lord, all occurring in St John's writings; and in the Prologue of the Gospel the change took place very early.

These facts would prove, if any proof were needed, that υἱός was the reading of the MS. or MSS. from which the Old Latin version was originally made; for *unicus Deus*[1] could never

---

renders it not unlikely that Irenæus is following a similar double reading when he speaks of Abraham (233) as τὸν ἴδιον μονογενῆ καὶ ἀγαπητὸν παραχωρήσας θυσίαν τῷ θεῷ, ἵνα καὶ ὁ θεὸς εὐδοκήσῃ...τὸν ἴδιον μονογενῆ καὶ ἀγαπητὸν υἱὸν θυσίαν παρασχεῖν κ.τ.λ. In Jud. xi 34 the Alex. and other MSS add to μονογενής without a conjunction αὐτῷ ἀγαπητή, and others αὐτῷ ἀγαπητή, περίψυκτος αὐτῷ.

[1] In Dr Swainson's *History of the Creeds* attention is called to a "not infrequent punctuation" of MSS. by which *unicum* is strangely separated from the preceding *Filium ejus* and joined to the following *Dominum nostrum* (pp. 163, 166, 365). He points out that this construction occurs in two sermons wrongly attributed to St Augustine: in one (240 in t. v p. 394 Ap.) it is at variance with the interpretation, and must be due to a scribe; in the other (t. vi p. 279 Ap.), a very late cento, it belongs to an extract from Ivo of Chartres, a pupil of Lanfranc. It is indeed, I find, as old as Rufinus, for he labours (*Com. in Symb.* 8 p. 71) to justify it, though evidently preferring (6 ff.) to take *unicum* with *Filium*. But *unicum Dominum nostrum* can hardly be more than a Latin

IN SCRIPTURE AND TRADITION

have been a designation of our Lord, and moreover it was actually applied to the Father in the Creed of Carthage in Tertullian's time (*De Virg. vel.* 1; *Adv. Prax.* 2 f.). But they also give additional interest to the almost uniform rule that *unicus* belongs to native Latin Creeds, *unigenitus* to comparatively late Greek Creeds translated into Latin, both alike having but one original, the μονογενής of St John's third chapter, if not also his first. It is needless to enumerate the various forms of what we call the Apostles' Creed, which have been several times collected. They all have *unicus*[1], (mostly in the order *Filium ejus unicum* as John iii 16, but the Aquileian form given by Rufinus[2] *unicum Filium ejus* as iii 18, and the Poictiers form used by Venantius Fortunatus [Hahn, *Bibl. d. Symb.* 33; Heurtley, *Harm. Symb.* 55] *unicum Filium* only) with the exception of two peculiar Gallican documents, closely related to each other, which have *unigenitum sempiternum* (Hahn, 35 f.; Heurtley, 68 f.)[3]. In Tertullian we have seen *unigenitus* (cf. *De An.* 12; *Scorp.* 7), possibly a word of his own coinage, side by side with *unicus*. But the influence of the Creed remained strong: a century and a half later Lucifer seems to have only *unicus*, which he repeats incessantly. Augustine vacillates between the Creed and his Latin MSS of the 'Italian' revision. Writing *de Fide et Symbolo* in 393 he puts *unigenitus* into the Creed but promptly explains it by the equivalent to which his hearers were more accustomed

---

blunder, arising from the separation of *unicum* from *Filium* by the genitive *ejus* and the immediate proximity of *Dominum*, together with the latitude of sense in *unicus*. In some Spanish Creeds the insertion of *Deum et* before *Dominum* (Swainson 164, 323) brings *unicum* and *Deum* into contact: but the resemblance to μονογενῆ θεόν can be only fortuitous.

[1] So also the Latin original of the Sirmium formulary of 357 (Hil. *De Syn.* 11 p. 466 A), notwithstanding the Greek cast of its language.

[2] This order cannot be safely assumed for the Roman and 'Eastern' forms to which he sometimes refers.

[3] In the *Te Deum* we have *verum et unicum Filium* in the common text, probably rightly: but in the present state of knowledge *unigenitum* must be admitted as an alternative reading. The *Gloria in excelsis* has *Domine Fili Unigenite Jesu Christe*, without apparent variation.

("*credimus* etiam *in Jesum Christum Filium Dei*, Patris unigenitum, id est *unicum*, *Dominum nostrum:* c. 3 t. vi p. 153 A), and twice afterwards repeats *unigenitus*. Nearly thirty years later in the *Enchiridion* he employs *unicus* (34, 35, 36 bis) till he has to quote John i 14, when he takes up for a moment the *unigenitus* of his version (36 s. f.), but in the next sentence slips back to the Creed by again combining both words, *unigenitus id est unicus:* and in the rest of the treatise he uses only *unicus* when commenting on the Creed (38, 56), *unigenitus* only with *Verbum* (41) or else absolutely (49, 56, 103, 108). But the influence of the Greek controversies of the fourth century upon Latin theology, the convenience of the antithesis to *ingenitus*, and the revision of Latin biblical texts secured the ultimate victory for the more explicit term *unigenitus*, except in the Creed itself. It is the word adopted in several private formularies, all imbued with the results of Greek thought; those of Pelagius (but with *Deum*, Hieron. *Opp.* xi 202 Vall.), Auxentius of Milan[1] (Hil. *Lib. c. Aux.* 14: cf. Caspari, *Quellen u. s. w.* ii 301), and Ulfilas (in Caspari 303)[2]. And from the fourth century onwards it is the constant rendering of μονογενής in all the Latin translations of Greek Creeds or other formularies, with hardly any exceptions and those in secondary authorities. Thus ten out of the eleven versions, or recensions of versions, of the original Nicene Creed collected by Walch (*Bibl. Symb.* 80 ff.) have *natum ex Patre unigenitum*, the eleventh[3] omitting the word: and five[4] out of the seven ver-

---

[1] The closely related formulary of Germinius of Sirmium has however *unicus* (Hil. *Op. Hist.* XIII—XV: cf. Caspari 302).

[2] Another attributed to Damasus and several other Fathers (Hahn 185) has *unigenitus*, but it appears to be a translation.

[3] As given by Lucifer (*De non parc.* p. 204 Col.). Singularly enough *unicus* occurs in what can be only a quotation from the Nicene Creed following on the already cited use of *uni-*genitus by Augustine in the *De fide et symbolo* (6 p. 154 B): "naturalis ergo Filius de ipsa Patris substantia unicus natus est, id exsistens quod Pater est, Deus de Deo, lumen de lumine." So also Gregory of Eliberis, if he is the author of the treatise *De fide orthodoxa* in the Appendix to Ambrose's works (ii 845).

[4] Dionysius Exiguus omits; the Code of Canons &c. of the Roman Church printed with Leo's works substitutes *unicum*.

sions or recensions of the 'Constantinopolitan' Creed, as quoted by Hahn (113), have *Filium Dei unigenitum*. The two renderings of μονογενής were unconsciously retained by Latin Christianity in the two Creeds throughout the Middle Ages, and the double tradition is still preserved by corresponding renderings in our own tongue.

Note E

On ΜΟΝΟΓΕΝΗC ΘΕΟC *in the Nicene Creed*

The second part of the original Nicene Creed begins thus:—
καὶ εἰς ἕνα κύριον Ἰησοῦν Χριστόν, τὸν υἱὸν τοῦ θεοῦ, γεννηθέντα ἐκ τοῦ πατρὸς μονογενῆ, τοῦτ' ἐστὶν ἐκ τῆς οὐσίας τοῦ πατρός, θεὸν ἐκ θεοῦ, φῶς ἐκ φωτός, θεὸν ἀληθινὸν ἐκ θεοῦ ἀληθινοῦ, γεννηθέντα, οὐ ποιηθέντα, ὁμοούσιον τῷ πατρί.
Then follows the recital of the Incarnation.

If now we withdraw the parenthetic clause τοῦτ' ἐστὶν ἐκ τῆς οὐσίας τοῦ πατρός, the words μονογενῆ and θεόν become contiguous. Is this contiguity accidental, so that μονογενῆ alone goes with γεννηθέντα, and a new clause in apposition is formed by θεὸν ἐκ θεοῦ, or should the eight words γεννηθέντα ἐκ τοῦ πατρὸς μονογενῆ θεὸν ἐκ θεοῦ be all read continuously, so that μονογενῆ belongs to θεόν? Neither alternative presents any grammatical difficulty; and thus the question must be decided by analogy and sense. The first step evidently is to investigate the probable origin of the passage. The enquiry must occupy a space disproportionately great if μονογενὴς θεός alone be considered: but it has to do with matters of sufficient historical interest to reward minute examination on other grounds.

It is certain (1) that the bulk of the Nicene Creed was taken from earlier formularies, one or more; and (2) that the three[1] clauses τοῦτ' ἐστὶν ἐκ τῆς οὐσίας τοῦ πατρός, γεννηθέντα οὐ ποιηθέντα, and ὁμοούσιον τῷ πατρί were novelties introduced by the Council with the special purpose of excluding ambiguity.

---

[1] Three for some purposes, howsoever the second and third may be grammatically related.

Athanasius in his old age, nearly half a century later, explained how the introduction of the new phrases had arisen (*De Decr. Nic. Syn.* 19 ff.; *Ad Afr.* 5 f.), and justified them, as he or others had evidently done at Nicæa, by reference to similar language of Theognostus, Dionysius of Rome, and Dionysius of Alexandria respectively (*De Decr.* 25 f.) : and this anxious appeal to theological writers sets in strong relief the absence of authority derived from public Creeds. In a different quarter the unwonted language of the three clauses elicited from Eusebius a somewhat reluctant apology in the epistle which he addressed to his own diocese shortly after the Council (*Ep. ad Caes.*, preserved by Athanasius *De Decr.* pp. 238 ff. and Socrates *H.E.* i 8). The testimony thus doubly borne renders it highly unlikely that the Nicene Creed contained other novelties not mentioned; and however modified in arrangement, the whole of its remaining contents may be assumed to have been taken from Creeds already in use.

The scattered and confused memorials of the Council afford little information as to the Creeds brought forward in the course of the discussions. Theodoret (*H.E.* i 6) mentions an exposition (ὑπαγορεύσαντες δὲ πίστεως διδασκαλίαν) which was presented to the assembly by the small group of bishops comparatively friendly to Arius, led by Eusebius of Nicomedia; and which was at once torn up. Eustathius of Antioch, an eye-witness, cited in Theodoret's next chapter, tells the same story of "the writing (γράμμα) of Eusebius's blasphemy," meaning evidently the same document[1], which was probably an elaborate private statement of doctrine. From the above-mentioned pastoral letter of Eusebius of Cæsarea, the leader of the middle party, we learn more. Its purpose is to explain the circum-

---

[1] Identical also, it would seem, with the "epistle" of Eusebius of Nicomedia from which Ambrose (*De Fide* iii 125) cites a sentence as having furnished the term ὁμοούσιος to his opponents. What is said by Philostorgius (*H.E.* i 7), or rather by Photius abridging his words, about the winning over of Hosius and other bishops by Alexander at Nicomedia before the Council has no necessary reference to the term itself.

stances which had led him after some hesitation to subscribe the Conciliar Creed, as he was afraid that incorrect rumours might cause misunderstanding[1]. "We first," he says, "transmit "to you the writing concerning the faith which was put forward "by us, and then the second, which they have published after "putting on additions to our expressions[2]. Now the writing "presented by us, which when read in the presence of our most "religious emperor was declared to have a right and approved "character (εὖ τε ἔχειν καὶ δοκίμως ἀποφανθέν), was as follows. "'As we received from the bishops before us both in our first "'catechetical instruction and when we were baptized, and as "'we have learned from the Divine Scriptures, and as "'we both believed and taught in the presbyterate and in the "'office of bishop itself, so now likewise believing, we offer to "'you our faith; and it is this.'" Eusebius then transcribed a Creed, to which he added a few lines of explanation and protestation[3]. When "this faith", he tells his diocese, had been set

---

[1] This is not the place to examine the characters and beliefs of the actors in the great Council. But it is worth while here to observe that though Eusebius differed on a grave point of doctrine from Athanasius, and probably yet more from Athanasius's non-Alexandrine allies, the difference which determined the attitude of the two men respectively in regard to the proceedings of the Council was not of doctrine but of policy. When the policy of Eusebius had at length been clearly overruled, he had to decide how he could most nearly conform to its spirit; by giving in his adhesion to the conclusion of the majority, or by recording his protest against it. He decided that the former course was the best now open, provided that he could receive sufficient assurance that the new terms were not meant to carry a sense inconsistent with his own belief, misgivings having perhaps been raised in his mind by wild language on the part of such men as Marcellus. The assurance was given, his conscience was relieved, and the accession of his name furnished a guarantee that the new Creed was not to be understood as a rejection of the elder theology. It was quite consistent with this decision that he should desire, on public and on private grounds, to be known as still regretting the eclipse of the policy which he represented.

[2] Διεπεμψάμεθα ὑμῖν πρῶτον μὲν τὴν ὑφ᾽ ἡμῶν προταθεῖσαν περὶ τῆς πίστεως γραφήν, ἔπειτα τὴν δευτέραν, ἣν ταῖς ἡμετέραις φωναῖς προσθήκας ἐπιβαλόντες ἐκδεδώκασιν.

[3] The defensive tone of this document implies accusations flung about in the previous debates. The later controversy with Marcellus may well have had a prelude at Nicæa; nor is it likely that the animosity of Eustathius (Socr. i 23) began after the Council.

forth by him (ταύτης ὑφ' ἡμῶν ἐκτεθείσης τῆς πίστεως), there was no room for gainsaying. The emperor, followed apparently by others[1], declared his entire agreement with it, and "urged all the bishops to give their assent to it and to subscribe to its articles and to express concurrence with them in this very form, with the insertion of the one single word ὁμοούσιος"; which word he proceeded to interpret by rejecting various erroneous senses[2]. Such, Eusebius says, was the wise discourse of the emperor; "but they, under pretext of the addition of ὁμοούσιος, have made the following writing[3]," i.e. the Nicene Creed. He then relates how, as soon as the Creed had been propounded, he or his party (the pronouns 'we' and 'they' are throughout ambiguous) enquired minutely about the intended meaning of the new phrases, and on receiving satisfactory answers thought it right to give consent, having peace always in view.

From this narrative it plainly appears that Eusebius presented a declaration of his own faith as his namesake of Nicomedia had done; that the kernel of this private declaration was a public Creed, the same with which he had been conversant in his own Church at all stages of his life; the Creed therefore of Caesarea from at least the latter part of the third century; that

[1] This seems to be involved in the words αὐτός τε πρῶτος ὁ...βασιλεύς, although no second corresponding clause is extant. The shape of Constantine's proposal was probably suggested by the debates which had followed the reading of the exposition by Eusebius of Nicomedia. But much may have been due to the advice of Hosius, who enjoyed his special confidence, and who, whatever may have taken place at Nicomedia (see p. 55 n. 1), had doubtless not returned without instruction from his previous confidential mission to Alexandria (Eus. V. Const. ii 63—73; Socr. i 7 1; Soz. i 16 5).

[2] Such must be the force of the evidently careful though ungainly language, καὶ ταύτῃ τοὺς πάντας συγκατατίθεσθαι ὑπογράφειν τε τοῖς δόγμασι καὶ συμφωνεῖν τούτοις αὐτοῖς παρεκελεύετο, ἑνὸς μόνου προσεγγραφέντος ῥήματος τοῦ ὁμοουσίου. Following ὑπογράφειν, and joined with τούτοις αὐτοῖς, συμφωνεῖν must as usual denote some express act of agreement or compact.

[3] Καὶ ὁ μὲν σοφώτατος ἡμῶν καὶ εὐσεβέστατος βασιλεὺς τοιάδε ἐφιλοσόφει· οἱ δὲ προφάσει τῆς τοῦ ὁμοουσίου προσθήκης τήνδε τὴν γραφὴν πεποιήκασιν. Late usage would allow πρόφασις to express the mere connexion of facts without implication of motive: but the equally common stricter sense is suggested by the context, as also by the form of the sentence.

58 ON THE WORDS ΜΟΝΟΓΕΝΗC ΘΕΟC

Constantine advised the Council to be satisfied with adopting this Creed as it stood, inserting only the term ὁμοούσιος, this addition being evidently proposed in consequence of a previous discussion; that the Council, under colour of following the advice, did in effect go much further in the way of composition, so that the resulting document could be called a "writing" which they "made"; and yet that it might with equal correctness be described as the Creed of Cæsarea with additions.

The truth of the principal statements is confirmed by historic probability and by internal evidence. An appeal to a venerable existing document, such as the traditional Creed of Cæsarea, was exactly in the spirit of the conservative policy espoused by Eusebius; nor could he easily find a better resource in endeavouring to draw to his side the greater part of the Council. In like manner the adoption of this Creed as a basis by the Council would naturally ensue, in approximate compliance with the emperor's recommendation. The Creed which Eusebius transcribes is simple in form, unlike the personal profession which encloses it[1]. Echoes of its phrases can moreover be distinctly identified in references made by Eusebius elsewhere to a testimony of "the Church [of God]", which must be a public Creed, and is not the Nicene[2]. Its verbal coincidences with

---

[1] By a curious oversight Hahn (46 ff.) has included in the Creed part of this personal profession, and so been led to unfounded doubts as to the public character of the Creed as it stands.

[2] These coincidences appear to have been overlooked. The variations are only of order, and that among complete clauses, and they have no perceptible significance. The passages are as follows: Οὒς ἐκτραπεῖσα ἡ ἐκκλησία τοῦ θεοῦ τῷ τῆς ἀληθείας εὐαγγελικῷ κηρύγματι σεμνύνεται, ἕνα μὲν τὸν ἐπὶ πάντων θεὸν ἔχειν αὐχοῦσα ἕνα δὲ καὶ υἱὸν μονογενῆ, θεὸν ἐκ θεοῦ, Ἰησοῦν Χριστὸν ἐπιγραφομένη (De Eccl. Theol. p. 62 c). Διά τοι τούτων ἁπάντων ἀπο-καθαίρουσα τὴν πλάνην ἡ ἐκκλησία τὸν ἕνα θεὸν κηρύττει, αὐτὸν εἶναι καὶ πατέρα καὶ παντοκράτορα διδάσκουσα, ...οὕτω καὶ υἱὸν θεοῦ μονογενῆ Ἰησοῦν Χριστὸν παραδίδωσι, τὸν πρὸ πάντων αἰώνων ἐκ τοῦ πατέρος γεγεννημένον, οὐ τὸν αὐτὸν ὄντα τῷ πατρί, καθ' ἑαυτὸν δὲ ὄντα καὶ ζῶντα, καὶ ἀληθῶς υἱὸν συνόντα, θεὸν ἐκ θεοῦ, καὶ φῶς ἐκ φωτός, καὶ ζωὴν ἐκ ζωῆς (p. 66 A, B). Διὸ πιστεύειν παρείληφεν [ἡ ἐκκλησία τοῦ θεοῦ] εἰς ἕνα θεὸν πατέρα παντοκράτορα, καὶ εἰς τὸν κύριον ἡμῶν Ἰησοῦν Χριστὸν, τὸν μονογενῆ τοῦ θεοῦ υἱὸν (p. 108 B). Another probable trace occurs in the *Demonstratio Evangelica*, p. 215 B,

the Nicene Creed, as is well known, are at least too large to be accidental[1].

But it is equally certain that one or more other Creeds furnished their quota to the result. Prominent among the leaders of the majority were the representatives of important sees, as Eustathius of Antioch, Hellanicus of Tripolis, Macarius of Jerusalem[2], and Marcellus of Ancyra, not to speak of Alexander of Alexandria; and there would be an obvious fitness on such an occasion in combining with the Cæsarean confession well chosen forms of language consecrated by the use of other great churches. Indeed two of these sees possessed rights which their bishops could not willingly compromise by allowing Cæsarea to furnish alone a standard for universal use, merely because Eusebius was in favour with the emperor: all Palestine was subject to the supremacy of Antioch; and the metropolitan jurisdiction of Cæsarea over the rest of Palestine was balanced by privileges peculiar to Jerusalem, which were ratified by the seventh canon of the Council. The silence of Eusebius as to the employment of any additional Creeds by the Council is of little moment, for his narrative is palpably incomplete, though sufficient for his purpose of shewing first how he had made the best stand he could for the old Creed of his church, and then how it was that he had nevertheless in good faith subscribed the Conciliar Creed. It is at least possible that the omission of certain phrases used at Cæsarea, as elsewhere, πρωτότοκον πάσης κτίσεως (Col. i 15) and πρὸ πάντων τῶν αἰώνων (1 Cor.

ἀλλ' ὡς μονογενὴς υἱὸς μόνος πρὸ πάντων τῶν αἰώνων ἐκ τοῦ πατρὸς γεγεννημένος: and doubtless others might be found.

[1] At the end of these Dissertations will be found the Creed of Cæsarea in full, and also the Nicene Creed printed so as to shew its coincidences with the Cæsarean base by diversity of type. The concordances and differences are exhibited in another way by Dr Swainson, pp. 65 f.

[2] The prominent part taken by Macarius against the Arians in the Council is attested by Theodoret (H. E. i 18; cf. 2, 4) and Sozomen (H. E. i 13 2; ii 20): he was moreover apparently on terms of friendship with Constantine and Helena (Sozom. ii 1 7; 4 7; Theodoret i 15 f.; Euseb. V. Const. iii 29 ff.).

ii 7: cf. Eph. iij 11; Heb. i 2), arose from a dread of their lending themselves too easily to suspected interpretations. But the insertions and alterations in the latter half of the Creed all correspond with fair exactness to extant phraseology of Syrian and Palestinian Creeds[1], though they cannot be traced to any one of the very few extant formularies. It is of course possible that other lost formularies of a similar type may likewise have supplied materials[2].

These facts enable us to understand the manner in which the Council changed those articles of the Creed that touched on the immediate subject of controversy. The Cæsarean Confession ran,

καὶ εἰς ἕνα κύριον Ἰησοῦν Χριστόν, τὸν τοῦ θεοῦ λόγον, θεὸν ἐκ θεοῦ, φῶς ἐκ φωτός, ζωὴν ἐκ ζωῆς, υἱὸν μονογενῆ, πρωτότοκον πάσης κτίσεως, πρὸ πάντων τῶν αἰώνων ἐκ τοῦ πατρὸς γεγεννημένον.

Not only were the phrases mentioned above omitted, and

---

[1] Apostolic Constitutions and Jerusalem (compare Antioch in all forms) τὰ πάντα ἐγένετο for καὶ ἐγένετο τὰ πάντα; Ap. Const. insertion of τά τε ἐν τῷ οὐρανῷ καὶ τὰ ἐπὶ τῆς γῆς; Antioch (at least Cassianus and Eusebius of Dorylæum have δι' ἡμᾶς) insertion of δι' ἡμᾶς τοὺς ἀνθρώπους; Ap. Const. and Antioch (Lucianus and Eus. Doryl.) insertion of κατελθόντα; Jerusalem ἐνανθρωπήσαντα for ἐν ἀνθρώποις πολιτευσάμενον; Ap. Const., Jerusalem, and Antioch (Lucianus and Cassianus) εἰς τοὺς οὐρανούς for πρὸς τὸν πατέρα; Jerusalem ἐρχόμενον for ἥξοντα πάλιν (ἐν δόξῃ being likewise omitted by Cassianus); and Ap. Const. and Antioch (Lucianus) τὸ ἅγιον πνεῦμα (at least these Creeds have τὸ πνεῦμα τὸ ἅγιον) for ἓν ἅγιον πνεῦμα. In the above enumeration 'Eusebius of Dorylæum' means the author of the Διαμαρτυρία against Nestorius, printed in the Acts of the Council of Ephesus (Mansi *Conc.* iv 1109): see Caspari, *Quellen* u.s.w. i 78, 80; and Dissertation II.

[2] It would be rash to assume that there were no clauses on the Church, Baptism, &c. in the Cæsarean or other similar formularies. It is more likely that Eusebius presented only so much of his native Creed as related to the Persons of the Godhead, as sufficient for the special purpose of the Council; and that the Council kept within the same lines. Compare the language of the 'First' Formulary of the Synod of Antioch in 341 (ap. Ath. *De Syn.* 22 p. 735 E), εἰ δὲ δεῖ προσθεῖναι, πιστεύομεν καὶ περὶ σαρκὸς ἀναστάσεως καὶ ζωῆς αἰωνίου. The Anathematism (doubtless suggested by a precedent in the closing exposition of Eusebius, as Mr Lumby points out, p. 50), being evidently intended as part of the Creed, rounds off what would otherwise be an abrupt termination.

with them τὸν τοῦ θεοῦ λόγον and ζωὴν ἐκ ζωῆς, but the surviving language reappeared in a different arrangement, including a new phrase[1] θεὸν ἀληθινὸν ἐκ θεοῦ ἀληθινοῦ, in addition to the three clauses which were the special creation of the Council. This arrangement bears no trace of having been devised with the sole purpose of carrying the new clauses. The rather loose and clumsy order of the Cæsarean Formulary might seem to invite the substitution of a compact and methodical paragraph supplied out of other existing Creeds: and such a procedure would be in analogy with the course seen to have been pursued in the later articles. The first step would be to set the simple fact of our Lord's Divine Sonship[2] in the forefront immediately after His name, in accordance with most precedents. Next would follow the declaration of the nature of His Sonship. Here even our imperfect evidence suffices to exhibit in outline what probably took place. The construction by which γεννηθέντα ἐκ τοῦ πατρός is followed by a predicate, in this case μονογενῆ [θεόν], is borrowed from the Jerusalem Creed, which has in like manner τὸν γεννηθέντα ἐκ τοῦ πατρὸς θεὸν ἀληθινὸν πρὸ πάντων τῶν αἰώνων[3]. Probably the con-

---

[1] New, that is, in relation to the Cæsarean Creed, but doubtless taken wholly or in part from another source, for otherwise it would probably have been mentioned as new by Athanasius and Eusebius. The complete phrase occurs in the *Expositio Fidei* of Athanasius himself (c. 1 p. 99 B: cf. *Or. c. Ar.* iii 9 p. 558 c, ὅτι τοῦ ἀληθινοῦ πατρὸς ἀληθινόν ἐστι γέννημα); but so do similar forms not adopted at Nicæa, as ἄτρεπτος ἐξ ἀτρέπτου, γέννημα ἐκ τελείου τέλειον, τὸν ἐκ τοῦ μόνου μόνον. On the presence of θεὸν ἀληθινόν in the Jerusalem Creed at this time see note 3.

[2] The extrusion of the clause setting Him forth as the Word, and the transfer of the following clauses to the Sonship, would find justification in almost universal precedent.

[3] Touttée, the editor of Cyril of Jerusalem, in an excellent dissertation on the Creed of Jerusalem (p. 80), conjectures θεὸν ἀληθινόν to have been introduced into the Creed from the Nicene Creed between 325 and the time, some quarter of a century later, when Cyril's lectures were delivered. The supposition is surely gratuitous. The presence of πρὸ πάντων τῶν αἰώνων affords no grammatical argument, as our other evidence shews; the suggestion is sustained by no other Nicene echo in the Creed of Jerusalem; had anything been interpolated from the work of the great Council, it would hardly have been a phrase so little conspicuous or characteristic; and any early Creed might easily take it at once from 1 Jo. v 20.

struction is the same in the Antiochian Creed of Lucianus[1], τὸν γεννηθέντα πρὸ τῶν αἰώνων ἐκ τοῦ πατρὸς θεὸν ἐκ θεοῦ. But at all events the Antiochian diction passes with great facility into the Nicene. It stands thus:—

τὸν υἱὸν αὐτοῦ, τὸν μονογενῆ θεόν, δι' οὗ τὰ πάντα, τὸν γεννηθέντα πρὸ τῶν αἰώνων ἐκ τοῦ πατρὸς θεὸν ἐκ θεοῦ, ὅλον ἐξ ὅλου, μόνον ἐκ μόνου, τέλειον ἐκ τελείου κ. τ. λ.

When once the evidently premature clause δι' οὗ τὰ πάντα had been deferred till the place which it held at Cæsarea and Jerusalem alike, and the inconvenient[2] phrase πρὸ τῶν αἰώνων had been omitted, it was an obvious gain to shift μονογενῆ θεόν from its isolated position, now rendered doubly conspicuous by the removal of δι' οὗ τὰ πάντα, deprive it of its dangerous article, and employ it, in strict analogy with St John's own usage, as the chief predicate to γεννηθέντα ἐκ τοῦ πατρός, combining it with the already present θεὸν ἐκ θεοῦ into the single phrase μονογενῆ θεὸν ἐκ θεοῦ[3].

The other alternative now claims attention. The simple τὸν μονογενῆ of Jerusalem may have been preferred to the τὸν

The exact date of Cyril's lectures cannot, I think, be determined, but it seems to lie shortly before 350: see Pearson *De Succ.* ii 21 2; Tillemont viii 779 f.; Touttée *Diss.* cxx ff. The most probable year is 348, which is preferred by Touttée, though partly on untenable grounds.

[1] The doubt of course arises from the bare possibility of taking πρὸ τῶν αἰώνων as the sole predicate (ἐκ τοῦ πατρός being excluded from direct predication by the sense), in which case θεὸν ἐκ θεοῦ would become an addition in apposition. But this construction is virtually condemned, if I mistake not, by the order of the words. In both the local Creeds πρὸ τῶν αἰώνων seems to hold a weak place, as a secondary predicate only, though the places are not identical. The omission of these words at Nicæa, whether suggested by dogmatic prudence or not, was an undoubted gain as regards grammatical clearness. It may also be owing to a grammatical impulse that Hilary omits them in his version of Lucianus' Creed (*De Syn.* 29 p. 478 c).

[2] See last note.

[3] What follows hardly needs comment. θεὸν ἐκ θεοῦ is succeeded by two clauses of similar form, as in both the Cæsarean and the Antiochian Creeds; but no actual phrases are borrowed from Antioch, and but one, φῶς ἐκ φωτός, retained from Cæsarea. The other, θεὸν ἀληθινὸν ἐκ θεοῦ ἀληθινοῦ, whether then first put together or not, had the advantage of taking up for better use what at Jerusalem had stood after γεννηθέντα ἐκ τοῦ πατρός.

μονογενῆ θεόν of Antioch; and μονογενῆ may have been intended, when transposed, to stand alone after γεννηθέντα ἐκ τοῦ πατρός, with θεὸν ἐκ θεοῦ as a fresh clause in apposition. It is impossible to disprove this rival supposition: but it is weighted with several improbabilities. First, it involves a somewhat wide departure from the real force of both the assumed precedents: in both of them the primary predicate to γεννηθέντα ἐκ τοῦ πατρός is a strong term containing θεόν, in the one case θεὸν ἀληθινόν, in the other, θεὸν ἐκ θεοῦ. It is not likely therefore that both these phrases would be deposed into a secondary position, and their room occupied solely by an adjective not in itself implying Deity. Secondly, the bare phrase γεννηθέντα ἐκ τοῦ πατρὸς μονογενῆ is redundant and artificial[1], if μονογενής retains its true usual sense of an only son or offspring. The rare secondary sense (see p. 17) in which it casts off the idea of parentage, and comes to mean only "unique", receives no support from Athanasius or, as far as I can discover, any writer of the Nicene generation[2]. Thirdly, it is difficult to believe that a collocation so naturally suggesting the combination μονογενῆ θεόν to the many ears already familiar with it would have been chosen or retained except with the deliberate intention that it should be so understood[3]. On the other hand the one tangible ground for supposing the

[1] The circumlocution would be all the more improbable because the obvious form τὸν υἱὸν αὐτοῦ (or τοῦ θεοῦ) τὸν μονογενῆ was not only directly Scriptural (John iii 16; 1 Jo. iv 9) but stood already in the Creeds of Jerusalem and (by the easy omission of θεόν) of Antioch. But in the case of μονογενῆ θεόν there would be no circumlocution, partly on account of the sense and the weight of the phrase, partly because of the need of introducing it only in a predicative position.

[2] This seemingly stronger sense would in effect have served the purpose of the Council less; for no Arian would have hesitated to affirm the *uniqueness* of our Lord's Sonship. The point for which at least Athanasius repeatedly contends, as involving all else, is the strict and primary sense of the terms *Father* and *Son;* and this argument would have received no help from μονογενής as a Scriptural designation of the Son, if it did not by recognised usage imply actual parentage.

[3] The transfer of *unicum* from *Filium* to *Dominum* by transcribers of Latin Creeds (see p. 50 n. 1) can afford no real analogy for the skilful Greek theologians of Nicæa.

two words to have been intended to belong to different clauses, namely the position of the Nicene parenthesis, requires careful consideration. But first, a few more words must be said in illustration of the continuous construction γεννηθέντα ἐκ τοῦ πατρὸς μονογενῆ θεὸν ἐκ θεοῦ.

Apart from the unfamiliarity of μονογενῆ θεόν, the prevalent habit of treating θεὸν ἐκ θεοῦ as a complete and independent formula may probably at first disincline a reader to accept its suspension, so to speak, on a preliminary participle. The absolutely independent use of θεὸν ἐκ θεοῦ has undoubtedly sufficient authority in ancient theological writers; but on the other hand this use is virtually unknown in Creeds; for popular intelligibility the help of γεγεννημένον ἐκ τοῦ πατρός or some equivalent was apparently felt to be needed. Setting aside the Creed of Cæsarea, where θεὸν ἐκ θεοῦ follows τὸν τοῦ θεοῦ λόγον with probably the same effect as to sense, and perhaps the Creed recited by Charisius of Philadelphia at Ephesus in 431, where θεὸν ἐκ θεοῦ follows τὸν υἱὸν αὐτοῦ τὸν μονογενῆ[1], I can find no exceptions; for it is impossible to count as such the highly technical Confession of Gregory Thaumaturgus (ed. Paris 1622 p. 1 A, εἷς κύριος, μόνος ἐκ μόνου, θεὸς ἐκ θεοῦ, χαρακτὴρ καὶ εἰκὼν τῆς θεότητος, λόγος ἐνεργής κ.τ.λ.), or the still more elaborate Exposition of Athanasius (p. 99 B), in which θεὸν ἀληθινὸν ἐκ θεοῦ ἀληθινοῦ is isolated among texts of Scripture[2]. On the other hand the rule is observed by the Antiochian baptismal Creed in all its extant forms[3]; the 'Third' Formulary of the

---

[1] It is at least equally probable that here too τὸν μονογενῆ θεὸν ἐκ θεοῦ should be taken together; and then μονογενῆ would have the same effect as a participle.

[2] A similar Exposition of uncertain authorship (ad calc. Greg. Naz. i 906 &c.: cf. Walch, *Bibl. Symb.* 172 ff.; Hahn, *Bibl. der Symbole* 185 ff.), has "Patrem verum qui genuit Filium verum, ut est Deus de Deo, lumen de lumine, vita ex vita" &c. Yet here too the aid is given by the context, though not formally by the grammar.

[3] As represented by Lucianus, Eusebius of Dorylæum, Cassianus. The last two writers doubtless represent the same form, which shews signs of Nicene influence: see Dissertation II. I venture to cite Eusebius of Dorylæum, although the words in question precede his express quotation from the μάθημα of Antioch. He certainly began to interweave the diction of

Synod of Antioch, by Theophronius[1]; the 'Fourth' of the same (ap. Ath. *De Syn.* 25 p. 737 E, &c.; the 'Fifth' (A.D. 345), known as Ἔκθεσις μακρόστιχος (ap. Ath. ib. 26 p. 738 c &c.); the Formulary of the Synod of Philippopolis, miscalled 'Sardica', in 347 (ap. Hil. *De Syn.* 34, p. 482 D: the only probable construction in the lost Greek is a little disguised in the Latin version); the 'First' Formulary of the Synod of Sirmium in 351 (ap. Ath. ib. 27, p. 742 A &c.); the 'Second' in 357 (ap. Hil. ib. p. 466 A &c.); the 'Third' in 358 (ap. Ath. ib. 8 p. 721 c &c.), with the peculiar form γεγεννημένον δὲ μονογενῆ, μόνον ἐκ μόνου τοῦ πατρός, θεὸν ἐκ θεοῦ, ὅμοιον τῷ γεννήσαντι αὐτὸν πατρί, which was copied, with variations of perfect and aorist only, at the Synod of Nicé in Thrace in 359 (ap. Theodoret. *H. E.* ii 16 [al. 21]) and at that of Constantinople in 360 (ap. Ath. ib. 30 p. 747 A)[2]; and lastly by what is known as the 'Constantinopolitan' Creed[3]. Hence abundant analogy leads to the conclusion that θεὸν ἐκ θεοῦ, whether forming part of the direct predicate to γεννηθέντα ἐκ τοῦ πατρός or not in the Nicene Creed, is at least dependent on it, so that on either construction ἐκ θεοῦ *presupposes* γεννηθέντα: and when thus much is established, there can be no intrinsic difficulty, μονογενῆ and the parenthesis apart, in the closer construction which makes θεὸν ἐκ θεοῦ part of the main predicate.

The chief external evidence for joining to γεννηθέντα a the Creed before he made formal appeal to it. The words are, ἀλλ' ἕνα τὸν πρὸ πάντων αἰώνων γεννηθέντα θεὸν ἐκ θεοῦ καὶ πατρός, θεὸν ἀληθινὸν ἐκ θεοῦ ἀληθινοῦ, κ.τ.λ.

[1] Cf. pp. 22 f. The words are, τὸν γεννηθέντα ἐκ τοῦ πατρὸς πρὸ τῶν αἰώνων θεὸν τέλειον ἐκ θεοῦ τελείου, καὶ ὄντα πρὸς τὸν θεὸν ἐν ὑποστάσει, ἐπ' ἐσχάτων δὲ τῶν ἡμερῶν κατελθόντα κ.τ.λ. The position of πρὸ τῶν αἰώνων allows θεὸν τέλειον κ.τ.λ. to be taken either predicatively or in apposition, though the former is the more probable construction, as two other participial clauses follow at once. For the present purpose the difference is immaterial.

[2] We are not here concerned with the theological position of these various Synods, but solely with their incidental testimony to a traditional habit of language.

[3] That is, in the clauses φῶς ἐκ φωτός, θεὸν ἀληθινὸν ἐκ θεοῦ ἀληθινοῦ, as this Creed does not contain the simple θεὸν ἐκ θεοῦ. In all the other Creeds cited, that of Theophronius excepted (note 1), θεὸν ἐκ θεοῦ stands unmodified.

predicate containing θεόν has been already given, namely the probable analogy of the Creeds of Antioch and Jerusalem. To this must be added the Epistle to Paul of Samosata by the bishops assembled at Antioch in 260—270, if the correction already suggested is right[1]. The whole sentence must be quoted here. Τοῦτον δὲ τὸν υἱόν, γεννητὸν μονογενῆ υἱόν (read θεόν), εἰκόνα τοῦ ἀοράτου θεοῦ τυγχάνοντα, πρωτότοκον πάσης κτίσεως, σοφίαν καὶ λόγον καὶ δύναμιν θεοῦ πρὸ αἰώνων ὄντα, οὐ προγνώσει ἀλλ' οὐσίᾳ καὶ ὑποστάσει, θεὸν θεοῦ υἱόν, ἔν τε παλαιᾷ καὶ νέᾳ διαθήκῃ ἐγνωκότες ὁμολογοῦμεν καὶ κηρύσσομεν. As soon as θεόν is substituted for the unmeaning second υἱόν, the two preceding words acquire a clear force, the verbal γεννητόν being equivalent to a passive participle. Possibly however this ought not to be accounted independent evidence, but only as a reproduction of the Creed of Antioch[2]. The second required combination, that of μονογενῆ with θεὸν ἐκ θεοῦ, had undoubtedly an actual existence. In the *Demonstratio Evangelica* (p. 149 A) Eusebius speaks of our Lord as τῷ πατρὶ ὡς υἱὸν διὰ παντὸς συνόντα καὶ οὐκ ἀγέννητον ὄντα γεννώμενον δ' ἐξ ἀγεννήτου πατρός, μονογενῆ ὄντα λόγον τε καὶ θεὸν ἐκ θεοῦ. The position of τε proves a reference to two distinct forms, the familiar μονογενῆ λόγον, not seldom used by Eusebius (as by Athanasius), and μονογενῆ θεὸν ἐκ θεοῦ: the only other grammatical construction, that which makes μονογενῆ and λόγον two distinct terms, would give λόγον an inappropriate position, imply an arbitrary distribution of the conjunctions, and enfeeble the

---

[1] See pp. 4, 19, 39. Even if υἱόν is right, which seems incredible, we should still have as the predicate of γεννητόν a combination of μονογενῆ with a substantive.

[2] The construction of the Nicene Creed here advocated receives illustration, rather than direct confirmation, from the language of the Third Sirmian Formulary (quoted above, p. 65), adopted at Nicé in Thrace and at Constantinople in the two following years: it will be observed that μόνον ἐκ μόνου, an accepted gloss on μονογενῆ (see p. 17), occupies the place of the Nicene parenthesis. The parallel language of Cyril of Jerusalem (iv 7) is instructive, τὸν ἐκ τοῦ θεοῦ θεὸν γεννηθέντα, τὸν ἐκ ζωῆς ζωὴν γεννηθέντα, τὸν ἐκ φωτὸς φῶς γεννηθέντα, τὸν ὅμοιον κατὰ πάντα τῷ γεννήσαντι (iv 7): ὅμοιος γὰρ ἐν πᾶσιν ὁ υἱὸς τῷ γεγεννηκότι, ζωὴ ἐκ ζωῆς γεννηθείς, καὶ φῶς ἐκ φωτός, δύναμις ἐκ δυνάμεως, θεὸς ἐκ θεοῦ (xi 18: cf. 4).

whole of the last clause as a climax. The same form, slightly resolved, occurs a little earlier (p. 147 B), καὶ ἕνα τέλειον μόνον γεννητὸν θεὸν ἐκ θεοῦ; and, slightly extended, in the *Panegyric on Constantine* (xii 7: cf. *Theophan.* i 24), οὗτος μονογενὴς θεὸς ἐκ θεοῦ γεγεννημένος λόγος[1]. It reappears in the Formulary of the Synod of Seleucia in Isauria (A.D. 359) θεὸν λόγον, θεὸν ἐκ θεοῦ μονογενῆ, φῶς, ζωήν κ.τ.λ. (ap. Ath. *De Syn.* 29 p. 746 C; Epiph. *Haer.* 873 C). And in the next century it is employed by Cyril in his commentary on St John, σημεῖον... τοῦ εἶναι βασιλέα καὶ δεσπότην τῶν ὅλων τὸν ἐκ θεοῦ πεφηνότα θεὸν μονογενῆ (viii 35 p. 541 C), and again, ἐπείπερ ὑπάρχων [ὁ υἱὸς] ἐκ θεοῦ θεὸς μονογενὴς ἄνθρωπος γέγονεν (x 15, p. 653 C); as also in his *Third* (Second Œcumenical) *Epistle to Nestorius* (p. 24 Pusey) ὁ ἐκ θεοῦ πατρὸς γεννηθεὶς υἱὸς καὶ θεὸς μονογενής. It is immaterial whether these forms of speech were derived from the Nicene Creed or independent of it[2]. In either case they shew the naturalness of the combination in the eyes of theologians of the fourth and fifth centuries. Doubtless it was felt that each of the two elements associated with θεόν in μονογενῆ θεὸν ἐκ θεοῦ would sustain and illustrate the other.

Thus far the discussion has left out of account the Nicene parenthesis τοῦτ' ἐστὶν ἐκ τῆς οὐσίας τοῦ πατρός. Were it absent, the evidence would all, as far as I can see, be clearly in favour of taking μονογενῆ θεὸν ἐκ θεοῦ as an unbroken predicate of γεννηθέντα ἐκ τοῦ πατρός. It remains to consider whether we are driven to a different conclusion by the position of the

---

[1] The added γεγεννημένος increases the resemblance to the Nicene language, though inverted in order.

[2] Yet it can hardly be doubted that at least Cyril had the Nicene Creed definitely in view; for in his *Ep.* 55, which is a commentary on the Creed, he says that the Fathers of Nicæa, τῆς ὠδῖνος [the Paternity] τὸ γνήσιον ... εὖ μάλα σημαίνοντες, θεὸν ἔφασαν ἐκ θεοῦ γεγεννῆσθαι τὸν υἱόν (p. 178): and again, οὐ γάρ τοι ἀπόχρη ... φρονεῖν ὡς θεὸς ἐκ θεοῦ γεγέννηται τοῦ πατρός, ...ἀλλ' ἦν ἀναγκαῖον εἰδέναι πρὸς τούτοις ὡς τῆς ἁπάντων ἕνεκα σωτηρίας κ.τ.λ.· διὰ τοῦτό φασι Τὸν δι' ἡμᾶς τοὺς ἀνθρώπους κ.τ.λ. (p. 180). Both passages lose their force if θεὸν ἐκ θεοῦ was not part of the main predicate.

parenthesis. It matters little for our purpose whether the Nicene Fathers were here simply copying an earlier (lost) Creed, or, as the extant language of Jerusalem and Antioch has rather suggested, to a certain extent modifying in combination and arrangement the traditional materials. In either case the sense and the place of their own entirely new parenthesis must be taken into account in order to ascertain the meaning which they attached to their completed work.

A reader examining the passage merely as a piece of Greek, unaided by extraneous knowledge, could hardly fail to take μονογενῆ as the one weighty word interpreted by the parenthesis. Yet this supposition cannot be more than partially true at most, if we are to trust the concurrent testimony of the two men who had the best means of knowing the facts, who moreover regarded them from different points of view. Eusebius and Athanasius represent ἐκ τῆς οὐσίας τοῦ πατρός as the interpretation of ἐκ τοῦ πατρός[1]. Eusebius passes μονογενῆ over altogether, and Athanasius alludes to it with a slightness and indirectness which throw it completely into subordination[2].

---

[1] Καὶ δὴ ταύτης τῆς γραφῆς ὑπ' αὐτῶν ὑπαγορευθείσης, ὅπως εἴρηται αὐτοῖς τό 'Ἐκ τῆς οὐσίας τοῦ πατρός καὶ τό Τῷ πατρὶ ὁμοούσιον, οὐκ ἀνεξέταστον αὐτοῖς κατελιμπάνομεν· ἐπερωτήσεις τοιγαροῦν καὶ ἀποκρίσεις ἐντεῦθεν ἀνεκινοῦντο, ἐβασάνιζέν τε ὁ λόγος τὴν διάνοιαν τῶν εἰρημένων· καὶ δὴ τό 'Ἐκ τῆς οὐσίας ὡμολογεῖτο πρὸς αὐτῶν δηλωτικὸν εἶναι τοῦ ἐκ μὲν τοῦ πατρὸς εἶναι, οὐ μὴν ὡς μέρος ὑπάρχειν τοῦ πατρός· ταύτῃ δὲ καὶ ἡμῖν ἐδόκει καλῶς ἔχειν συγκατατίθεσθαι τῇ διανοίᾳ τῆς εὐσεβοῦς διδασκαλίας κ.τ.λ. Eus. Ep. ad Caes. 5. Οἱ περὶ Εὐσέβιον [of Nicomedia]...ἐβούλοντο τό 'Ἐκ τοῦ θεοῦ κοινὸν εἶναι πρὸς ἡμᾶς [i. e. mankind]...ἀλλ' οἱ πατέρες θεωρήσαντες ἐκείνων τὴν πανουργίαν...ἠναγκάσθησαν λοιπὸν λευκότερον εἰπεῖν τό 'Ἐκ τοῦ θεοῦ, καὶ γράψαι ἐκ τῆς οὐσίας τοῦ θεοῦ εἶναι τὸν υἱόν, ὑπὲρ τοῦ μὴ τό 'Ἐκ τοῦ θεοῦ κοινὸν καὶ ἴσον τοῦ τε υἱοῦ καὶ τῶν γενητῶν νομίζεσθαι. Ath. De Decr. 19 p. 224 DE. And so in the parallel narrative Ad Afr. 5 p. 895 B, ἀλλ' οἱ ἐπίσκοποι θεωρήσαντες τὴν κ.τ.λ. λευκότερον εἰρήκασι τό 'Ἐκ τοῦ θεοῦ, καὶ ἔγραψαν ἐκ τῆς οὐσίας τοῦ θεοῦ εἶναι τὸν υἱόν.

[2] The possible allusions in the Ep. de Decretis to μονογενῆ (represented by μόνος) are in the two sentences ὁ δὲ λόγος, ἐπεὶ μὴ κτίσμα ἐστίν, εἴρηται καὶ ἔστι μόνος ἐκ τοῦ πατρός, τῆς δὲ τοιαύτης διανοίας γνώρισμα τὸ εἶναι τὸν υἱὸν ἐκ τῆς οὐσίας τοῦ πατρός, οὐδενὶ γὰρ τῶν γενητῶν ὑπάρχει τοῦτο, and διὰ τοῦτο γὰρ καὶ ἡ ἁγία σύνοδος λευκότερον εἴρηκεν ἐκ τῆς οὐσίας αὐτὸν εἶναι τοῦ πατρός, ἵνα καὶ ἄλλος παρὰ τὴν τῶν γενητῶν φύσιν ὁ λόγος εἶναι πιστευθῇ, μόνος ὢν ἀληθῶς ἐκ τοῦ θεοῦ (225 A—C). The Ep. ad Afros has likewise the word itself, but in an ambiguous context, ὁ δὲ υἱὸς μόνος ἴδιος τῆς τοῦ

But the more the stress is shifted back from μονογενῆ to ἐκ τοῦ πατρός, the less reason is there to regard the clause as so terminating in μονογενῆ as to make θεὸν ἐκ θεοῦ a fresh clause in apposition. It would seem in fact that μονογενῆ was put to double duty, combined alike with ἐκ τοῦ πατρός and with θεὸν ἐκ θεοῦ; just as we have already found reason provisionally to recognise θεόν as doing double duty, combined alike with μονογενῆ and with ἐκ θεοῦ. Thus there would be no real pause between the seven words ἐκ τοῦ πατρὸς μονογενῆ θεὸν ἐκ θεοῦ. Yet the parenthesis had to be inserted somewhere. It could not be placed at the end, for τοῦ πατρός was too distant; nor before ἐκ θεοῦ, partly for the same reason, partly because θεὸν ἐκ θεοῦ could not be severed. If placed before μονογενῆ, it would have been close to ἐκ τοῦ πατρός, but at the cost of depriving ἐκ τοῦ πατρός of any additional force or clearness which it could derive from association with μονογενῆ, including perhaps the reminiscence of John i 14 (δόξαν ὡς μονογενοῦς παρὰ πατρός). Placed as it actually was, the parenthesis, while chiefly limiting the sense of ἐκ τοῦ πατρός, limited also the sense of μονογενῆ, as against the Homœousians, and at the same time compelled μονογενῆ into a subsidiary limitation of ἐκ τοῦ πατρός, as against the Anomœans. No doubt in the process μονογενὴς θεός was disguised: but it was not possible to introduce the parenthesis without some sacrifice somewhere. Probably it was thought that μονογενὴς θεός was too well known and accepted to lose instant recognition despite the parenthesis. But at all events its acceptance by Arius himself deprived it of controversial value for the special purpose of the Council; whereas in the eyes of at least Athanasius it must have been of primary importance to secure to the interpretation ἐκ τῆς οὐσίας τοῦ πατρός

πατρὸς οὐσίας, τοῦτο γὰρ ἴδιον μονογενοῦς καὶ ἀληθινοῦ λόγου πρὸς πατέρα (895 c). These incidental references are of no force as compared with the express statements of fact cited in the last note. Indeed elsewhere (*De Syn.* 51), assuming ἐκ τῆς οὐσίας as the universal criterion of true parentage and filiation, Athanasius argues from Jephthah's daughter and the son of the widow of Nain that a child is *not less* ὁμοούσιος with its parent because it is likewise μονογενής.

the utmost possible force[1]. Thus μονογενὴς θεός, though retained like other traditional forms too little stringent for the present need[2], might have to suffer partial obscuration through the necessity of the case.

No other explanation than this appears to account for all the facts, and to do justice alike to the language of the Creeds of Antioch and Jerusalem, to the statements of Eusebius and Athanasius, and to the actual order of words in the Nicene Creed. There is the less difficulty in accepting a single long clause made up of closely combined terms, if we remember the evident purpose to give continuity of form to the entire declaration respecting the nature of the Divine Sonship, the other Creeds having been more or less disjointed hereabouts, the Creed of Cæsarea to an extreme degree[3]. Where all the clauses

---

[1] Innumerable passages of his writings shew that the form of language adopted in this clause was the test on which he relied above all others for the exclusion of Arianism. On the other hand, loyally as he defends ὁμοούσιος when needful, he shews no great inclination to use it when left to himself: Dr Newman has noticed its almost total absence from the great treatise made up by what are called his first three *Orations against the Arians* (*Sel. Treat. of Ath.* 500, 210 d, 264 g), as also his use of the term ὁμοίας οὐσίας (210 e: cf. 136 g): cf. *Tracts Theol. and Eccl.* 291. The final result in the Creed may have been a combination of the expedients proposed by different sections of the majority in the Council.

[2] Athanasius dwells on the desire of the Council to use only scriptural terms, till it was found that the party of Eusebius of Nicomedia was ready to accept them all (*De Decr.* 19 ff. p. 224 ff.; *Ad Afr.* 5 f. p. 894 ff.). Among such terms he includes the following, evidently described somewhat vaguely, ὅτι ἐκ τοῦ θεοῦ τῇ φύσει μονογενής ἐστιν

ὁ λόγος, δύναμις, σοφία μόνη τοῦ πατρός κ.τ.λ. (895 A).

[3] To this purpose must probably be referred the omission of τόν before the first γεννηθέντα, and the emphatic repetition of γεννηθέντα, first to set forth the contrast οὐ ποιηθέντα, and then to carry ὁμοούσιον τῷ πατρί without another participle. Then comes a fresh start on the relation of the Son to created things, δι᾽ οὗ τὰ πάντα ἐγένετο; and the added clause τά τε ἐν τῷ οὐρανῷ καὶ τὰ ἐπὶ τῆς γῆς, wanting at Cæsarea, Antioch, and Jerusalem (it is found in the Apostolic Constitutions), at once gives weight to this division of the second article of the Creed and constitutes a parallel to the first article, on the Father, πάντων ὁρατῶν τε καὶ ἀοράτων ποιητήν. The resumptive force of the second γεννηθέντα, as connecting οὐ ποιηθέντα with the earlier clause, is distinctly recognised in the later Antiochian Creed (Cassianus), which has been modified by Nicene influence, *ex eo natum ante omnia saecula, et non factum, Deum verum ex Deo vero;* as also, by exactly the same collocation,

bearing on a single subject are so carefully shaped into a whole, it is only natural that the series of terms relating to one portion of the subject should be knit together with unusual closeness. The arrangement may be exhibited as follows:—

Καὶ εἰς ἕνα κύριον Ἰησοῦν Χριστόν,
  τὸν υἱὸν τοῦ θεοῦ·
    γεννηθέντα ἐκ τοῦ πατρὸς μονογενῆ -
      τοῦτ' ἐστὶν ἐκ τῆς αὐτῆς οὐσίας -
      θεὸν ἐκ θεοῦ,
      φῶς ἐκ φωτός,
      θεὸν ἀληθινὸν ἐκ θεοῦ ἀληθινοῦ,
    γεννηθέντα, οὐ ποιηθέντα,
    ὁμοούσιον τῷ πατρί,
    δι' οὗ τὰ πάντα ἐγένετο,
      τά τε ἐν τῷ οὐρανῷ καὶ τὰ ἐπὶ τῆς γῆς·
  τὸν δι' ἡμᾶς τοὺς ἀνθρώπους κ.τ.λ.

We have, it is to be feared, no means of knowing with any certainty how the sentence was understood in the following years. The remarkable form of the Creed noticed above (p. 23) as employed by Eustathius and others in 366 might be due either to an attempt to express more clearly the assumed sense of the Nicene language, or to a conscious reintroduction of a combination assumed to have been set aside. The concise Philadelphian Creed recited by Charisius, in borrowing the Nicene phraseology, omits the Nicene parenthesis, and thus removes the only hindrance in the way of reading τὸν υἱὸν αὐτοῦ τὸν μονογενῆ θεὸν ἐκ θεοῦ continuously: but the other construction remains possible; and again the authors of this Creed may have intended to improve rather than to interpret. Yet the growing favour of the phrase μονογενὴς θεός with the friends and successors of Athanasius, in spite of its controversial uselessness, during the time that the distinctive terms of the Nicene Creed were the watchwords of every struggle, suggests the operation of some

in the (Syriac) Mesopotamian Creed examined in the following Dissertation, which rests on an Antiochian foundation.

more potent and universal cause than the influence of scattered local Creeds, or of Synods of doubtful orthodoxy which borrowed their language. The Nicene Creed itself would evidently be such an adequate cause, if it was understood as containing μονογενὴς θεός: and if such was the retrospective view taken in the fourth century, such also, we may not unreasonably believe, was the intention of the Council.

Against this evidence there is, as far as I am aware, nothing to set. A Cappadocian Creed formed on the base of the Nicene Creed at a date not far from 370, of which some account will be given in the next Dissertation, merely repeats this part of the Nicene language unchanged. No other known Creed can be said with any propriety to be a revised form of the Nicene Creed. That the 'Constantinopolitan' Creed had no such origin, it is easy to shew: but a position so much at variance with commonly received views requires to be illustrated in some detail, and must therefore be treated separately. It is enough here to say that the history of μονογενὴς θεός in ancient times virtually closes with the gradual supersession of the Nicene Creed. As its primary apostolic sanction had been lost long before through the increasing degeneracy of biblical texts, so its ecclesiastical sanction, such as it was, died out by an equally fortuitous process. Neither in 381 nor at any other date was the phrase μονογενὴς θεός removed from the Nicene Creed. If it had a place there from 325, as we have found good grounds on the whole for concluding, it was never displaced while the authority of the Nicene Creed was in force. It passed away only when the Nicene Creed itself completely yielded place to another Creed which never possessed it.

ON THE 'CONSTANTINOPOLITAN' CREED AND OTHER EASTERN CREEDS OF THE FOURTH CENTURY

In the last Note appended to the preceding Dissertation the origin of the Nicene Creed was incidentally brought under a fresh examination. The chief subject of the present Dissertation is the origin of the Creed which has taken its place and its name. Were the common account of the later history of the Nicene Creed true, we should have to believe that the 150 bishops who composed the Council of Constantinople in 381 not only added new clauses to meet new doctrinal errors, but revised the existing text in such a manner as to shatter the most elaborate handiwork of their predecessors in 325. To abolish the specially Athanasian definition τοῦτ' ἐστὶν ἐκ τῆς οὐσίας τοῦ πατρός, to erase the time-honoured form θεὸν ἐκ θεοῦ[1], and to remove μονογενῆ from the post in which it

---

[1] This single omission is usually explained on the ground that θεὸν ἐκ θεοῦ is contained in θεὸν ἀληθινὸν ἐκ θεοῦ ἀληθινοῦ. Yet surely there is a distinct force in the unaccompanied substantives, especially as preceding φῶς ἐκ φωτός, though on other grounds (see p. 83 n. 2) there is likewise force in the close association of φῶς ἐκ φωτός with the participial clause: nor could the conciseness gained by dropping three such words have seemed a compensation for the loss of a form both Nicene and Antenicene. But indeed it is impossible to separate the loss of this clause from that dissipation of the whole sentence which the common story implies.

contributed to a careful exposition of the Divine Sonship into its old place in less distracted days, as a simple Scriptural affix (with τόν) to τὸν υἱὸν τοῦ θεοῦ, are operations which it is difficult to understand as performed upon a formulary undergoing a dogmatic enlargement in the midst of fierce controversy by men professing to guard the Nicene bequest with jealous care.

Part of the difficulty has been removed by recent criticism[1], starting from the well known fact that in his *Ancoratus*, written about 374, Epiphanius transcribes under the name of the Nicene Creed[2] a formulary differing only by the accession of two clauses[3] from the Creed as alleged to have been renovated at Constantinople seven years later. It is now certain that we have no evidence of any public recognition of the 'Constantinopolitan' Creed before the Council of Chalcedon in 451, when it was read by Aetius a deacon of Constantinople as the "Creed of the 150", and accepted as orthodox, but not in any way placed on a level with the Nicene Creed, the "Creed of the 318", (which was likewise read,) much less accepted as taking its place. The short records of the Council of Constantinople illustrate indeed the watchfulness with which the sufficiency of the Nicene Creed was maintained; but throw no direct light on the foundation of

---

[1] See especially Mr Lumby, pp. 67—84, and Dr Swainson, pp. 86—96, 111—131.

[2] At the outset he calls it ταύτην τὴν ἁγίαν πίστιν τῆς καθολικῆς ἐκκλησίας, ὡς παρέλαβεν ἡ ἁγία καὶ μόνη πάρθενος τοῦ θεοῦ ἀπὸ τῶν ἁγίων ἀποστόλων τοῦ κυρίου φυλάττειν; and after an appended Anathematism, a loose copy of the Nicene, he adds Αὕτη μὲν ἡ πίστις παρεδόθη ἀπὸ τῶν ἁγίων ἀποστόλων, καὶ ἐν ἐκκλησίᾳ τῇ ἁγίᾳ πόλει [sic] ἀπὸ πάντων ὁμοῦ τῶν ἁγίων ἐπισκόπων, ὑπὲρ τριακοσίων δέκα τὸν ἀριθμόν. A strange statement: but Epiphanius's own remarks upon his priceless materials are often strange.

[3] In addition to the Anathematism. They are both Nicene, τοῦτ' ἐστὶν ἐκ τῆς οὐσίας τοῦ πατρός and τά τε ἐν τοῖς οὐρανοῖς καὶ τὰ ἐν τῇ γῇ: τοῖς οὐρανοῖς is substituted for τῷ οὐρανῷ and ἐν τῇ γῇ for ἐπὶ τῆς γῆς, the latter at least, and apparently both, of these variations being found in ancient copies of the Nicene Creed (see Hahn p. 106 n. 2, 108 f. n. 8); indeed they both stand in the Nicene text embodied in Epiphanius's own 'Second' Creed. The only other Epiphanian variations from the Chalcedon copy, both slight, the insertion of τε after οὐρανοῦ in the first article and the change of τὸ ζωοποιόν to καὶ ζωοποιόν, (together with the omission of τό before κύριον, if Petau's text is right,) are probably in like manner accidental.

the tradition which seventy years later associated the new form of Creed in some way with the 150 Bishops then assembled, and which does not seem likely to have been a mere invention[1]. It is not however an unreasonable conjecture that the Creed was submitted to the Council by some one of its members, and accepted as legitimate[2], without any idea of its becoming in any sense an œcumenical Symbol, regulating the faith of many lands. However this may be, it was certainly in existence some years before the Council met, and already included those clauses which in a later age were specially said to have been introduced by the Council[3].

The responsibility for the 'Constantinopolitan' Creed is thus shifted from the Council of 381, in which various distinguished men took part, to an unknown person, synod, or church at an earlier date, possibly a much earlier date, than 374. Yet it would still be difficult to understand how the Nicene Creed could be treated with such remarkable freedom in a revision which, upon any view, bears marks of having

---

[1] It is quite possible, as has been suggested, that the presentation of the Creed by Aetius was connected with the efforts made by a Constantinopolitan party in the Council of Chalcedon to secure the supremacy of their city, which had been maintained by a canon of the Council of 381. But the Creed would hardly have served their purpose, unless it were already in some way associated with the proceedings of 381. That it had become the local Creed of the imperial city is not likely. In a homily preached at Constantinople in 399 (on Col. ii 14, p. 369 F) Chrysostom appeals to the words εἰς ζωὴν αἰώνιον as part of the Creed which his hearers knew (cf. Caspari i 93 f.); words absent from the 'Constantinopolitan' Creed but present in that of Antioch. And *a priori* we should expect Constantinople to have received its Creed from Antioch, its ecclesiastical mother. Reasons will however be presently given for concluding that the 'Constantinopolitan' Creed was in some manner known or used at Constantinople early in the fifth century; and this ill defined currency may possibly date from 381, though we have no evidence for the fact.

[2] Its presentation and acceptance on this occasion would thus bear a resemblance to what took place afterwards with the same Creed at Chalcedon, with the Creed of Cæsarea on its first presentation by Eusebius at Nicæa (see p. 56), and probably with the (Philadelphian) Creed presented by Charisius at Ephesus. Some other indirect confirmations of this conjecture will be noticed further on.

[3] Not only the additional clauses on the Holy Spirit, but οὗ τῆς βασιλείας οὐκ ἔσται τέλος, which stands in the Creed of the Apostolic Constitutions as well as in that of Jerusalem.

been conducted by men fully alive to theological requirements. In the attempt however to trace the chief sources of the variations introduced, I have been led to observe that the Epiphanian or 'Constantinopolitan' Creed is not a revised form of the Nicene Creed at all, but of the Creed of Jerusalem[1]. A comparative exhibition of the Epiphanian Creed on the two bases, marking those words and clauses which occur already in the Nicene and Jerusalem Creeds respectively, will dispense with the need of lengthened argument[2]: but a few explanatory remarks may place the bearing of the evidence in a clearer light.

Whichever base is assumed, most of the changes and insertions in the latter part may easily be explained by the influence of the Creeds of Antioch and the Apostolic Constitutions, or, it may be, lost Creeds of a similar type[3]: this feature therefore must be taken as common to both theories. In all other particulars the difference is striking. The first 6 lines, ending with πρὸ πάντων τῶν αἰώνων, are copied exactly from the Jerusalem Creed, with the one exception that θεὸν ἀληθινόν is omitted from the sixth, being reserved for its Nicene place

---

[1] The confusion was the more natural, since the Nicene revision of the Cæsarean Creed made considerable use either of the Creed of Jerusalem or of some closely allied formulary; and moreover the Creeds of Cæsarea and Jerusalem not rarely coincide, both being Palestinian. The similarity of the Jerusalem and 'Constantinopolitan' Creeds was noticed, I find, by Gerard Voss (*De trib. Symb.* 32—38), and evidently perplexed him much: he took refuge in the crazy suggestion that the Lectures of Cyril and the contained Creed may have been interpolated after 381, forgetting that the supposed 'interpolation' would have involved not the addition or alteration of words or sentences here and there, but the total rewriting of large masses of the Lectures.

[2] See the comparison at the end of the volume. The Creed of Jerusalem is given nearly in accordance with Hahn's careful revision of Touttée's work.

[3] The citations given in this paragraph and elsewhere from the Cappadocian, Mesopotamian, or other late Creeds are not intended to suggest that these Creeds were themselves the sources of any 'Constantinopolitan' language. Conversely it is highly unlikely that they owe anything to the 'Constantinopolitan' Creed, as in that case they would assuredly have borrowed from it more freely. It follows that, where they depart from Nicene language, they supply evidence partly for lost Creeds prior to Nicene admixture, partly for new phrases analogous to the new 'Constantinopolitan' clauses.

lower down. At this point the scanty language of Jerusalem is enlarged by a long insertion from the Nicene Creed; first (but only in the Epiphanian copy) the parenthesis explanatory of ἐκ τοῦ πατρός; then above 7 lines without change and almost without interruption[1], from φῶς ἐκ φωτός to κατελθόντα, to which last word is added ἐκ τῶν οὐρανῶν nearly as in the Apostolic Constitutions[2] and the Cappadocian and Mesopotamian Creeds. Henceforward to the end there is not a trace of unquestionable Nicene influence. It is true the παθόντα of the Nicene Creed is *added* to the σταυρωθέντα of Jerusalem; but μετὰ τὸ παθεῖν stands in the Apostolic Constitutions, the Creed of which has apparently supplied the intervening words ὑπὲρ ἡμῶν ἐπὶ Ποντίου Πιλάτου (ἐ. Π. Π. being in the Mesopotamian Creed likewise), and παθόντα itself was used at Cæsarea and Antioch (Lucianus)[3]: and again τὸ πνεῦμα τὸ ἅγιον is nearer to τὸ ἅγιον πνεῦμα (Nicene) than to ἐν ἅγιον πνεῦμα (Jerusalem)[4]; but it is supplied exactly by the Apostolic Constitutions, the Cappadocian Creed, and at least the early or Lucianic Creed of Antioch. Thus the 'Constantinopolitan' Creed in its Conciliar form owes nothing to the Nicene except one long extract,

---

[1] The exception is the dropping of τά τε ἐν τῷ οὐρανῷ καὶ τὰ ἐπὶ τῆς γῆς in the 'Constantinopolitan' recension, though not in the Epiphanian. But of this more presently.

[2] It stands also in the Latin *Libellus Fidei* of Phœbadius (p. 49 c Migne).

[3] The following are the Eastern forms used here, variations of articles and conjunctions being neglected: 'Sy.' is prefixed to the synodical formularies of 341—360. Παθόντα Cæs.; Nic.; Arius; Sy.Ant. 1 and 3: παθ. ὑπὲρ ἡμῶν Ant.(Luc.): παθ. ὑπὲρ τῶν ἁμαρτιῶν ἡμῶν Sy.Sel.: παθ. ἐπὶ Π. Π. Iren.. Παθόντα, ἀποθανόντα Smyrn.; Orig.. Σταυρωθέντα Jerus.; 'Adamantius' (?): σταυρ. ἐπὶ Π. Π. Ant.(Eus.Dor. and Cass.). Σταυρωθέντα, ἀποθανόντα Alexander; Ath.; Sy.Ant.4 and 5; Sy.Philip.; Sy.Sirm.1 and 3; Sy.Nic.Thrac.; Sy.CP. of 360: σταυρ. ὑπὲρ ἡμῶν, ἀποθανόντα Philad. Παθόντα, σταυρωθέντα Capp.: καὶ παθόντα καὶ σταυρωθέντα ἐπὶ Π. Π. Mesop. Καὶ σταυρωθέντα ἐπὶ Π. Π. καὶ ἀποθανόντα ὑπὲρ ἡμῶν καὶ ... μετὰ τὸ παθεῖν κ.τ.λ. Ap. Const. Σταυρωθέντα τε ὑπὲρ ἡμῶν ἐπὶ Π. Π. καὶ παθόντα 'Constantinop.' It will be observed (1) that the combination of the participles παθόντα and σταυρωθέντα is confined to three late Creeds, the Cappadocian, Mesopotamian, and 'Constantinopolitan', though the Apostolic Constitutions append μετὰ τὸ παθεῖν; and (2) that this irregular arrangement in Ap. Const. will account for the unique 'Constantinopolitan' position of καὶ παθόντα at the end.

[4] See however p. 81, n. 1.

with a single clause omitted; this clause, and also the Athanasian parenthesis and the Anathematism, being retained in the Epiphanian recension. Moreover this long Nicene extract incorporates the whole parallel language of Jerusalem, namely θεὸν ἀληθινόν, as reserved from above, and δι' οὗ τὰ πάντα ἐγένετο.

If on the other hand we start from the Nicene Creed as far as it proceeds, we find changes at almost every point till we reach φῶς ἐκ φωτός; namely οὐρανοῦ [τε] καὶ γῆς inserted, and πάντων and ποιητήν shifted, γεννηθέντα ἐκ τοῦ πατρὸς μονογενῆ exchanged for τὸν μονογενῆ τὸν ἐκ τοῦ πατρὸς γεννηθέντα, and πρὸ πάντων τῶν αἰώνων inserted to make a predicate to the denuded participle. After κατελθόντα, the end of the clearly Nicene passage, the contrast is even more striking. From a Nicene base we should have to suppose the insertion of καὶ ταφέντα (Jerusalem &c.), καὶ καθεζόμενον ἐκ δεξιῶν τοῦ πατρός (Jerusalem &c., with καθίσαντα), μετὰ δόξης after ἐρχόμενον (Jerusalem ἐν δόξῃ), and οὗ τῆς βασιλείας οὐκ ἔσται τέλος (Jerusalem and Apostolic Constitutions): whereas from a Jerusalem base we find nothing omitted, and nothing of any moment altered[1] except ἓν ἅγιον πνεῦμα already mentioned[2].

Comparison of course fails after the first words on the Holy Spirit, what follows being entirely new to the Nicene Creed. The Creed of Jerusalem is more altered here than elsewhere. In place of τὸν παράκλητον after πνεῦμα we have some important new clauses, to be examined in due time; and ἐν τοῖς προφήταις is exchanged for διὰ τῶν προφητῶν. The order of the clauses on Baptism and the Church is inverted, ὁμολογοῦμεν

---

[1] The changes are from καθίσαντα to καθεζόμενον, and from ἐν δόξῃ to μετὰ δόξης: the probable motive for the former change will be noticed in another place (pp. 90 f.).

[2] A passing word must suffice for the not unimportant accompanying additions new alike to the Nicene and Jerusalem Creeds, as by the nature of the case they do not concern us. Besides ἐκ τῶν οὐρανῶν (see p. 77), they are ἐκ πνεύματος ἁγίου καὶ Μαρίας τῆς παρθένου after σαρκωθέντα (see p. 89 n. 3, and for M. τ. π. compare Ap. Const., Antioch, and Mesop.), ὑπὲρ ἡμῶν ἐπὶ Ποντίου Πιλάτου after σταυρωθέντα τε (see p. 77 n. 3), κατὰ τὰς γραφάς after ἡμέρᾳ (Antioch according to Cassianus [followed by Mesop.] and in an earlier place Lucianus), and πάλιν before ἐρχόμενον (Cæsarea, Ap. Const., Antioch, Mesop., Philad.).

being prefixed to ἓν βάπτισμα[1]: καὶ ἀποστολικήν (Apost. Const., Ueltzen's text[2]) is inserted after καθολικήν, and μετανοίας omitted

[1] The form taken by the clause on the Church (εἰς τὴν κ.τ.λ.) is not a little surprising. We should have expected it either to come under ὁμολογοῦμεν or, as the last article under πιστεύομεν, and as following a group of three clauses on the Holy Spirit, to be introduced by καί. The combination of this clause with λαλῆσαν, which has been defended, as a friend points out, by M. Valetta, is too artificial to be consistent with the diction of this or any other known Creed. Moreover the corresponding clause in the earlier Creed of Jerusalem to all appearance stands independently, and certainly was so taken by Cyril in his Lectures (xviii 22, 26). Yet the combined construction has the support of other formularies. The Creed of the Apostolic Constitutions, which has some remarkable coincidences with the 'Constantinopolitan' Creed, ends its diffuse article on the Holy Spirit with the words καὶ μετὰ τοὺς ἀποστόλους δὲ [ἀποσταλὲν] πᾶσι τοῖς πιστεύουσιν ἐν τῇ ἁγίᾳ καὶ ἀποστολικῇ ἐκκλησίᾳ, followed at once by εἰς σαρκὸς ἀνάστασιν κ.τ.λ. The baptismal interrogation in the Coptic (probably Alexandrian) Constitutions (as translated by Bötticher in Bunsen's *Anal. Antenic.* ii 467), ends with Πιστεύεις εἰς τὸ ἅγιον πνεῦμα, τὸ ἀγαθόν, τὸ ζωοποιοῦν, τὸ πάντα καθαῖρον ἐν τῇ ἁγίᾳ ἐκκλησίᾳ; the previous jussive form appends to the Names of the Trinity μίαν κυριότητα, μίαν βασιλείαν, μίαν πίστιν, ἓν βάπτισμα ἐν τῇ καθολικῇ ἀποστολικῇ ἐκκλησίᾳ, καὶ εἰς ζωὴν αἰώνιον. The Creed of Seleucia (359) has δι' οὗ [sc. τοῦ ἁγίου πνεύματος ὁ σωτὴρ] καὶ ἁγιάζει τοὺς ἐν τῇ ἐκκλησίᾳ πιστεύοντας καὶ βαπτιζομένους ἐν ὀνόματι πατρὸς καὶ υἱοῦ καὶ ἁγίου πνεύματος, four of its predecessors (Ant.3, Ant.4, Philippop.,

Sirm.1: cf. Sirm. 2) having had simply, with hardly any variation, δι' οὗ καὶ ἁγιάζονται αἱ τῶν εἰλικρινῶς εἰς αὐτὸν πεπιστευκότων ψυχαί. Another combined construction is supplied by the Latin Creed of N. Africa, where *per sanctam ecclesiam* follows *vitam aeternam* at the end. The authorities are Cyprian, Augustine (*Serm.* 215: he usually expounds the Creed of Milan or Rome, as Caspari has shown, ii 264 ff.), the unknown authors of three sermons ascribed to Augustine (cf. Heurtley *H. S.* 44 ff.), and Fulgentius (Caspari ii 257). Tertullian's references (*De Bapt.* 6, 11) suit this arrangement at least as well as any other, and it is implied in two Latin sermons attributed to Chrysostom (Caspari ii 229 f., 241 ff.: cf. Pearson *On the Creed* p. 334 notes). Thus a subordinate introduction of the Church in the Creed must have existed in various regions: and in particular the Spirit was sometimes set forth as given to the believing or the baptized *in the Church*. Any Creed of this form (and the Creed of the Apostolic Constitutions with peculiar ease) might give rise to the 'Constantinopolitan' arrangement if it were hastily assumed that the previous article ended with πιστεύουσιν (virtually as in the four or five synodic formularies cited above), and that ἐν τῇ κ.τ.λ. was a fresh beginning (going back to the initial Πιστεύομεν), needing only to be changed to the more correct εἰς τὴν κ.τ.λ. On the history of the subsequent removal of *in* from the Latin 'Constantinopolitan' Creed, resulting from its absence in the Western Creed and the distinction drawn between *Credo in* and *Credo*, much evidence is given by Caspari i 220—234.

[2] It occurs in the Nicene *Anathe-*

after βάπτισμα as in the Mesopotamian Creed. In place of σαρ ὸς ἀνάστασιν we have ἀνάστασιν νεκρῶν (so the Cappadocian, Mesopotamian, and Philadelphian Creeds, νεκρῶν ἀνάστασιν the Antiochian in Chrysostom[1]), with προσδοκῶμεν prefixed; and in place of καὶ εἰς ζωὴν αἰώνιον we have καὶ ζωὴν τοῦ μέλλοντος αἰῶνος (Apost. Const.)[2], followed by Ἀμήν. Unfortunately only a fragment of this part of the Antiochian Creed has survived, and nothing of the Cæsarean Creed, supposing it to have contained corresponding clauses (see p. 60 n. 2); so that we know very little of the source or sources of the changes. But notwithstanding their number, which would have left the matter in uncertainty but for the clear light cast by the earlier parts of the Creed, there is no sufficient reason to doubt that the base is still supplied by Jerusalem. None of the Jerusalem materials are missing except τὸν παράκλητον, replaced by the new clauses, and itself absent from the Cappadocian and Mesopotamian Creeds, and μετανοίας, absent from the Mesopotamian Creed: and the only change of order places the Church naturally next to the Holy Spirit. Thus, with these two exceptions of τὸν παράκλητον and μετανοίας, the entire Creed of Jerusalem from beginning to end is reproduced in the 'Constantinopolitan'.

The new clauses on the Holy Spirit were doubtless inserted in consequence of the Pneumatomachian controversy, as is commonly said. For the present it is enough to observe their simplicity of form. The adoption of the extended phrase τὸ πνεῦμα τὸ ἅγιον is accompanied by the addition of two adjectives similar to ἅγιον, so as to make a triad of epithets desig-

---

matism in most of the early texts, though not in that of Eusebius appended to Athanasius *De Decretis* as edited by Montfaucon; and though accordingly omitted in some reprints, it is probably genuine. It stands in the body of the Cappadocian, the Mesopotamian, and apparently the Alexandrian Creeds.

[1] On 1 Cor. xv 29 p. 380 c (Heurtley *Harm. Symb.* 39; Caspari i 83 ff.). So also the Apostolic Constitutions a little further on in the Blessing of the Water (vii 43), κηρύξαι βασιλείαν, ἄφεσιν ἁμαρτιῶν, νεκρῶν ἀνάστασιν. Νεκρῶν appears likewise to have been the Alexandrian reading (Origen and Alexander).

[2] This peculiar phrase occurs likewise in the Confession of Arius and Euzoius (ap. Socr. i 26; Sozom. ii 27).

nating the One Spirit within the Godhead, "the Spirit which is Holy, which is Lord, which is Lifegiving"[1]. Another clause sets forth His relation to the Father; a third His equality with the Father and the Son as confessed in worship. But the clear purpose which may thus be traced was directed less to

---

[1] The four copies of the Creed in Mansi's *Concilia* have severally τὸ κύριον τὸ ζωοποιόν (A) iii 565, τὸ κύριον καὶ ζωοποιόν (B) vii 111 and xi 633, τὸ κύριον καὶ τὸ ζωοποιόν (C) vi 957: Routh (*S. E. O.* i 454) cites two with A. The Epiphanian copy in Dindorf's text (probably taken from the Jena MS., but perhaps due only to the editor) has B, in Petau's text (founded on the Paris MS.) it has only κύριον καὶ ζωοποιόν (D): both MSS. are bad. Almost all Latin copies have *et* (B, C, or D), as was natural with the substantival rendering of κύριον: A however stands in the Mozarabic Liturgy (p. 231 = 557 Migne). D is virtually impossible, and C must have been derived from A or less probably B. Authority slightly favours B: but on a small point so liable to variation, and in the absence of MSS. of ascertained excellence, one authority is nearly as good as another. B makes good sense, but was not likely to be altered: A gives a better yet a less obvious sense, while familiarity would tempt scribes to take τὸ πνεῦμα τὸ ἅγιον as a single name. On the whole the original text seems likely to have had three articles without a conjunction: and if so, the true arrangement is almost certainly that given in the text. Had τὸ κύριον τὸ ζωοποιόν been intended to be taken apart from what precedes, or had B been the true reading, the form selected would surely have been τὸ ἅγιον πνεῦμα, which is nearer to the ἓν ἅγιον πνεῦμα of Jerusalem, and actually stands in the Nicene text. The Cappadocian Creed has a similar triad of attributes, τὸ πνεῦμα τὸ ἅγιον τὸ ἄκτιστον τὸ τέλειον, "the Spirit which is Holy, which is Uncreate, which is Perfect"; confirmed by three other triads occurring in other clauses. All the chief writers of the period dwell on ἅγιον in a manner which shews that they did not regard it merely as part of a compound name.

Touttée (p. 83: cf. Hahn, p. 11, and Caspari *ZS. f. Luth. Th.* 1857 p. 654) notices the curious fact that several late writers connected with Jerusalem retain ἕν, which he supposes to be a remnant of the Creed as given in Cyril's Lectures. We might be tempted to surmise rather that the purest text of the revised Creed, as preserved at Jerusalem itself, read καὶ εἰς ἓν πνεῦμα τὸ ἅγιον τὸ κύριον τὸ ζωοποιόν, in conformity with ἕνα θεόν, ἕνα κύριον, μίαν... ἐκκλησίαν, ἓν βάπτισμα, and 1 Cor. xii 13; Eph. iv 4, &c. Unfortunately those who have ἓν omit τό, and none of them are quite clearly quoting the Creed. It is not easy to see why ἓν should have been expelled from its old place, to the loss of symmetry if not of doctrine; and though ἓν πνεῦμα τὸ ἅγιον by itself might be pedantic, the addition of the two other articles and adjectives would restore simplicity by clearly marking ἅγιον as an attribute, not a name: the unfamiliar combination would naturally in transcription succumb to grammatical smoothness in two different ways, here becoming ἓν πνεῦμα ἅγιον, and there τὸ πνεῦμα τὸ ἅγιον. But in the absence of any external evidence for ἓν πνεῦμα τὸ ἅγιον the existing text must be allowed its rights.

accurate definition than to pregnant instructiveness[1]; and the rhythm of devotional recitation is never lost.

These clauses inserted in the third division bear a close analogy to the Nicene extract (with or without the parenthesis) in the second division. The two cases taken together suggest the probable origin of the 'Constantinopolitan' Creed. Either at Jerusalem or in some neighbouring part of Palestine[2], where the old local Creed was still in use for ordinary ecclesiastical purposes, a desire might be felt to furnish it with clauses, terse and popular in form but effectual in statement, which would guard the members of the local Church from the worst errors current on two great doctrines of the faith. For the second division the most obvious course was to appropriate so much of the Nicene definition as could be introduced without incongruity[3]; and the portion adopted would doubtless include ὁμοούσιος as a token of full Nicene communion, supposing such communion to be either now sought or already enjoyed. For the third division no such resource was available, and new clauses had to be compiled or devised. The opportunity might be taken

---

[1] Κύριον, ζωοποιόν, and πορευόμενον come from Scripture, changed in inflexion only: συνπροσκυνούμενον and συνδοξαζόμενον for all their cogency are not technical. The consecration which ὁμοούσιος had acquired in the second division of the Creed was not allowed to introduce it into the third, though here too the greatest theologians, from Athanasius (*Ep. ad Ser.* i 27 p. 676 CD) onwards, attested its truth, and used it where there was need with more or less freedom: and so with other terms of the schools. The third clause is not unlikely to be original; hardly the second, or any member of the first.

[2] Epiphanius's long residence in Palestine, or even the proximity of Cyprus, the seat of his episcopal activity from about 367, may explain how the Creed reached his hands. He shews local knowledge of circumstances not otherwise recorded, relating to Jerusalem, Eleutheropolis (in Judæa), and Cæsarea, the dates being about 359, 360 (p. 97 n. 1) and 366, 367 (p. 93 n. 4), both in the early period. But there is reason to think that he always kept up a connexion with his own former monastery at his birth-place near Eleutheropolis (see Tillemont x 498 f.). He has a list of bishops of Jerusalem extending through the troubled times to the date of his writing, 375 (*Haer.* 637). About 377 we find him in correspondence with Basil on the dissensions among the brethren on the Mount of Olives (Bas. *Ep.* 258), noticed further on for another purpose.

[3] If a single employment of οὐσία (as contained in ὁμοούσιος) could be made to suffice, it was clearly better to avoid a second. See also note 1.

to effect other lesser improvements in the Creed, suggested by intercourse with sister churches: but there would be a natural desire not to obliterate the identity with the formulary handed down from earlier generations. For such a purpose as this the Nicene Creed itself would evidently have been useless[1]. The requirements of a local congregational or baptismal Creed will likewise account for the absence of the earlier part of the Nicene definition. That carefully compacted sentence was not in itself fitted for popular recitation, nor was it in rhythm and diction in harmony with the existing Creed of Jerusalem.

The same consideration goes far towards shewing that Epiphanius has preserved a less pure copy of the Creed, as originally formed, than that which was read at Chalcedon, and which alone acquired general authority. It is doubtless possible that the Athanasian parenthesis was from the first picked out of its surroundings for insertion, to be followed immediately by the longer extract: but it is hard on this view to explain the omission of the intervening θεὸν ἐκ θεοῦ[2], and the technical form of the parenthesis itself agrees ill with the supposed use. The presence of the Anathematism in the Epiphanian recension points at least as strongly towards the same conclusion. Moreover if the Chalcedonian recension was the original, the Epiphanian variations are at once explained by the common tendency to approximate more closely, especially by addition, to a familiar verbal standard with which there is accordance

---

[1] If the 'Constantinopolitan' Creed was only the Creed of Jerusalem enlarged and improved, we need no further explanation of the absence of the Anathematism which closes the Nicene Creed. The trivial variations in the Anathematism of the Epiphanian 'Constantinopolitan' Creed, like its previous insertion of τέ, are evidently accidental errors of transcription, due either to Epiphanius's habitual inaccuracy of quotation or to discrepancies in current copies of the Nicene Creed, such as certainly existed: on ῥευστόν see A. Jahn *Method. Plotiniz.* p. 75.

[2] If the insertion of the parenthesis was not original, there would be nothing strange in beginning the extract with φῶς ἐκ φωτός, more especially as the illustration of the eternal generation of the Son by the analogy of light (ἀπαύγασμα τῆς δόξης Heb. i 3), to which Origen had given currency, would thus be brought into prominence. Conciseness (see p. 73) would justify non-insertion where it would not justify excision.

already: whereas no reason can be found here for a change in the opposite direction. Analogous extensions of an originally incomplete adoption of Nicene language took place, as will be shown further on, in contemporary enlarged Greek recensions of the Cappadocian Creed. It may therefore be accepted as reasonably certain that the explicit analysis of πάντα supplied after δι' οὗ τὰ πάντα ἐγένετο, the Athanasian parenthesis, and the Anathematism formed no part of the original appropriation of Nicene language, but were secondary additions from the same source[1], made either by Epiphanius or by those from whom he received the Creed.

So far as the ascertainment of the true character of the 'Constantinopolitan' Creed is concerned, the investigation might stop here. Yet a supplementary enquiry into its probable authorship and date, though unavoidably resting on more doubtful grounds, will hardly be out of place. As the 'Constantinopolitan' Creed took its origin from the Creed of Jerusalem, conjecture naturally turns first to the Church of Jerusalem as the body for whose use it may have been framed. Now the legitimate bishop of Jerusalem, during the whole period within the limits of which the construction of the Creed must of necessity be placed, was Cyril, to whose Lectures, written in youth[2], we owe our knowledge of his Church's Creed towards the middle of the fourth century. His Lectures are remarkable for the combination of Nicene doctrine with an avoidance of the specially Nicene language; and similarly his episcopate was more than once interrupted by expulsion at the hands of Arians, while in its earliest years he chiefly associated himself with men who were commonly regarded as Semiarians. On the other hand he is distinctly stated to have sub-

---

[1] They would thus constitute an exact parallel to the late Latin *Deum de Deo* of the Western form of the 'Constantinopolitan' Creed; which was indeed a more harmonious interpolation. On the other hand *Filioque*, in its primary character as intended for Spanish use, bears some analogy to the new clauses on the Holy Spirit.

[2] "Extant ejus κατηχήσεις, quas in adolescentia composuit." Hieron. *De vir. ill.* 112.

sequently accepted the term ὁμοούσιον, though the time of change is not clearly marked. Thus his personal history is in some sort parallel to a transition from the Creed of Jerusalem to that which we call Constantinopolitan; and the tone of the later phrases is in harmony alike with his firm hold of doctrine and with his dread of excessive definition in theological statement.

Again comparison of the 'Constantinopolitan' phrases with the language previously employed by Cyril of Jerusalem, in expounding the earlier form of Creed, yields some interesting though hardly decisive results. Of the three most distinctive clauses, those on the Holy Spirit, the first, καὶ εἰς τὸ πνεῦμα τὸ ἅγιον τὸ κύριον τὸ ζωοποιόν, is made up entirely of Scriptural terms (Jo. xiv 26 &c.; 2 Co. iii 6, 17, 18; Jo. vi 63; Rom. viii 11), and thus attests nothing more than selection. Τὸ κύριον, evidently inserted as an expression of the truth denied by those who said μὴ μόνον κτίσμα ἀλλὰ καὶ τῶν λειτουργικῶν πνευμάτων ἓν αὐτὸ εἶναι, καὶ βαθμῷ μόνον αὐτὸ διαφέρειν τῶν ἀγγέλων (Ath. *Ep. ad Serap.* i 1 p. 648 A), does not occur in Cyril or even, I think, in Athanasius; but the idea expressed by it is set forth by Cyril with much force more than once (iv 16 οὗ καὶ χρείαν ἔχουσι θρόνοι καὶ κυριότητες, ἀρχαὶ καὶ ἐξουσίαι; xvi 23 at some length, ending καὶ τὰ μέν ἐστιν εἰς λειτουργίαν ἀποστελλόμενα, τὸ δὲ ἐρευνᾷ καὶ τὰ βάθη τοῦ θεοῦ)[1]. Again, τὸ ζωοποιόν[2], fully propounded by Athanasius (ib. 23 p. 671: cf. 19 p. 668 A), is indirectly anti-

---

[1] Cyril's statement is happily condensed in a fragment interpolated into his 16th Lecture in one MS. (p. 262 Touttée), τὸ κυριεῦον καὶ βασιλεῦον πάσης τῆς γεννητικῆς (? γενητῆς) οὐσίας ὁρατῶν τε καὶ ἀοράτων φύσεων, τὸ δέσποζον ἀγγέλων τε καὶ ἀρχαγγέλων, ἐξουσιῶν, ἀρχῶν, κυριοτήτων, θρόνων. Cyril's use of 1 Cor. ii 10 finds an exact parallel in Athanasius's own Confession (2 p. 100 B), in which it supplies the only attribute assigned to the Holy Spirit: Πιστεύομεν ὁμοίως καὶ εἰς τὸ πνεῦμα τὸ ἅγιον, τὸ πάντα ἐρευνῶν καὶ τὰ βάθη τοῦ θεοῦ, ἀναθεματίζοντες τὰ παρὰ τοῦτο φρονοῦντα δόγματα.

[2] Its force is given by Athanasius l. c., τὰ δὲ κτίσματα...ζωοποιούμενά ἐστι δι' αὐτοῦ, τὸ δὲ μὴ μέτεχον ζωῆς, ἀλλ' αὐτὸ μετεχόμενον καὶ ζωοποιοῦν τὰ κτίσματα, ποίαν ἔχει συγγένειαν πρὸς τὰ γενητά, ἢ πῶς ὅλως ἂν εἴη τῶν κτισμάτων, ἅπερ ἐν ἐκείνῳ παρὰ τοῦ λόγου ζωοποιεῖται;

cipated by Cyril in a doxology (ᾧ ἡ δόξα σὺν τῷ μονογενεῖ κ.τ.λ. σὺν τῷ ἁγίῳ καὶ ζωοποιῷ πνεύματι, vii 16)[1], as by earlier writers[2]. In like manner Cyril has nothing answering to the second clause, τὸ ἐκ τοῦ πατρὸς ἐκπορευόμενον, which is undoubtedly Athanasian[3]: but he would probably have no difficulty, in the presence of a new controversy, in adopting a phrase which, in spite of the change of preposition, might pass as only a free quotation from Scripture[4], and which had long enjoyed some currency[5]. The third and weightiest clause,

---

[1] So also one of Cyril's answers to the question why our Lord (John iv 14) compared the Spirit to water is Ἐ-πειδὴ...ζωοποιόν ἐστι τὸ ὕδωρ (xvi 12).

[2] The Coptic and Æthiopic baptismal confessions (given by Caspari ii 12 f. from Assemani *Cod. Liturg.* i 159 [see likewise the Coptic Constitutions translated by Bötticher in Bunsen's *Anal. Antenic.* ii 467, for both the jussive and the interrogative forms], and Bibl. Max. Patr. [Lugd. 1677] xxvii 636 a D) contain *Spiritum Sanctum vivificantem*, which probably has an ancient origin not 'Constantinopolitan'. The revised Mesopotamian Creed also has τὸ πνεῦμα τὸ ζωοποιόν.

[3] Athanasius uses it often, but the following passages are of primary importance as fixing his meaning. Ἑνὸς γὰρ ὄντος τοῦ υἱοῦ, τοῦ ζῶντος λόγου, μίαν εἶναι δεῖ τελείαν καὶ πλήρη τὴν ἁγιαστικὴν καὶ φωτιστικὴν ζῶσαν ἐνέργειαν αὐτοῦ καὶ δωρεάν, ἥτις ἐκ πατρὸς λέγεται ἐκπορεύεσθαι, ἐπειδὴ παρὰ τοῦ λόγου τοῦ ἐκ πατρὸς ὁμολογουμένου ἐκλάμπει καὶ ἀποστέλλεται καὶ δίδοται· ἀμέλει ὁ μὲν υἱὸς παρὰ τοῦ πατρὸς ἀποστέλλεται,...ὁ δὲ υἱὸς τὸ πνεῦμα ἀποστέλλει. *Ep. ad Ser.* i 20 p. 669 c d. Τὸ δὲ ἅγιον πνεῦμα, ἐκπόρευμα ὂν τοῦ πατρός, ἀεί ἐστιν ἐν ταῖς χερσὶ τοῦ πέμποντος πατρὸς καὶ τοῦ φέροντος υἱοῦ, δι' οὗ ἐπλήρωσε τὰ πάντα. *Exp. Fid.* 4 p. 102 a: the phrase ἐν τ. χερσὶ κ.τ.λ. comes from Dionysius of Alexandria (ap. Ath. *De sent. Dion.* 17 or Routh *R.S.* iii. 395, cf. Montf. *Praef.* xviii).

[4] Athanasius dwells so much on ἐκ τοῦ θεοῦ as applied to the Spirit in Scripture (quoting 1 Cor. ii 12), and connects it so distinctly with his favourite idea of ultimate derivation from the Father through the Son, that he probably regarded τὸ ἐκ τοῦ πατρὸς ἐκπορευόμενον not as a free transcript of Jo. xv 26 but as a combination of the two texts; that is, he took τὸ ἐκ τοῦ πατρός as the fundamental formula, qualified by ἐκπορευόμενον. See *Ep. ad Ser.* i 22, 25; iii 2.

[5] Athanasius writes of it as though it were an old phrase that he was interpreting rather than a new one that he was inventing (*Ep. ad Ser.* i. 15 p. 663 e). It occurs 7 times in a single short passage of Marcellus (ap. Eus. *E. T.* iii 4 p. 168), who apparently confuses it with the words in St John, παρὰ τοῦ πατρὸς ἐκπορεύεται, which he quotes once at the outset: and Eusebius, in answering him, equally assumes it as recognised (p. 169 ac), probably (λέγεται, εἴρηται) with the same confusion. This free use in two different camps is hardly consistent with a recent origin. On the other hand the phrase is absent to all appearance from Origen's extant writings: at least it is impossible to determine whether he or Rufinus wrote the sentence in the commen-

τὸ σὺν πατρὶ καὶ υἱῷ συνπροσκυνούμενον καὶ συνδοξαζόμενον,

tary on Romans (viii 14 p. 593 Ru.), "sed unus est [spiritus] qui vere ex ipso Deo procedit." It was probably constructed by one of the Origenists who adorned the latter half of the third century. Dionysius of Alexandria (ob. 264 or 5) might easily arrive at it in his development of the doctrine of the Trinity due to his controversy with Sabellius: a fragment of his has already been mentioned (p. 86 n. 3) as supplying Athanasius with another peculiar phrase on the Holy Spirit (the words being Ἐν τε ταῖς χερσὶν αὐτῶν [Father and Son] ἐστὶ τὸ πνεῦμα, μήτε τοῦ πέμποντος μήτε τοῦ φέροντος δυνάμενον στέρεσθαι, and the same fragment has also the sentence Ἅγιον πνεῦμα προσέθηκα, ἀλλ' ἅμα καὶ πόθεν καὶ διὰ τίνος ἦκεν ἐφήρμοσα. The Exposition of Gregory Thaumaturgus (p. 1), another contemporary Origenist, has Καὶ ἓν πνεῦμα ἅγιον, ἐκ θεοῦ τὴν ὕπαρξιν ἔχον καὶ διὰ υἱοῦ πεφηνός, δηλαδὴ τοῖς ἀνθρώποις, εἰκὼν τοῦ υἱοῦ, τελείου τελεία, ζωὴ ζώντων αἰτία κ.τ.λ. Theognostus, a third eminent Origenist of an apparently somewhat later date, has also to be noticed, as the subject of the third book of his *Hypotyposes* was the Holy Spirit (Phot. Cod. 106 p. 86 a 12). It will be remembered (see p. 55), that Dionysius was the authority cited by Athanasius for the early acceptance of ὁμοούσιος, and Theognostus for ἐκ τῆς οὐσίας τοῦ πατρός. The conception common to Dionysius, Gregory Thaumaturgus, and Athanasius is ultimately derived from Tertullian, for whom as a Montanist the subject had especial interest: the first of the two following passages is likewise the source of ἐκ τῆς οὐσίας τοῦ πατρός. "Ceterum qui Filium non *aliunde* deduco, sed *de substantia Patris*, nihil facientem sine Patris voluntate, omnem a Patre consecutum potestatem, quomodo possum de fide destruere monarchiam, quam a Patre Filio traditam in Filio servo? Hoc mihi et in tertium gradum dictum sit, quia *Spiritum non aliunde* puto quam *a Patre per Filium.*" *Adv. Prax.* 4. (Cf. 3, " in Filio et in Spiritu Sancto, secundum et tertium sortitis locum., tam *consortibus substantiae Patris*.") "Omne quod prodit *ex aliquo* secundum sit ejus necesse est de quo *prodit*, non ideo tamen est separatum. Secundus autem ubi est, duo sunt, et tertius ubi est tres sunt. Tertius enim est *Spiritus a Deo* †et† *Filio* [surely the sense requires *ex Filio*], sicut tertius a radice fructus ex frutice, et tertius a fonte rivus ex flumine, et tertius a sole apex ex radio. Nihil tamen a matrice alienatur a qua proprietates suas ducit. Ita trinitas per consertos et conexos gradus a Patre decurrens et monarchiae nihil obstrepit et οἰκονομίας statum protegit." *Ib.* 8. (Cf. *ib.* " Nam et istae species [sc. frutex, fluvius, radius] προβολαὶ sunt earum *substantiarum ex quibus prodeunt.*") It is unlikely that Tertullian meant *prodit* to represent ἐκπορεύεται, though (written as *prodiit*) it is the rendering in *e* (alone of Old Latin authorities); for in that case he must have at least made some clear allusion to the original verse, which he has done nowhere in his writings. But his pregnant treatise against Praxeas would naturally be studied by those who had to controvert the more refined 'Monarchianism' of Sabellius. Among these Dionysius of Rome, the third authority for Nicene diction, holds a place: and he may be included among the possible authors of the 'Constantinopolitan' phrase. Purely 'Constantinopolitan' it is not, expresses ideas common to all stages of the controversy[1], and especially suits the comparatively late time when the evils of excessive elaboration of doctrine came to be strongly felt[2]: but it agrees likewise with what Cyril wrote when as yet the controversy had not visibly risen. Thus he begins the corresponding article in his preliminary summary of doctrine (iv 16) with the decisive words, Πίστευε καὶ εἰς τὸ πνεῦμα τὸ ἅγιον, καὶ τὴν αὐτὴν ἔχε περὶ αὐτοῦ δόξαν ἣν παρέλαβες ἔχειν περὶ πατρὸς καὶ υἱοῦ, and repeats after a few lines ὅπερ σὺν πατρὶ καὶ υἱῷ τῇ τῆς θεότητος δόξῃ τετίμηται, the last word being explained by a similar passage in the fuller exposition (xvi 4), τῷ μετὰ πατρὸς καὶ υἱοῦ τετιμημένῳ, καὶ ἐν τῷ καιρῷ τοῦ ἁγίου βαπτίσματος ἐν τῇ ἁγίᾳ τριάδι συμπεριλαμβανομένῳ: and again he says, προσκυνοῦντες τὸν ἀποσταλέντα κύριον καὶ ὑπὲρ ἡμῶν σταυρωθέντα, προσκυνοῦντες καὶ τὸν ἀποστείλαντα πατέρα θεὸν σὺν ἁγίῳ πνεύματι[3] (xiii 41). The impression produced by the three clauses taken together is, that they were compiled under the influence of Athanasius's

---

for it occurs in the revised Mesopotamian Creed, with τὸ πνεῦμα τῆς ἀληθείας prefixed in accordance with John xv 26.

[1] For Athanasius see *Ep. ad Ser.* i 31 p. 679 D (cf. 9 p. 657 AB), τὸ συνδοξαζόμενον πατρὶ καὶ υἱῷ καὶ θεολογούμενον μετὰ τοῦ λόγου. In his Epistle to Jovianus (A.D. 363), 4 p. 782 BC, he treats the inclusion of the Spirit in the Nicene Creed as amounting to 'conglorification'.

[2] Εἰ δὲ πατὴρ καὶ υἱὸς καὶ ἅγιον πνεῦμα εὐσεβῶς δοξάζοιτο καὶ προσκυνοῖτο παρὰ τῶν πιστευόντων ἐν ἀσυγχύτῳ καὶ διακεκριμένῃ τῇ ἁγίᾳ τριάδι μίαν εἶναι καὶ φύσιν καὶ δόξαν καὶ βασιλείαν καὶ δύναμιν καὶ τὴν ἐπὶ πάντων ἐξουσίαν, ἐνταῦθα ὁ πόλεμος τίνα εὔλογον αἰτίαν ἔχει; ..."Ἕως γὰρ οὖν ἐξ ὅλης καρδίας τε καὶ ψυχῆς καὶ διανοίας προσκυνεῖται (so we must read for προσκυνῆται) ὁ μονογενὴς θεός, ἐκεῖνο εἶναι πεπιστευμένος ἐν πᾶσιν ὅπερ ἐστὶν ὁ πατήρ, ὡσαύτως δὲ καὶ τὸ πνεῦμα τὸ ἅγιον ὁμοτίμῳ προσκυνήσει δοξάζεται (ed. -ζηται), οἱ τὰ περισσὰ σοφιζόμενοι ποίαν τοῦ πολέμου εὐπρόσωπον ἔχουσιν ἀφορμήν, κ.τ.λ.; Greg. Nyss. *Ep. ad Eust.* (iii 1017 CD Mi.), probably about A.D. 381: see p. 103. In 372 Basil had written to the Western bishops, Λαλείσθω καὶ παρ' ἡμῖν μετὰ παρρησίας τὸ ἀγαθὸν ἐκεῖνο κήρυγμα τῶν πατέρων, τὸ καταστρέφον μὲν τὴν δυσώνυμον αἵρεσιν τὴν Ἀρείου, οἰκοδομοῦν δὲ τὰς ἐκκλησίας ἐν τῇ ὑγιαινούσῃ διδασκαλίᾳ, ἐν ᾗ ὁ υἱὸς ὁμοούσιος ὁμολογεῖται τῷ πατρί, καὶ τὸ πνεῦμα τὸ ἅγιον ὁμοτίμως συναριθμεῖταί τε καὶ συλλατρεύεται (*Ep.* 90 p. 182 BC).

[3] Two MSS. have καὶ τὸ ἅγιον πνεῦμα, but the sense is the same. To these passages might be added others, e.g. vi 6; xvi 24, which presuppose a similar belief.

Epistles to Serapion, or at least of Athanasian ways of thought, by some one exercising a cautious and independent judgement, and sedulous in confining the Creed within the lines of Scriptural diction and traditional usage. This character at least agrees with what we know of Cyril, though it may be equally applicable to others; and the expansion of doctrine as compared with his earlier teaching answers well to that moderated growth which seems to have distinguished his career. Intimate affinities of belief[1], too fundamental to be obscured by different estimates of conflicting expediencies, must have throughout attached Cyril in mind to Athanasius, and thus disposed him to accept suggestions from the great theologian's writings. Indeed the language on the Holy Spirit already quoted from Cyril's own Lectures is singularly clear and emphatic for the time when it was spoken. Much vacillation is attested by Gregory of Nazianzus and others to have still existed a few years later, when the controversy had already begun, as has often been noticed[2].

We may next examine the other 'Constantinopolitan' phrases which belong neither to the earlier Creed nor to the Nicene insertion. No stress can be laid on so obvious an addition as ἐκ τῶν οὐρανῶν after κατελθόντα: but it is not absent from Cyril's summary exposition of the Incarnation, διὰ τὰς ἁμαρτίας ἡμῶν ἐξ οὐρανῶν κατῆλθεν ἐπὶ τῆς γῆς (iv 9). The same passage supplies a more important parallel to ἐκ πνεύματος ἁγίου καὶ Μαρίας τῆς παρθένου as added to σαρκωθέντα[3], in the

---

[1] Under this third division of the Creed τὸ πάντων ἁγιαστικὸν καὶ θεοποιόν (iv 16) may be compared with *Ep. ad Ser.* i 25 p. 674 BC; and ὁ πατὴρ δι' υἱοῦ σὺν ἁγίῳ πνεύματι τὰ πάντα χαρίζεται (xvi 24) with various expressions of the same thought by Athanasius, who substitutes ἐν for σύν (as virtually Cyril likewise in xviii 29), e.g. ib. 14 p. 663 B; 24 p. 673 B; 28 p. 676 F; iii 5 p. 694 D. In the same chapter Cyril has καὶ πατὴρ μὲν δίδωσιν υἱῷ, καὶ υἱὸς μεταδίδωσιν ἁγίῳ πνεύματι.

[2] See *e.g.* Gieseler *K.G.* i 2 69 ff. Münscher (*HB. Dogmengesch.* iii 485) justly observes that Hilary, though a Homoousian, shews less decision on this head than Cyril: cf. Meier, *Lehre v. d. Trinität* i 192.

[3] In extant Creeds this combination is, I believe, unique: the revised Mesopotamian Creed however contains the more remarkable part of it, σαρκωθέντα

90 ON THE 'CONSTANTINOPOLITAN' CREED

words γεννηθεὶς ἐξ ἁγίας παρθένου καὶ ἁγίου πνεύματος, followed after two lines by σαρκωθεὶς ἐξ αὐτῆς ἀληθῶς[1]: and the longer exposition has ἐκ παρθένου καὶ πνεύματος ἁγίου κατὰ τὸ εὐαγγέλιον ἐνανθρωπήσαντα (xii 3). Nor can much be inferred from the comparative prominence given by Cyril to the first (iv 10; xiii 1 ff.) and third (xiii 4) elements of ὑπὲρ ἡμῶν ἐπὶ Π. Π. καὶ παθόντα following σταυρωθέντα. It is more worthy of notice that he devotes 19 out of his 23 chapters (xiv 2—20) on the Resurrection to the illustration of κατὰ τὰς γραφάς in 1 Cor. xv 4. The change from καθίσαντα to καθεζόμενον coincides exactly with his repeated contention (xi 17;

ἐκ πνεύματος ἁγίου. The form γεννηθέντα ἐκ ... καὶ ..., employed by Cyril before he advances to σαρκωθέντα ἐξ αὐτῆς ἀληθῶς, occurs in Origen's Rule of Faith, in the problematical Greek rendering of a Latin Creed sent by Marcellus to Julius (Epiph. *Haer.* 836), and a similar Creed in Athelstan's Psalter (Heurtley *H. S.* 79 ff.); in the formulary of Nicé (A.D. 359) repeated at Constantinople in 360; and in the confession of Julianus of Eclanum (Hahn 201): Paulinus of Antioch uses it in assenting to the Tome of the Council of Alexandria in 362 written by Athanasius (Ath. *Tom. ad Ant.* 777 B); as also virtually Athanasius himself some years later (*c. Apoll.* i 20 p. 938 E, ἐξ ἁγίας παρθένου καὶ ἐκ πνεύματος ἁγίου γεννηθέντα υἱὸν ἀνθρώπου, and ii 5 p. 943 D, γεννηθεὶς ἐκ Μαρίας τῆς παρθένου καὶ πνεύματος ἁγίου), though he usually omits ἐκ πν. ἁγίου. In the *natus de Sp. S. et (ex) V. M.* of the early Latin Creeds *et*, though as old as Augustine (cf. Caspari ii 275 f., 279 f.), seems to be a corruption of the at least equally well attested *ex*. In Mat. i 20 all Latin versions have *de Sp. S.*, while *ex ea* is a not infrequent Old Latin rendering of ἐν αὐτῇ, occurring as early as Cyprian; so that both parts of the combination were derived from the same verse: the influence of ἐξ ἧς ἐγεννήθη in Mat. i 16 is questionable, since after Tertullian (*De carne Chr.* 20) the Old Latin, except in two of its later types, followed a paraphrastic reading containing the active ἐγέννησεν, as did other ancient versions.

[1] It is not necessary to suppose the combination of σαρκωθείς with ἐκ Μαρίας in the Creed to have been directed against any heresy. But if it were, an obvious motive would be suggested by Cyril's frequent warnings against Docetic doctrines, and especially those of the Manicheans, colonies of whom were to be found in Palestine: see Touttée's note on vi 20 p. 99 E. Another possible but not probable occasion has been found in the theory of a heavenly origin for our Lord's body which was sometimes associated with doctrines resembling those of Apollinaris from 362 onwards, but for which Apollinaris himself was apparently not responsible, and which he certainly disclaimed (Walch *Ketzerhistorie* iii 190 ff.; cf. Dorner *Person Christi* i 978 ff.). Indeed σαρκωθείς (σάρκωσις) ἐξ ἁγίας παρθένου Μαρίας occurs repeatedly in the epistles bearing the name of Julius of Rome, but suspected to be of Apollinarian origin.

xiv 27—30), enforced by the constant use of the present tense (even in such a phrase as ὁ καταβὰς καὶ ἀναβὰς καὶ τῷ πατρὶ συγκαθεζόμενος, c. 30), that the Session did not begin at the Ascension but was from eternity. In the clause of the future Advent πάλιν answers to the subject of the first two chapters of the corresponding Lecture (xv 1 f.), and μετὰ δόξης, not ἐν δόξῃ, is at least the form adopted by Cyril when he uses his own words (xv 3)[1]. Lastly the substitution of νεκρῶν for σαρκός with ἀνάστασιν is in striking agreement with the, I believe, invariable diction of his 21 chapters on the future resurrection (xviii 1—21), confirmed by a final interpretation, καὶ εἰς σαρκὸς ἀνάστασιν, τοῦτ' ἐστὶ τὴν τῶν νεκρῶν (cf. 22, 28[2]). The remaining 'Constantinopolitan' changes in the contents of the Creed, which find apparently no support in Cyril's Lectures, are the insertion of ἐπὶ Ποντίου Πιλάτου (1) and καὶ ἀποστολικήν (2), the substitution of ζωὴν τοῦ μέλλοντος αἰῶνος for ζωὴν αἰώνιον (3), and the omission of τὸν παράκλητον (4) and μετανοίας (5); of which the first three might come from the Creed of the Apostolic Constitutions (possibly the source of ἐκ τῶν οὐρανῶν, ὑπὲρ ἡμῶν, παθόντα, πάλιν, and μετὰ δόξης likewise)[3], (5) is supported by the Mesopotamian Creed, and (4) was almost necessitated by the form of the accompanying enlargement[4]. Of the introduced verbs, ὁμολογοῦμεν

---

[1] Still more trivial is the agreement between ὁ λαλήσας ἐν πνεύματι ἁγίῳ διὰ τῶν προφητῶν in his last chapter on the Holy Spirit (xvii 38) with the 'Constantinopolitan' variation from ἐν τοῖς προφήταις. The Creed of Irenæus, following many Scriptural precedents, has διά: ἐν probably came from Heb. i 1.

[2] Cyril's successor, John of Jerusalem, is severely rebuked by Jerome (Lib. c. Jo. Jer. 25—28 pp. 430 ff. Vall.; cf. Caspari i 176 f.) because in his Exposition of Faith he nine times spoke of the resurrection of the body, never of the resurrection of the flesh, as was prescribed by "the Symbol of our faith and hope, handed down by the Apostles," &c. (c. 28), i.e. by a Latin Creed. However Cyril equally avoided σαρκός at a time when it was certainly in the Creed of his church and in that of the Apostolic Constitutions; and σαρκός is absent (see p. 80) from all known revised Eastern Creeds.

[3] Indeed (2) had probably Nicene authority, though not in this place: see p. 79 n. 2.

[4] It is also possible that the omission of τὸν παράκλητον was partly due to the manner in which it was used in Arian and 'Semiarian' Creeds, dating from

and προσδοκῶμεν, the former occurs in the Mesopotamian Creed. Thus the various coincidences suggest that the 'Constantinopolitan' changes in the Creed of Jerusalem were due to compilation, and that the predilections of the compiler bore no little resemblance to those of Cyril.

On the supposition that he was the author of the revision of the Creed, the incidents of his life give a clue to the probable date. His predecessor Maximus, by whom he had been ordained presbyter (Hier. *Chron.* an. Abr. 2364), and as whose deputy he apparently delivered his Lectures (Schröckh *K. G.* xii 344 f.), had taken some part in the Synod of Tyre in 335, at which Athanasius was deposed (Socr. ii 8; Soz. ii 25 20), but afterwards repenting held aloof from the Dedication Synod of Antioch in 341 (Socr. l.c.; Soz. iii 6 6), and eventually in a synod at Jerusalem, about 349, welcomed Athanasius on his return (Ath. *Ap. c. Ar.* 57; Socr. ii 24; Philostorg. iii 12; cf. Ath. *Hist. Ar.* 25). This act evidently displeased his Arian metropolitan, Acacius of Cæsarea; and there can be no reasonable doubt that either on his death (Theodoret. ii 26; Hier. l.c.), or by his expulsion (Soz. iv 20 1), Cyril succeeded him as Acacius's nominee. It is equally clear that Cyril kept himself independent of Acacius and his party. No reliance can be placed on a phrase of doubtful genuineness as it now stands, τὴν ἁγίαν καὶ ὁμοούσιον τριάδα, τὸν ἀληθινὸν θεὸν ἡμῶν, at the end of a letter which he addressed to the emperor Constantius in 351.

341 to 360. It is the single term denoting the temporal mission of the Holy Spirit, on which alone they lay stress, observing silence as to His eternal or even prior being. At a later time Gregory of Nyssa (*c. Eun.* ii 485 ff. [549 f.]) censures the Eunomian profession Πιστεύομεν εἰς τὸν παράκλητον τὸ πνεῦμα τῆς ἀληθείας, on the ground that it casts off the Divine associations belonging to τὸ πνεῦμα τὸ ἅγιον, and divorces τὸ πνεῦμα τῆς ἀληθείας from the words which our Lord subjoins, ὃ παρὰ τοῦ πατρὸς ἐκπορεύεται; though on the other hand he claims the name *Paraclete* as belonging to the Son, and even implicitly to the Father, and so itself implying Deity. The criticism is not worth much, but it shews the direction which suspicions might take: the form used by Eunomius is best illustrated by the Philadelphian Creed, in which it is evidently a relic of older times. It is conceivable that Gregory had in mind a Creed in which both the phrases from John xv 26 were consecutively represented, as in the revised Mesopotamian Creed.

But during no small part of his long episcopate he was at war with Acacius, partly no doubt on matters of jurisdiction or precedence, yet also for doctrinal reasons[1]. Being deposed by Acacius, apparently early in 358[2], he joined the Homœousian chiefs in Asia Minor, Silvanus of Tarsus, Basil of Ancyra, and George of Laodicea (Theodoret. ii 26; Soz. iv 25 1), who were striving to make a stand against the Arian tyranny under Constantius. After a short restoration[3], which seems to have followed on the deposition of Acacius by the Council of Seleucia in the autumn of 359, he was again banished, like several of his associates, and there is no trace of his return till after the death of Constantius in November 361. Up to this time it is highly unlikely that he had adopted the Nicene watchword: all indications mark him out as an unwavering Homœousian of the higher type, declining to adopt the one critical term, and therefore divided from Athanasius, but as steadily refusing all complicity with the dominant Arianism. Restored to his bishopric by the accession of Julian, he ruled it prosperously for some years[4]. Once more he was driven out, probably by the edict of Valens in 367 for the expulsion of the bishops released from banishment by the death of Constantius (Soz. vi 12 5); nor was he allowed to return till the death of Valens in 378. By that time the *Ancoratus* of Epiphanius was already written; so that if Cyril's acceptance of the ὁμοούσιον now first took place, he cannot be responsible for the revision of the Creed of Jerusalem. The language of the historians, in relating

---

[1] Ἀλλήλους διέβαλον ὡς οὐχ ὑγιῶς περὶ θεοῦ φρονοῖεν· καὶ γὰρ καὶ πρὶν ἐν ὑπονοίᾳ ἑκάτερος ἦν, ὁ μὲν τὰ Ἀρείου δογματίζων, Κύριλλος δὲ τοῖς ὁμοιουσίον τῷ πατρὶ τὸν υἱὸν εἰσηγουμένοις ἑπόμενος. Soz. iv 25 2.

[2] Theodoret. ii 22; Sozom. iv 25. Compare Touttée *Diss.* i c. 7.

[3] Reasonably inferred by Tillemont viii 432.

[4] On the death of Acacius about 366 he was even able to place two nominees of his in the see of Cæsarea; first Philumenus, and then (after an intervening episcopate of another Cyril, a nominee of his rival Eutychius) his own nephew Gelasius (Epiph. *Haer.* 885 CD). But all three terms of office were evidently short, and for a while Euzoius came in by Arian influence, though ultimately Gelasius was restored, and apparently justified Cyril's choice (cf. Tillemont viii 438 f.).

his appearance at the Council of Constantinople in 381, might suggest that his change of position was then recent[1]: but as they shew hardly any knowledge of his doings in the preceding 20 years[2], and the peculiar recognition accorded to him probably by the Council in 381, certainly by its leading members in 382, would seem to need a word of justification in this place, their vague statements cannot be taken to fix the date.

On the other hand, when the circumstances of the Church at the accession of Julian are taken into account, it becomes highly probable that Cyril's adoption of the Nicene language belongs to this time, that is to about 362 or 3. The heavy hand of the Arian emperor Constantius had accomplished a great work. The faith and constancy shewn by the better Homœousians were not lost upon Athanasius and men like him, themselves purified and softened by endurance of the same sufferings. To this period (late in 359) belong the often quoted words of Athanasius, "Towards those who accept all else that was written at Nicæa, but doubt about the ὁμοούσιον only, we ought not to behave as though they were enemies;...but we argue with them as brethren with brethren, seeing they have the same mind (διάνοιαν) as ourselves but only question the name," &c., Basil of Ancyra (see above, p. 93) being specially mentioned (*De Syn.* 41 p. 755 DE). A few months earlier Hilary had likewise written his treatise *De Synodis* with a conciliatory no less than a doctrinal purpose. When the per-

---

[1] Συνῆλθον οὖν τῆς μὲν ὁμοουσίου πίστεως ἐκ μὲν Ἀλεξανδρείας Τιμόθεος, ἐκ δὲ Ἱεροσολύμων Κύριλλος, τότε ἐκ μεταμελείας τῷ ὁμοουσίῳ προσκείμενος (Socr. v 8 3). Καὶ Κύριλλος ὁ Ἱεροσολύμων, μεταμεληθεὶς τότε, ὅτι πρότερον τὰ Μακεδονίου ἐφρόνει (Soz. vii 7 3). Macedonius stands here of course as the representative of Semiarianism generally, not of the particular doctrine associated with his name in later times. In this passage, as often, Sozomen had probably no independent evidence, but merely copied Socrates with modifications of language.

[2] Socrates mentions his interpretation of prophecy on the occasion of Julian's attempt to rebuild the Temple of Jerusalem in 363 (iii 20 7), and his possession of the see at Jovian's death in 364 (iv 1 13): both historians briefly record the successions in the episcopate (Socr. ii 45 17; Soz. iv 30 3). Casual statements of Epiphanius supply the rest of our knowledge (p. 97 n. 1; p. 93 n. 4).

secution was stopped for a while by the accession of a heathen emperor who had once been a Christian, the impressiveness of the crisis must have powerfully quickened the desire of peace. The Council assembled at Alexandria by Athanasius soon after his return proposed with a view to this end, on which they repeatedly insist, to admit all dissidents to communion without any other requirement than that they should "anathematise the Arian heresy, and confess the faith" of Nicæa, "and also anathematise those who say that the Holy Spirit is a creature, and divided from the substance of Christ" (Ath. *Tom. ad Ant.* 3 p. 772 A: cf. 8f. p. 775). In the Conciliar Tome or epistle the express condemnation of this doctrine on the Holy Spirit is accompanied by a censure of a wholly new doctrine akin to what was afterwards called Apollinarianism. In order to carry out the purposes of the Council Eusebius of Vercelli went first to Antioch. There he found that during the sitting of the Council Lucifer's intolerant zeal had frustrated the hope of terminating a long standing schism; for he had made Paulinus bishop, refusing to acknowledge Meletius, because he had received Arian ordination. This untoward event had lasting consequences, for Athanasius did not feel himself justified in repudiating Paulinus; and thus, in spite of the efforts of mediators like Basil the Great, Egypt continued divided from the rest of the Catholic East. But the work begun by the Council of Alexandria was not abandoned. We read in particular how Eusebius of Vercelli left Antioch in sorrow, though he did not venture to pronounce any judgement in his own name, and travelled about the East "like a good physician", winning back many to the faith (Socr. iii 9; Soz. v 13).

Various indications in the following years point to this juncture as the time when many relinquished the Homœousian position. Among them was Meletius, the friend of Cyril as of other greater men; who early in 361 had been set over Antioch by the influence of Acacius and Eudoxius, both of them political Arians, as Cyril had been set over Jerusalem by Acacius, but had soon been banished by Constantius in consequence of a sermon which proved his sympathies to be with the Nicene faith[1], though he had avoided the one watchword (Epiph. *Haer.* 876 ff.; Soc. ii 44; Soz. iv 28). Returning on Julian's accession, he must have taken the decisive step in or before[2] the autumn of 363, when the Nicene Creed was formally accepted in a memorial to the emperor Jovian by a synod at Antioch[3], with an explanation of ὁμοούσιον which combined the old Homœousian formula with the ἐκ τῆς οὐσίας of Athanasius[4] (Soc. iii 25; Soz. vi 4).

Thus we may reasonably take 362-4 as the most probable date for Cyril's decisive adoption of the Nicene standard in its integrity[5]. His return to his diocese under such circumstances

---

[1] Socrates (ii 44 4) and Sozomen (iv 28 6) speak as though he on this occasion taught the ὁμοούσιον: but the sermon itself, as preserved by Epiphanius, proves them to be in error. See Möller in Herzog *R.E.* ix 306 f. In this twofold character the sermon of Meletius affords an instructive parallel to the Lectures of Cyril.

[2] Socrates indeed says, ὃς μικρὸν ἔμπροσθεν αὐτῶν (the Acacians) χωρισθεὶς τῷ ὁμοουσίῳ προσέθετο: but he may be only referring to the sermon preached two years before. Philostorgius (v 1) evidently regards the change as virtually synchronous with his going to Antioch, but his language is vague. The same must be said of Chrysostom's statement (*Or. in Melet.* p. 519).

[3] The probable insincerity of Acacius and perhaps others who signed the document does not affect Meletius; whose credit with the new emperor Jovian is said to have induced them to come to terms with him on this occasion (Socr. l.c.).

[4] With this explanation may be compared Hilary's long exposition in his book *De Synodis* (67 ff.). A few words may be cited. "Dicturus *unam* catholicus *substantiam* Patris et Filii non inde incipiat, neque hoc quasi maximum teneat, tamquam sine hoc vera fides nulla sit. Tuto unam substantiam dicat cum ante dixerit, 'Pater ingenitus est, *Filius* natus est, *subsistit ex Patre*, Patri similis est virtute, honore, natura, Patri subjectus est ut auctori, nec se per rapinam Deo cujus in forma manebat aequavit, obediens usque ad mortem fuit'," &c. (69). "Potest *una substantia* pie dici et pie taceri. Habes nativitatem, habes *similitudinem*. Quid verbi calumniam suspiciose tenemus rei intellegentia non dissidentes? Credamus et dicamus esse *unam substantiam:* sed per naturae proprietatem, non ad significationem impiae unionis. *Una* sit *ex similitudine,* non ex solitudine" (71).

[5] Tillemont (viii 433) comes virtually to the same conclusion, chiefly on the evidence of the undoubted fact that Cyril was with Meletius in the perilous days of Julian's stay at Antioch, and accepted from him the charge of conveying away into Palestine by night a young convert, son of a heathen priest high in favour with the emperor (Theodoret. iii 10). Julian was at Antioch from June 362 to March 363 (Clinton *F.R.* i 448). The incident is of real importance as proving the

would be a natural occasion for revising its public Creed by skilfully inserting some of the Conciliar language, including the term which proclaimed the restoration of full communion with the champions of Nicæa, and other phrases and clauses adapted for impressing on the people the positive truth the denial of which was declared at Alexandria in 362 to be incompatible with Catholic communion. Of such conditions the Creed which we call 'Constantinopolitan' might easily be the result, and there would be ample time for it to be established in use at Jerusalem long before Epiphanius placed a slightly augmented form of it in his *Ancoratus* in 374[1].

To these speculations about the origin of the Creed may be added another respecting its possible recognition as a Creed of Cyril by the Bishops assembled at Constantinople in 381 or 382. The Council as summoned together by Theodosius in the spring of 381, "to confirm the Nicene faith and ordain a bishop for Constantinople," was a signal triumph for men in Cyril's position. The cause of Meletius was the cause of Cyril and probably not a few others. The constancy with which the Catholic chiefs of Asia, led by Basil in his lifetime and now by the Gregories and their friends, upheld Meletius as the lawful bishop of Antioch was a sore offence to the West. Yet the emperor, imbued though he was with Western prepossessions[2],

friendship of Cyril and Meletius to have existed as early as this date. In 359 and perhaps 360, if we may trust Epiphanius (*Haer*.870f., 875), Meletius consorted with Acacius and a party said to have separated from Cyril's friends Basil of Ancyra &c. on account of an enmity between Cyril and one of their number, Eutychius of Eleutheropolis, Epiphanius's own city. If the two parties really differed theologically, the names shew Cyril to have been on the side nearest to Nicene doctrine; but Epiphanius seems to say that Eutychius affected to be more Arian than he actually was, in order to win favour with Constantius: of Meletius nothing special is said.

[1] The date 362—4, it will be observed, falls well within the time of Epiphanius's residence near Eleutheropolis, the metropolis of the region to the S.W. of Jerusalem; for 367 is the probable date of his removal to Cyprus. For the date of the *Ancoratus* see Tillemont x 804 f. Athanasius's *Epistles to Serapion* were written either during his exile in the wilderness (356—362) or shortly after.

[2] In February 380, about a year after he had been raised to the throne of the East by Gratian, Theodosius had set

had treated him with marked attention, and the honour which his memory received, when he died during the session of the Council, bore witness to the prevailing mind of that first great gathering of the Catholic East after the long Arian desolation. What followed proved that this demonstration was more than a personal tribute to his virtues: in spite of the remonstrances of Gregory of Nazianzus, it was decided to recommend that Flavianus, one of his presbyters, should succeed at once to his see, rather than that Paulinus, the bishop acknowledged by the West, should be left in sole possession till his death[1]. The Egyptian bishops, who held with the West, were out of harmony with the Council as to what had been done before their arrival in the matter of the see of Constantinople, and probably in other matters likewise. The only written monument of the Council's work is a body of canons with an introductory letter to the emperor[2]. The first canon decided that the Creed

up Damasus and Peter of Alexandria as the standards of Catholicity in an edict addressed "to the people of the city of Constantinople": "cunctos populos quos clementiae nostrae regit temperamentum in tali volumus religione versari quam divinum Petrum apostolum tradidisse Romanis religio usque nunc ab ipso insinuata declarat, quamque pontificem Damasum sequi claret et Petrum Alexandriae episcopum virum apostolicae sanctitatis." Cod. Theod. xvi 1 2. Himself a Spanish soldier, Theodosius had been just receiving baptism and instruction from Ascholius of Thessalonica, a Cappadocian by birth and a friend of Basil, but at this time closely allied with Damasus and Ambrose.

[1] It is beside our purpose to consider the merits of this perplexing transaction, in which it was easy for good and highminded men to take different sides at the time. Whether as a right act or as an accomplished fact, it was accepted by nearly all the Asiatic Churches (Soz. vii 11 2), and maintained, as we shall see, by the Council of the following year.

[2] The letter sums up the proceedings thus (Mansi iii 557). Συνελθόντες εἰς τὴν Κωνσταντίνου Πόλιν κατὰ τὸ γράμμα τῆς σῆς εὐσεβείας, πρῶτον μὲν ἀνανεωσάμεθα τὴν πρὸς ἀλλήλους ὁμόνοιαν· ἔπειτα δὲ καὶ συντόμους ὅρους ἐξεφωνήσαμεν, τήν τε τῶν πατέρων πίστιν τῶν ἐν Νικαίᾳ κυρώσαντες, καὶ τὰς κατ' αὐτῆς ἐκφυείσας αἱρέσεις ἀναθεματίσαντες· πρὸς δὲ τούτοις καὶ ὑπὲρ τῆς εὐταξίας τῶν ἐκκλησιῶν ῥητοὺς κανόνας ὡρίσαμεν· ἅπερ ἅπαντα τῷδε ἡμῶν τῷ γράμματι ὑπετάξαμεν. It is possible that the second head relates to the 'first canon' and the third head to the other canons. But the 'first canon' is not naturally described by the term σύντομοι ὅροι, which better designates a series of short dogmatic judgements like the recent Anathematisms of Damasus, in which Pneumatomachian doctrines were chiefly condemned. Probably a somewhat similar docu-

of Nicæa should not be set aside (ἀθετεῖσθαι) but should remain valid (κυρίαν)[1], and anathematised "every heresy", six being named. The second at some length forbad the interference of bishops with distant dioceses to the "confusion of Churches", citing the authority of the Nicene canons. The third claimed for the bishop of Constantinople, as New Rome, the second place after the bishop of Rome. The fourth repudiated the claims of Maximus "the Cynic" (an impostor) to be bishop of Constantinople: the Egyptians had rashly committed themselves to his cause, and for a while he was supported by the West against Nectarius, whom the emperor and Council had placed in the see on Gregory's final refusal. It is a moot question, and of no great consequence for our purpose, whether the next two canons found in the Greek MSS. (they are wanting in the Latin) belong to 381 or 382. The fifth says concisely, "As touching the Tome (synodical letter) of the Westerns, we further accept those of Antioch who confess one Deity of Father and Son and Holy Ghost"[2]: in other words, they refused to discuss old Arian ordinations or even old Arian opinions, and therefore recognised Meletius, his present orthodoxy being unquestioned. The sixth canon at great length imposes restrictions on the accusation of bishops. The pre-

ment was composed by the Council (see also p. 101, n. 2), and then the result summed up in the first canon for purposes of discipline. The 'Constantinopolitan' Creed, unlike the Nicene, evidently differs from both the σύντομοι ὅροι and the first canon in containing no anathemas.

[1] There can be no doubt that both the emperor and the leading bishops sincerely desired to admit to communion every one who would now acquiesce in the Nicene faith, subject to the Alexandrian interpretation of the one clause on the Holy Spirit. Thirty-six bishops of the 'Semiarian' remnant assembled for the Council, and were entreated to remember their own proposals to Liberius in 366 (see p. 23) and to accept the present terms: but they gave a decided refusal, and left the Council (Socr. v 8 2·9; Soz. vii 7 2-5). The ratification of the Nicene Creed was thus the act which defined the doctrinal position of the Council both positively and negatively. It is difficult to see how on such an occasion an enlargement of the Creed as a standard of communion could have been carried out without suicidal inconsistency.

[2] Περὶ τοῦ τόμου τῶν δυτικῶν καὶ τοὺς ἐν Ἀντιοχείᾳ ἀπεδεξάμεθα τοὺς μίαν ὁμολογοῦντας πατρὸς κ.τ.λ.

amble states that "many purposing to confuse and subvert ecclesiastical order (εὐταξίαν) in a hostile and frivolous (συκοφαντικῶς) manner fabricate certain charges against the orthodox bishops who administer the Churches, having no other endeavour than to stain the reputations of the priests (ἱερεῖς, i.e. bishops[1]) and to excite disturbances among the flocks (λαῶν) that are at peace". Moreover when "heretics" are forbidden to bring accusations against "the orthodox bishops about ecclesiastical affairs", heretics are defined to be not only those who have been formerly or lately banished from the communion of the Church, but also, "in addition to these, those who claim to confess the sound faith, but have separated themselves and form congregations in opposition to our canonical bishops" (ἀποσχισθέντας καὶ ἀντισυνάγοντας τοῖς κ. ἡ. ἐ.). Such persons as are qualified to act as accusers are to bring their charges before all the bishops of the eparchy, and then, if need be, before a larger synod of the bishops of the province (διοικήσεως), after giving written security for the penalties of frivolous accusation. At the end all right of accusation is taken away from any one who in contempt of these decisions "shall dare either to trouble (ἐνοχλεῖν) the emperor's ears or to disturb (ταράσσειν) the courts of worldly magistrates or an œcumenical synod, thereby dishonouring all the bishops of the province"[2]. Finally in confirmation of the acts of the Council Theodosius published a constitution addressed to the proconsul of Asia, dated July 30 381, in which he named eleven bishops, with Nectarius of Constantinople and Timothy of Alexandria at the head[3], as standards of Catholic communion, pronouncing "all dissentients from the communion of their faith" to be manifest heretics[4].

[1] See Schweizer *Thes.* s.v. § 2; Hussey on Soz. ii 21 3.

[2] The seventh canon, wanting in some Greek as well as in the Latin authorities, and referring to a different subject, seems to belong to a later time. See Beveridge *Synod. Annot.* 100 f.; Hefele *Conciliengeschichte* ii 13 f., 27.

[3] The silent substitution of Nectarius of Constantinople for Damasus of Rome (see p. 97, n. 2), could not be misunderstood. On the other hand the inclusion of Timothy of Alexandria attested the absence of factiousness in this construction of an independent Greek unity.

[4] Cod. Theod. xvi 1 3.

AND OTHER EASTERN CREEDS 101

The proceedings at Constantinople in 381 caused no little uneasiness in the West. Ambrose pleaded with the emperor for the assembling of a "General Council" at Alexandria, or, he subsequently urged, at Rome (*Epp.* 12 f.). When the greater number of the bishops who had met in 381 met again at Constantinople in the summer of 382, they received a synodical epistle from the Western bishops[1], exhorting them to come to Rome and take part in a specially great (μεγίστης) synod about to meet there (Theodoret. *H. E.* v 8; Sozom. vii 11 4). It matters little whether the 'Tome of the Westerns' so curtly referred to in the fifth canon was this letter or some unknown document written at an earlier date, though the former seems the more probable alternative. Fortunately Theodoret (ib. 9) has preserved the answer of "the holy synod of the orthodox bishops gathered together in the great city of Constantinople to Damasus, Ambrose, &c. and the other holy bishops gathered together in the great city of Rome". They dwell much on the sufferings of the Eastern Churches and the need of manifold restoration now: they declare their inability to be absent from their dioceses without notice for a protracted journey beyond Constantinople, but depute three of their number to go to Rome on a friendly mission: they maintain their firm adherence to the Nicene Creed and to the faith in the coequal and coeternal Trinity, and the perfect Incarnation; referring to a 'Tome' written by the synod of Antioch, and to another written "last year" by "the œcumenical synod" at Constantinople, in which they had more diffusely (πλατύτερον) confessed their faith and recorded an anathematism of recent heresies[2]. At the end comes the sting. "Touching partial (or local) arrangements (τῶν οἰκονομιῶν τῶν κατὰ μέρος) in the

---

[1] According to Sozomen (vii 11 4) and the Eastern answer the emperor Gratian wrote to the same effect.

[2] Both these documents are lost. Indeed little is certainly known of the Council of Antioch, the historians being silent about it: but it appears to be the synod of 379 mentioned by Gregory of Nyssa in a letter referred to further on (p. 103 n. 1). By the confession and anathematism of 381 are probably meant the σύντομοι ὅροι referred to in the epistle to Theodosius. See p. 98, n. 2.

churches", they simply state it as their practice, in accordance alike with time-honoured custom and with the Nicene decree, that the ordinations (of bishops) in each eparchy should rest with those within the eparchy, though with the power of inviting the aid of neighbours. On these principles, they say, they "have accepted the 'priests' (bishops) of the most distinguished Churches"; and they give three examples (ὅθεν... κεχειροτονήκαμεν), Nectarius of Constantinople, Flavianus of Antioch, and Cyril of Jerusalem. In the two former cases they mention the various concurrences of support which confirmed the appointment: in the third they say, "Of the Church of Jerusalem, the mother of all the Churches, we recognise (γνωρίζομεν) the most venerable and pious (αἰδεσιμώτατον καὶ θεοφιλέστατον) Cyril to be bishop, he having been canonically appointed by them of the eparchy in former days, and having undergone many contests (ἀθλήσαντα) with the Arians in different places." With this practice, founded on custom and canons, they invite the Westerns to give cheerful concurrence (οἷς...συγχαίρειν παρακαλοῦμεν), setting the edification of the churches above individual preference. In this letter, remarkable alike for charity, wisdom, and patient firmness, the association of the three names cannot be accidental: Cyril must have been singled out for mention because, next to Nectarius and Flavianus, he was the bishop whose authority the Eastern bishops most cared to uphold against Western cavils.

Nor is direct evidence wanting that about this time Cyril had to undergo some such opposition. Two well known letters of Gregory of Nyssa relate to a visit which he paid to Jerusalem. In one of them (*Ep. de adeunt. Hier.*), while dissuading his Cappadocian brethren through a friend from undertaking a pilgrimage to the Holy Places, he explains how he came to make so long a journey himself. It became his duty, he says, to go as far as Arabia to help in correcting (διόρθωσιν) the state of the Arabian Church[1]. He refers in the same sentence to "the holy synod",

[1] Nothing is known with certainty about the Arabian troubles: but an extract is preserved (Beveridge *Synod.* i 678 f.) from the acts of a synod held

probably that of Constantinople in 381[1]; but the loss of one or more words in the text leaves uncertain the nature of the connexion between the synod and the journey[2]. Since Arabia was contiguous to the region of Jerusalem, he further undertook to go and "consult with those who presided over the holy Churches of Jerusalem, because their affairs were in confusion, and needed a mediator" (iii 1013 A Migne). In the other letter (*Ad Eustathiam &c.*), written soon after his return, he pours out his

[1] This is the view to which Casaubon inclines (on Greg. *Ep. ad Eust.* 43 ff.): it agrees best with the phrase "the holy synod", used absolutely, and with a statement in the *Ep. ad Eust.* (1017 c) about the true doctrine being now preached openly throughout the world. According to the other view, best maintained, though with some hesitation, by Tillemont (ix 734 ff.), the reference is to the synod held at Antioch in the autumn of 379 (Greg. Nyss. *De vita Macr.* 973 cD). Its chief support is found in an appeal made to Gregory a few weeks later by his sister Macrina on the strength of his fame being known to "cities and peoples and nations", and his being "sent and invited by churches for alliance and correction " (συμμαχίαν τε καὶ διόρθωσιν, ib. 981 b). But the mode of reference to the synod at Antioch implies its comparative obscurity (ἔννατος ἦν...μήν...καὶ σύνοδος ἐπισκόπων κατὰ τὴν Ἀντιόχου πόλιν ἠθροίζετο, ἧς καὶ ἡμεῖς μετέσχομεν); and the order of events required by this view is at least difficult of adjustment. The mission cannot have rested on the joint authority given to Gregory, Helladius, and Otreius in 381 (cf. *Ep. ad Flav.* 1007 D, ἴση παρὰ συνόδου καὶ μία γέγονεν ἀμφοτέρων [himself and Helladius] ἡ προνομία), for that was limited to the *Pontica Dioecesis*: but it need not have preceded the 'canon' of 381 against interference in other bishops' dioceses, for it might be sanctioned by invitation or by a special mandate from the synod. Even however if Gregory's journey to Jerusalem took place at the earlier date, neither Cyril's difficulties nor Gregory's readiness to obtain for him synodical support were likely to be at an end by 381 or 382.

[2] Ἐμοί, διὰ τὴν ἀνάγκην ταύτην ἐν ᾗ ζῆν ἐτάχθην παρὰ τοῦ οἰκονομοῦντος ἡμῶν τὴν ζωήν, ἐγένετο τῆς ἁγίας συνόδου διορθώσεως ἕνεκεν τῆς κατὰ τὴν Ἀραβίαν ἐκκλησίας μέχρι τῶν τόπων γενέσθαι. The assumed commission from the synod depends solely on the conjectural ὁρισάσης inserted after συνόδου, accepted by Tillemont from Casaubon; which after all only replaces impossible Greek by halting Greek. The sentence would run better with διαλυθείσης, which might be easier lost before διορθώσεως: this correction would quite change the sense, as would other possible but less likely emendations. The next sentence has no principal verb: but the meaning seems free from doubt.

anxieties to certain Christian ladies whom he had known at or near Jerusalem. "Hatred" is the evil on which he especially dwells as desolating the Church at Jerusalem. Two characteristics of the chief disturbers of peace may be clearly discerned through his guarded language[1]: they went beyond all reasonable bounds, Gregory thought, in exacting minute dogmatic correctness as against whatever might be interpreted as Semiarianism, and they set up rival 'altars' against those of the Church, treating Gregory and his friends as profane[2]. These particulars, obscure as they are, certainly suggest that Cyril's authority and orthodoxy were still disputed at Jerusalem[3].

---

[1] He calls them οἱ τὰ περισσὰ σοφιζόμενοι, ... σχίζοντες τὸν χιτῶνα τὸν ἄρρηκτον, ... καὶ τὸν προσεγγισμὸν τῶν τὸν χριστὸν προσκυνούντων βδελυκτὸν ἀποφαίνοντες, μόνον οὐ φανερῶς ἐκεῖνο βοῶντες τοῖς ῥήμασι, Πόρρω ἀπ' ἐμοῦ, μὴ ἐγγίσῃς μοι ὅτι καθαρός εἰμι. Δεδόσθω δέ, he adds, καὶ πλέον τι αὐτοῖς κατὰ τὴν γνῶσιν ἥνπερ αὐτοὶ οἴονται προσειληφέναι πρ..σεῖναι· μὴ πλέον τοῦ πιστεύειν ἀληθινὸν εἶναι θεὸν τὸν τοῦ θεοῦ ἀληθινὸν υἱὸν ἔχουσιν; τῇ γὰρ τοῦ ἀληθινοῦ θεοῦ ὁμολογίᾳ πάντα συμπεριλαμβάνεται τὰ εὐσεβῆ καὶ σώζοντα ἡμᾶς νοήματα (1017 D, 1020 A). The earlier part of the passage is quoted p. 88 n. 2. Towards the end he repeats, Εἰ οὖν ταῦτα βοῶμεν καὶ διαμαρτυρόμεθα, ... τί ἀδικοῦμεν καὶ ὑπὲρ τίνος μισούμεθα; καὶ τί βούλεται ἡ τῶν καινῶν θυσιαστηρίων ἀντεξαγωγή; ... Τί τοιοῦτον ἔχοντες ἐγκαλεῖσθαι φευκτοὶ ἐνομίσθημεν, καὶ ἄλλο παρά τινων ἀντεγείρεται ἡμῖν θυσιαστήριον, ὡς ἡμῶν βεβηλούντων τὰ ἅγια; (1024 AB)

[2] Gregory's accompanying exposition of doctrine points to the existence of an Apollinarian leaven among these persons (cf. Tillemont iv 583 f.); which is not inconsistent with the other facts. Gregory of Nazianzus had a similar embarrassment in his own diocese about the same time.

[3] About five years before this time we have traces of an earlier stage of what were probably the same troubles in the Church of Jerusalem in a letter (*Ep.* 258) of Basil to Epiphanius, apparently belonging to 376 or 7 (Tillemont ix 272 ff.; Prud. Maranus *Vita S. Bas.* xxxvi 6). It refers to a dissension among "the brethren" on the Mount of Olives, and records an answer given by Basil to two of their number, Palladius and Innocentius an Italian. He had disclaimed all power to add any thing, however small (καὶ τὸ βραχύτατον), to the Nicene faith except the doxology to (εἰς) the Holy Spirit, justifying the exception by the cursory treatment given to this article at Nicæa, the controversy on the subject not having yet been stirred. He had refused either to scrutinise or to accept certain additions (προσυφαινόμενα...δόγματα) to that faith, relating to the Incarnation, as being too deep for comprehension; knowing, he says, "that, as soon as we have once disturbed the simplicity of the faith, we shall find no end to the arguments when we are urged perpetually forward by contradiction; and moreover we shall harass the souls of the simpler sort by the introduction of matters that bewilder men" (393 D). It is hard to distinguish the voices of Basil and Gregory of Nyssa.

This glimpse into Cyril's difficulties at home confirms the obvious inference from the manner in which he is named with Nectarius and Flavianus in the synodical epistle of 382. At one or both the synods of 381 and 382 at Constantinople his authority must have been impugned and must have been vindicated. The language cited from the 'fifth canon' agrees closely with his case, though it was doubtless applicable to others; and the warning against 'disturbing an œcumenical synod[1]' must have been called forth by some actual incident of 381. Yet more, the responsibility of the Council of 381 for Nectarius and Flavianus was quite peculiar, for owing to a concurrence of external events they were in fact the nominees of the Council[2]; and accordingly it is reasonable to suppose that the Council had performed some equally definite act on behalf of Cyril. The records of the Council are too slight to cause

---

[1] The allusion, in itself sufficiently obvious, is confirmed by a pointed reference to the Council of 381 as τῆς οἰκουμενικῆς συνόδου made twice over in the Constantinople letter of 382. In the phrase οἰκουμενικὴ σύνοδος the adjective here, as probably always, follows the political sense of ἡ οἰκουμένη as the *orbis Romanus* or Empire, and means "imperial", partly as coextensive with the Empire, partly as summoned by the emperor's authority. Under Constantine the empire was undivided, and so it was easy for Athanasius to appropriate the term (already used by Eusebius, *V. Const.* iii 6, apparently in the twofold sense) to express simply the (theoretical) universality of the Nicene Council, which he regarded as contributing to its unique and inimitable character: and even he shews, by the language which he once employs (οἱ ἐν τῇ Νικαίᾳ συνελθόντες ἀπὸ πάσης τῆς καθ' ἡμᾶς οἰκουμένης *Ad Afr.* i p. 891 B), that he recognised the οἰκουμένη of the Council to be the Empire, not the world at large. In 381 Theodosius ruled one οἰκουμένη, and Gratian another; and the Council of Constantinople was not the less οἰκουμενικὴ because it was independent alike of Western emperor and Western bishops. In like manner Theodoret (*H.F.* iv 12, cited by Ducange) says that Nestorius ψήφῳ τῶν περὶ τὰ βασίλεια καὶ τοὺς θρόνους καὶ αὐτοῦ τοῦ τηνικαῦτα τῆς οἰκουμένης τὰ σκῆπτρα διέποντος was entrusted with the προεδρία of the Church of Constantinople, οὐδὲν δὲ ἧττον καὶ τῆς οἰκουμένης ἁπάσης, though certainly his patriarchate did not extend to the West.

[2] In both cases the epistle emphasises both the local and the œcumenical responsibility with much elaborateness. Thus Φλαβιανὸν οἵ τε τῆς ἐπαρχίας καὶ τῆς ἀνατολικῆς διοικήσεως συνδραμόντες κανονικῶς ἐχειροτόνησαν, πάσης συμψήφου τῆς ἐκκλησίας ὥσπερ διὰ μιᾶς φωνῆς τὸν ἄνδρα τιμησάσης, ἥνπερ ἔνδεσμον χειροτονίαν ἐδέξατο καὶ τὸ τῆς συνόδου κοινόν.

surprise at their silence on this point: a transaction that seemed to be only of local interest might easily be passed over among the proceedings that concerned the imperial see or the whole Church, more especially if it lacked the dramatic accompaniments under which the new bishops of Constantinople and Antioch assumed office. The charges against Cyril may have been presented either by envoys from Jerusalem or by the Egyptian bishops on their arrival: the latter alternative would account for the emphasis with which the Asiatic bishops in 382 vindicate Cyril to the Western allies of the Egyptians. That Gregory of Nyssa maintained his cause in the Council is at least not unlikely, when we remember the intimacy of both with Meletius, and the readiness of Gregory to attempt to reconcile to Cyril his opponents at Jerusalem: the fruitless mission of peace is a testimony of good will whether it preceded or followed the Council; but in the latter case it would be a natural sequel to a public release from unjust accusations.

However this may be, it seems tolerably certain that a vindication of Cyril took place at Constantinople either in 382 or, more probably, in 381. If so, the hypothesis already sketched as to the author of the 'Constantinopolitan' Creed may be carried a step further. If Cyril some twenty years before had provided his Church with an enlarged form of its ancient Creed, what more likely than that it should be produced before the Council when his own faith and authority were in question? And supposing the Council, in giving judgement in his favour, to have expressed their approval of his Creed, can it be held improbable that in the course of time, when the attendant circumstances were forgotten, the stately Creed so read and approved should be vaguely represented in tradition as the Creed of the Council itself? Nay, even the further tradition of a much later time[1], which makes Gregory of Nyssa the author

---

[1] In Nicephorus's compilation (xii 13), made in the fourteenth century, Gregory of Nazianzus is said to have been named as the author at the Council of Florence, but probably by a confusion of name. If Gregory of Nyssa had really been the author of the clauses on the Holy Spirit, it is

AND OTHER EASTERN CREEDS 107

of the new clauses on the Holy Spirit, may have had its origin in some appeal of his to their testimony on Cyril's behalf, if indeed he stood forth as Cyril's defender. No stress however can be laid on these bare possibilities. The supposition that Cyril had at least a principal share in the enlargement of the Creed has much greater probability, as on the one hand it stands in close relation with the Jerusalem base of the Creed, and on the other it agrees in several distinct points with what is known of Cyril, without, as far as I see, being liable to any objection. But of course it is by no means entitled to the same confidence as the fundamental fact that the 'Constantinopolitan' Creed is the old Creed of Jerusalem enlarged and revised; about which there can I think be no reasonable doubt.

It follows by necessary inference that the Creed long known as the Nicene Creed has no other title to the name than such as is given by the appropriation of a single passage of thirty-three words[1] from the true Creed of Nicæa. This result is negative only in form. It not merely nullifies the residue of the historical difficulty mentioned at the outset (pp. 73 f.), but justifies the usage of Christendom for many centuries. The liturgical or baptismal confession of faith recited in the congregations of East and West not only derived its first obscure elements from a popular Creed, for thus far all or nearly all are agreed, but was itself the Creed of the Mother Church of Christendom, to all appearance deliberately enlarged and

hardly credible that they should have left no trace in the many passages of his writings which deal with the same subject. He dwells much on the Scriptural epithet ζωοποιοῦν (e.g. *C. Eun.* i 351 AB [349 B Migne]; *Ep. ad Sebast.* [1032 B]; *Ep. ad Heracl.* [1093 A]), and on the conglorification (see p. 88 n. 2); but these are just the least characteristic points. The certainty that the other 'Constantinopolitan' terms express his belief makes it all the more significant that he gives them no clear verbal prominence even individually, still less brings them into combination.

[1] Out of 178: that is, less than a fifth of the whole. This reckoning of course excludes words found in both the Nicene and the Jerusalem Creeds, but proved by the preceding comparison not to have been in fact derived from the Nicene Creed.

fashioned into its present shape with an intention corresponding to its present popular mode of employment; incorporating indeed such terms as were thought needful for the guidance of faith in the midst of error under one or two fundamental heads, but studiously restrained within the bounds set by fitness for congregational use.

Such was not the function of the true Nicene Creed. By an unhappy necessity we have to use the one word "Creed" to express different purposes and to a certain extent different instruments. Indeed the Nicene Creed itself has a twofold character, arising out of the circumstances of its construction; and this twofold character exercised a confusing influence in the subsequent revision of Creeds, and still more in their use, as well as in its own use. External and internal evidence alike proclaim the Nicene Creed to be in intention a dogmatic standard, constructed for a particular emergency; much more than a popular Creed, if indeed a popular Creed at all. This is partly attested by the elaborate sentence on the Sonship; but emphatically by the Anathematism, that is, the recital of certain contemporary doctrinal propositions, the affirmation of which the Church pronounced to involve exclusion from her communion[1]. The circumstances already recounted explain why in other respects the Nicene Creed retained a popular form. It is enough here to refer to the political conservatism of Constantine, the risk of bringing into sight the latent differences among the majority of the Council, the widely prevailing dread of going beyond Scripture or innovating on existing tradition, and not least the wise instincts of Athanasius, too profound a theologian himself to be blind to the danger of strangling faith by overmuch theologising.

At length not only the crisis for which the Nicene Creed

---

[1] The absence of the clauses which probably followed the clause on the Holy Spirit in the Creed of Cæsarea might probably be added. It is to be observed that the Nicene Creed corresponds in the one characteristic to the exposition in which Eusebius enveloped his native Creed, in the other to the Cæsarean Creed itself. See p. 58 n. 1.

was framed passed away, but the period of deadlier conflict under Constantius in which it acquired a sanction which no Council could bestow. The short and antagonistic reigns of Julian and Jovian alike ushered in a time of reconstruction, invigorated if also checked and delayed by the renewed adversity under Valens. The last years of Athanasius forbid the dissociation of the two periods. The new work was set in motion by his own hands; and though his never wholly dissipated coolness towards the Antioch of Meletius might be truly read as a sign that another generation was beginning to need other chiefs, his blessing rested on their difficult enterprise. Asia now took the lead, as in earlier ages of the Church; and the Asiatic leaders were heirs of a double tradition, Homœousian as well as Nicene. On the one hand they had received their nurture and the substance of their faith from the associates or successors of Eusebius of Cæsarea, and they never disowned the debt: on the other they owed to Athanasius and the Nicene Creed a more perfect interpretation of their unaltered belief[1]. Time had proved the apprehensions of the middle party at the great Council to have had a true foundation. The dreaded inclination towards Sabellianism among some of Athanasius's allies had taken an ominous shape in Marcellus, and Photinus had opportunely shown what a disciple of Marcellus might come to at last: from a less suspected quarter among the stoutest champions of Nicene orthodoxy Apollinaris and his friends were fast occupying a position which would make the Incarnation of none effect. Time had not verified the fears of 325 respecting doctrinal dangers inherent in the term ὁμοούσιος, and it had amply justified the course chosen then and afterwards by the Church, in so far as it had to elect between two diverging ways.

[1] Οὕτω λογίζομαι καὶ ἐμοὶ τὸν αὐτὸν λόγον διὰ τῆς προκοπῆς ηὐξῆσθαι, οὐχὶ δὲ ἀντὶ τοῦ ἐξ ἀρχῆς ὄντος τὸν νῦν ὑπάρχοντα γεγενῆσθαι. Bas. *Ep.* 223 p. 338 E (see the whole passage): cf. p. 340 B, ἐκ προκοπῆς τινα αὔξησιν ἐπιθεωρεῖσθαι τοῖς λεγομένοις, ὅπερ οὐχὶ μεταβολή ἐστιν ἐκ τοῦ χείρονος πρὸς τὸ βέλτιον, ἀλλὰ συμπλήρωσις τοῦ λείποντος κατὰ τὴν προσθήκην τῆς γνώσεως.

It was to all appearance in this season of reconciliation and attempted restoration that several, possibly many, of the local popular Creeds underwent revision. Four of them are extant in their revised state, and a large part of a fifth[1]: but the greatest and most consummate among them is the revised Creed of Jerusalem. None carries such ample enrichment from Nicene and other sources with such an elastic and easy movement, and in none are the new phrases selected with such happy discernment. The formulary which approaches it most nearly in these respects is the Syriac Creed of Mesopotamia, now used by the Nestorian Churches. This highly eclectic formulary merely interweaves Nicene with the other materials which it introduces into the revised Creed of Antioch. The Cappadocian Creed, now used by the Armenian Churches, is constructed on a different plan. Here too the bulk of the local Creed is probably retained, but the Nicene Creed forms the base, the Anathematism being retained with the rest and itself enlarged. One evidently new clause on the Incarnation is somewhat elaborate, but neither here nor elsewhere is any technical term introduced without Nicene sanction, unless $ἄκτιστον$ ought so to be called[2]. The desire to keep the Creed popular is manifest, but it is thwarted by the precedence yielded to the Nicene structure. On the other hand the controversial spirit shews itself in Epiphanius's dealings with both the Creeds which he transcribed and recommended to his Pamphylian correspondents. The Cappadocian Creed reached him, as we shall find presently, somewhat overladen with doctrinal additions, and he encumbered it still further in the same manner,

---

[1] It is worthy of notice that the Fathers of Nicæa are claimed as the authors of all the three Creeds which have come into permanent ecclesiastical use, the Cappadocian and Mesopotamian as well as the 'Constantinopolitan'.

[2] The one condition of communion sanctioned by the Council of Alexandria (p. 95), over and above the acceptance of the Nicene Creed, was the excommunication of those who held the Holy Spirit to be a creature and divided from the substance of Christ. The latter words do not seem to have been long retained in practice: the condition as simplified by their omission meets us often, and here it is introduced into the body of a Creed by a single negative term.

unless, what is by no means likely, he received it already twice augmented. In like manner it was probably he who appended to the Creed of Jerusalem the Nicene Anathematism, perhaps under the influence of the Cappadocian precedent, besides reinserting two other Nicene clauses. The two other revised Creeds are much shorter than the three already mentioned. The revised Antiochian Creed, most of the latter part of which is lost, apparently borrows but three brief Nicene phrases, which it arranges in its own way: alone among these late formularies it retains an Antenicene type. The Creed read by Charisius at Ephesus is hardly longer in those parts in which comparison is possible; but it has drawn more freely on the Nicene store, though always keeping itself studiously simple and concise in diction. These last two Creeds, like that of Mesopotamia[1], have of course no Anathematism.

The history of the 'Constantinopolitan' Creed in the Eastern Churches has not yet been sufficiently investigated[2]. For the present purpose it will be enough to say a few words on certain facts which bear, or might be thought to bear, on the preceding enquiry. Subsequently to its early transcription by Epiphanius, the Creed, as has been already mentioned, first becomes visible 70 years after the Council of Constantinople. Apparently it then relapses into total obscurity for 85 years more: and 172 years have passed since the Council, so far as can be gathered

---

[1] Strictly speaking the inferior limit for the date of these three Creeds cannot be fixed earlier than about 431. But it is highly improbable that they are appreciably later than the two Creeds which Epiphanius transcribed into his work of 374.

[2] Considerable materials will be found in Dr Swainson's and Mr Lumby's books; as also in an essay by Caspari on the history of the baptismal confession in the Eastern Church from the fourth to the sixth century, in Rudelbach and Guericke's *Zeitschrift f. Lutherische Theologie* for 1857 pp. 634 ff. This essay shews that the 'Constantinopolitan' Creed, the traditional origin of which it does not occur to the writer to question, did not immediately succeed the ancient local Creeds as a baptismal confession, the original Nicene Creed having intervened till apparently some time in the sixth century. There is however but little evidence for the beginning of the period, and the final transition is not clearly marked.

from any clear evidence yet adduced, before it is found identified with the Nicene Creed, that is, treated as an improved recension of it[1]. There are however some obscure phenomena in the first half of the fifth century which cannot be passed over.

The existence of "additions" to the Nicene Creed, apparently in its second division, is acknowledged in a dialogue on the Trinity, of unknown authorship, written evidently before the Nestorian troubles of 429—431 (in Ath. *Opp.* ii 507 Montf., or Theodoreti *Opp.* v 991 f. Schulze). About 430 Nestorius in several places[2] quotes on his own behalf σαρκωθέντα ἐκ πνεύματος ἁγίου καὶ Μαρίας τῆς παρθένου as from the Nicene Creed[3], to the bewilderment of Cyril, who knew no such reading, whatever he might think of its doctrinal merits, and who took the

---

[1] Caspari interprets the Chalcedonian Definition as identifying the two Creeds, because, after reciting both, it refers to one only, and because that one Creed is said to teach the perfect doctrine (τὸ τέλειον) concerning Father, Son, *and Holy Ghost* and to establish *the Lord's Incarnation* for those who receive it faithfully. But the one Creed meant can be only the Nicene, and that in one form. The 150 stand in the same position towards the doctrine of the Holy Spirit as Cyril and Leo towards that of the Incarnation, as the subsequent context shews. Both appear merely as sound and now authorised interpreters of what the Nicene Creed contained already (it is even said, οὐχ ὥς τι λεῖπον τοῖς προλαβοῦσιν ἐπεισάγοντες); and in ratifying (κυροῖ) the Creed of the 150, the Council describes it simply as an "Instruction" (διδασκαλίαν), having just before "laid down as the primary matter" (ὥρισε προηγουμένως) that the "Faith" of the 318 is to remain "inviolate" (ἀπαρέγχείρητον). The whole passage falls into confusion if the single Creed is taken either as the "Constantinopolitan" or as that and the Nicene considered as one.

[2] *Oration* cited by Cyril of Alexandria (*Adv. Nest.* pp. 82, 84 Pusey = 22 Aubert = ix 45 BC, 49 A Migne) and Marius Mercator (770 A, 897 A, 925 B Migne); and again Cyril, p. 85, allusively, but M. Mercator completely, 771 A, 897 A; also (Latin only) Nest. *Ep. ad Caelest.* in Mansi *Conc.* iv 1022 c. This last passage, the reference to which I owe to Dr Swainson, p. 102, is worth quoting: "cum sancti illi et supra omnem praedicationem patres per (?) Nicaeam nihil amplius de Sancta Virgine dixissent nisi quia Dominus noster Jesus Christus incarnatus est ex Spiritu Sancto et Maria Virgine."

[3] The words ἐκ τῶν οὐρανῶν likewise stand in one of the two places where Cyril quotes the first passage (p. 82), but not in the other, nor in any of M. Mercator's quotations of either passage. Still they may possibly have lost their place in these texts merely by being unimportant to the argument. Μονογενῆ is likewise out of its true position; but the quotations hereabout are very lax.

pains to transcribe into his reply the whole Nicene Creed before discussing Nestorius's inferences from the words alleged (p. 85 Pusey). When Eutyches appealed to the Nicene Creed at the first session of the Council of Chalcedon, the same quotation was urged against him by Diogenes of Cyzicus, who accused him of omitting the last seven words on Apollinarian grounds[1], and stated that they had been added by "the holy fathers of a later time" to elucidate the Nicene ἐσαρκώθη[2]: the charge was not however allowed by the Egyptian bishops, who maintained that Eutyches had quoted the Creed rightly[3].

It is obvious at once that no œcumenical Symbol, in the large modern or Latin sense of the word, or even according to its proper Greek usage, can have contained the disputed words at this time: Cyril in 430 and his successors in 451 could never have been ignorant of its existence and contents, or have refused its authority. If Nestorius and Diogenes were quoting

[1] The printed text Δολερῶς προσέταξε τὴν...σύνοδον cannot be right. The verb is doubtless προέταξε: "It was crafty of him to set the Council in the front array," covering himself behind it.

[2] Οἱ γὰρ ἅγιοι πατέρες οἱ μετὰ ταῦτα τὸ 'Εσαρκώθη, ὃ εἶπον οἱ ἅγιοι ἐν Νικαίᾳ πατέρες, ἐσαφήνισαν εἰπόντες κ.τ.λ. It will be observed that the designation of the 'Fathers' is perfectly vague. It might mean the 150: but it might as easily mean the conjectured authors of observed additions, which would be assumed to have proceeded from some venerable authority.

[3] See Mr Lumby, pp. 78 f. and Dr Swainson, pp. 118 f. Caspari (661 ff.) uses this altercation at Chalcedon and the total silence about either the Council or the supposed Creed of Constantinople at Ephesus both in 431 and in 449 as evidence for a strange theory of his that the whole section of the Church who inclined to the Eutychian side were resolved to ignore altogether the Council of 381 and its Creed, partly on account of the addition to σαρκωθέντα, partly (after 451) as affording too good a precedent for the hated Definition of Chalcedon; and that the high esteem in which the 'Chalcedonian' section were similarly led to hold the 'Constantinopolitan' Creed eventually brought about the confusion of name with the proper Nicene Creed, and the substitution of the one for the other. It is difficult to represent to the imagination such a conspiracy of silence throughout a large proportion of Eastern Christendom; and not less difficult to understand why the other party should neither have exclaimed against the contumacious silence nor made appeal by name to the Creed and Council which they are supposed to have cherished. The Chalcedonian Definition puts them forward indeed for the interpretation of the doctrine of the Holy Spirit, but not for that of the doctrine of the Incarnation.

from the 'Constantinopolitan' Creed, it can have had only a very limited circulation. We have already seen (p. 75) that the circumstances under which it was presented at Chalcedon lead to the supposition that it had some kind of local currency at Constantinople. Now Nestorius was patriarch of Constantinople, and Cyzicus, the see of Diogenes, was brought practically near to Constantinople by the waters of the Propontis. Thus it is reasonable to look to the 'Constantinopolitan' Creed as the source of the phrase to which they appealed. But it by no means follows that the 'Constantinopolitan' Creed was the immediate source. The manner in which Nestorius and Diogenes treat their phrase as part of the Nicene Creed is difficult to reconcile with the recitation and acceptance of the "Creed of the 150" as a distinct document by the Council of Chalcedon, if the Council had the 'Constantinopolitan' Creed in view[1]. It would be at least easier to suppose that they were quoting from some local form of the Nicene Creed, into which under the influence of neighbourhood some phraseology of the longer Creed had informally crept.

This explanation is strikingly confirmed by the copy of the Nicene Creed embedded, with the "Creed of the 150" following it, in the "Definition" which the Council of Chalcedon put forth in its fifth session. This copy is conspicuously encrusted with a few of the 'Constantinopolitan' variations, including ἐκ πνεύματος ἁγίου καὶ Μαρίας τῆς παρθένου[2]. There is thus little room for doubt as to the conclusion, if the printed text of the Councils can be relied on; and there is no sufficient ground for impeach-

---

[1] No unquestionable trace of the 'Constantinopolitan' Creed has yet, as far as I am aware, been found in the writings of theologians throughout this period. It is certainly unnoticed and unused in numerous places where the results of an 'œcumenical' revision of the work of 325 were not likely to be ignored. The contrast in the writings of John of Damascus is significant.

[2] Special attention is drawn to this fact by Dr Swainson, 129 f. It is also noticed by Walch (77), by Caspari (i 103 ff.), and by Mr Lumby (81). Caspari refers to it only in his *Quellen*; just as in his previous article in the *Zeitschrift für Lutherische Theologie* he mentions only the incident of Eutyches and Diogenes.

AND OTHER EASTERN CREEDS 115

ing its integrity[1]. In any case it shews how easily the shorter Creed might become partially assimilated to the longer, at a time and place in which both were in use[2]. It was to all appearance reserved for a later time than the age of Chalcedon to confuse the "Creed of the 150" with the enlarged Nicene Creed, and thus to complete the fictitious history which was begun when the 150 Fathers of Constantinople were first reputed to be the authors of the Creed of which we may well believe that they had expressed approval.

Much more extensive confusions between a Creed proper and a dogmatic standard were involved, first in the gradual substitution of the Nicene for the local Creeds, and then in the treatment of the Constantinopolitan Creed as nothing else than a fuller and more precise statement of doctrine than the Nicene Creed. The one confusion however was eventually neutralised through the agency of the other, when the Nicene Symbol in its turn gave place to a Creed of yet more venerable ancestry, the worthiest of those that were called forth after a longer experience by the wants of a more auspicious time.

These observations on the origin of the 'Constantinopolitan' Creed may be fitly closed with a short account of the four other

---

[1] On referring to a Cambridge MS. (Ee 4 29) containing Greek conciliar documents, I have found ἐκ πνεύματος ἁγίου καὶ Μαρίας τῆς παρθένου to be absent from the Nicene text included in the 'Definition', as well as four other substantial 'Constantinopolitan' interpolations standing in the printed editions. On the other hand about as many more are retained: there are likewise several transpositions and other changes from which the printed text is free. I have no reason to suppose this authority to be of any peculiar value. Its existence merely suggests hesitation, so long as the manuscript sources of the conciliar texts are unexplored. Baluze's chief Latin MSS. of the Acts omit ἐκ πνεύματος κ.τ.λ., though they have other interpolations wanting in the Greek text: nor can the conformity of the printed Latin version with the Greek text be relied on, as it has apparently been retouched by the editors. But there is no evidence for Caspari's supposition that the Latin text is purer than the Greek.

[2] Many scattered 'Constantinopolitan' interpolations in copies and versions of the Nicene Creed are collected by Caspari, *Quellen* i 103 ff.

more or less similar Creeds which have been already noticed for purposes of illustration.

In 1866 Caspari rendered good service by pointing out the close resemblance between the Second Epiphanian Creed and a piece called *Interpretatio in Symbolum* published by Montfaucon (Ath. *Opp.* i 1278 f.) from two MSS., in one or both of which it is attributed to Athanasius. Caspari's enquiry into the origin and mutual relations of the two documents was less satisfactory, though it contained much useful matter. In 1869 he called attention to two other documents differing so slightly from each other that they may be treated as one, which correspond verbally with a large part of the two other pieces: they are the baptismal and eucharistic Creed of the Armenian Church proper and that of the Uniat Armenian Church. Caspari likewise quoted from two MSS. explored by himself at Venice and the Escurial a doctrinal exposition (διδασκαλία), attributed to Basil the Great in the Venice MS. and anonymous in the other, containing several passages agreeing approximately with language of the two other Greek expositions of faith.

The following results seem to me to suggest themselves conclusively on a careful collation and analysis of these several texts. The Armenian Creed[1] is a literal translation of a Greek

---

[1] The Armenian Creed proper was accessible to Caspari (ii 7 ff.) only in a somewhat loose dress, an English translation printed by Dr Neale (*Hist. of the East. Church* i 416 f.: cf. xvii, xxiv f., 379), chiefly made by Mr Blackmore from a Russian translation by Archbishop Dolgorouky published at St Petersburg in 1799. I have had the advantage of using the translation of *The Divine Liturgy of the Armenian Church* (pp. 32 f.) by Mr Malan, who has kindly answered some questions on doubtful points. His Armenian text is that printed at Constantinople in 1823, with the sanction of the Catholicos of Etchmiadzin (p. iv). The Uniat Armenian Creed was printed by Caspari (*ib.*) from an evidently accurate German translation by Steck; with which I have compared an English version published by the Venice Mechitarists in 1867. The original Armenian Creed may be recovered almost incorrupt from the versions of Steck and Mr Malan, which usually confirm each other. The other versions are more or less altered, chiefly by assimilation to the current 'Constantinopolitan' language. The Uniat Creed of course contains an interpolated clause, "proceeding from the Father and the Son," without which it must have lacked the *Filioque*, the badge of Latin communion.

Creed of the fourth century. This Greek Creed, soon after its composition, was enlarged and slightly modified, probably as the exposition of faith of a synod[1], and thus became the *Interpretatio in Symbolum*. The *Interpretatio* was still further enlarged and modified, apparently by Epiphanius[2] himself but perhaps by some other theologian, and in this shape was transcribed by Epiphanius into his *Ancoratus*, being what is called his Second Creed. At some later time the Epiphanian Creed, either as it

---

[1] This seems the natural inference from some of the words interpolated into the Anathematism, τούτους ἀναθεματίζομεν ὅτι αὐτοὺς ἀναθεματίζει ἡ καθολικὴ μήτηρ ἡμῶν καὶ ἀποστολικὴ ἐκκλησία. Moreover τοῦτ' ἐστίν is twice introduced before Cappadocian clauses which are not Nicene, so as to exhibit them as interpretations of the preceding Nicene clauses. It may be added that the Nicene Creed is strictly followed in the first case in which the later Cappadocian Creed had departed from it, the insertion of οὐρανοῦ καὶ γῆς. These characteristics, taken together, seem to indicate a public declaration on a particular occasion rather than either a Creed intended for repeated use or a private exposition of belief: but it is impossible to speak confidently.

[2] Caspari (i 5, 11ff.) has collected many striking coincidences between the language of Epiphanius himself and that of the *Interpretatio* and Second Epiphanian Creed. They chiefly concern the peculiarities of the Epiphanian formulary, but certainly comprise at least one important clause on the Incarnation common to the Armenian and both the Greek forms; and further there is a no less striking coincidence (*Haer.* 900 B), with a clause in the *Interpretatio* on the Holy Spirit, which in the Epiphanian formulary is replaced by totally different though concordant phraseology. But there is no difficulty in supposing that Epiphanius augmented his own stock of theological language from what he found in either of the Greek texts. He may have received the *Interpretatio*, and enlarged and altered it himself; or he may have received the later revision, and merely preserved it. The coincidences lend no support to the otherwise highly improbable view of Caspari that the Epiphanian Creed was composed as it stands by Epiphanius, and abridged into the *Interpretatio*, and that again into the Armenian Creed. Undoubtedly the choice lies between the two orders *Arm. Interp. Epiph.* and *Epiph. Interp. Arm.*; but *both* the processes performed seem to me to have been of enlargement, not abridgement. On the few cases in which the Epiphanian Creed has less than the *Interpretatio*, see next note: the change from the Armenian ἐν δόξῃ πατρός to ἐν δόξῃ must be taken along with the addition of a parallel ἐνδόξως to the clause on the Ascension. On any view the three forms contain matter suggested by the Apollinarian and Pneumatomachian controversies: both Greek forms have likewise a second anathematism evidently suggested by such doctrines on the Resurrection as we learn from Epiphanius (*Ancor.* 88 ff.; cf. *Haer.* lxiv, lxvii) to have been springing up or prevalent in his time in various quarters.

stood in the *Ancoratus* or more probably through an independent copy[1], furnished language to the author of the lately discovered exposition attributed to Basil. The Greek works thus enable us to restore with approximate exactness the original of the Armenian Creed.

Now the Armenian Church owed its origin at the beginning of the fourth century to the Cappadocian Church, and long retained the character of a daughter community. Till the end of the century its patriarchs were consecrated at Cæsarea the Cappadocian capital[2]; and the Armenian Liturgy is said to shew traces of a similar parentage by affinities to the Greek Liturgy which bears the name of St Basil of Cæsarea[3]. Thus it is improbable that its Creed came from any other region than Cappadocia, whether it originated in Cappadocia or not. The

---

[1] The second alternative is suggested by the absence from the Epiphanian Creed of certain phrases found in the *Interpretatio* which are not likely to have been intentionally omitted. They are ἀληθινῶς καὶ οὐ δοκήσει (after χωρὶς ἁμαρτίας) and τῇ τρίτῃ ἡμέρᾳ, both used in Caspari's Διδασκαλία (which certainly rests on the Epiphanian Creed), and καὶ ἀφέσεως ἁμαρτιῶν after βάπτισμα μετανοίας. But it is also possible that the defect is in our depraved text of the *Ancoratus*, depending virtually on two bad MSS. The remaining omission, that of [τοῦτ' ἐστὶ] σταυρωθέντα, ταφέντα, might easily be intentional; and indeed the removal of τῇ τρίτῃ ἡμέρᾳ, as Caspari remarks (i 52 f.), would combine the Resurrection and Ascension more distinctly under the one condition ἐν αὐτῷ τῷ σώματι; while so familiar a phrase might have come back into the Διδασκαλία from almost any source. No controversial word or phrase of the *Interpretatio* is absent from the Epiphanian Creed except ἀληθινῶς καὶ οὐ δοκήσει; and it is easier to explain its presence in the Διδασκαλία by supposing it to be absent from our text of the *Ancoratus* by an error of transcription than by supposing the Διδασκαλία to have used *both* the Greek formularies. The only other possible trace of the *Interpretatio* in the Διδασκαλία, the clause εἰς κρίσιν αἰώνιον, is quite uncertain: indeed its position at the end suggests that it is rather a fusion of two Epiphanian clauses than a single displaced clause of the *Interpretatio*.

[2] Neumann, *Versuch einer Gesch. d. armen. Liter.* 14 f., cited by Caspari. The literary and the political eminence of Cæsarea are alike asserted by Gregory of Nazianzus (*Or.* 43 p. 779 f.) in language too definite to be accounted for by his exuberant rhetoric: Prud. Maranus (*Vita S. Bas.* i 6) has completely proved the Cappadocian Cæsarea to be intended.

[3] Palmer *Orig. Liturg.* i 191 ff. E. Ranke in Herzog *R. E.* xi 382 f. draws a similar inference from certain remarkable coincidences between the Armenian Lectionary and passages in Basil's writings.

Creed itself on dissection proves to be exactly analogous to the 'Constantinopolitan', with the difference that in this case the true Nicene Creed does form the base. The Nicene Creed has been combined and filled out with the language of one or more traditional popular Creeds, and clauses have likewise been inserted with a view to the two great recent controversies, on the Incarnation (Apollinaris) and the Holy Spirit[1]. At first sight there is no little resemblance in parts to the 'Constantinopolitan' Creed: but the resemblance is deceptive, for the phrases in which the Cappadocian Creed agrees with the 'Constantinopolitan' against the Nicene Creed are all extant in other sources, and especially in the Creed of Jerusalem, while there is a significant absence of all the specially 'Constantinopolitan' statements on the Holy Spirit[2]. Whether one Creed or more was combined with the Nicene Creed cannot be determined: but it is likely that the early Creed either of Cappadocia or of some neighbouring region supplied at least the bulk of the supplementary matter; and it is interesting to find how much this primary source probably had in common with the Creed of Jerusalem. The following is an attempt to reconstruct the Cappadocian Creed[3], the evidence at all points where

---

[1] The rare formula γεννηθέντα...ἐκ Μαρίας τῆς ἁγίας παρθένου διὰ πνεύματος ἁγίου deserves notice. Dr Heurtley (p. 68) calls attention to *per* in two Latin Creeds; in Augustine, *De Fide et Symb.* 8, vi 155c (*qui natus est per Spiritum Sanctum ex Virgine Maria*); and after the Gallican Sacramentary in the Bobbio MS. (Muratori *Lit. Rom.* ii 967 or Migne lxxii 579: *natum de Maria Virgine per Spiritum Sanctum*). But Caspari (ii 264, 275) recalls Augustine's own warning in the *Retractations*, "in quo [libro de Fide et Symbolo] de rebus ipsis ita disseritur ut tamen non fiat verborum illa contextio quae tenenda memoriter competentibus traditur." The clause ὁρατά τε καὶ ἀόρατα is found in Basil's Confession, and in most of the formularies of 341—360.

[2] Caspari on the whole supposes the Armenian Creed to be a combination of the 'Constantinopolitan' Creed with an unknown Cappadocian Creed closely allied to the *Interpretatio* (ii 40ff.); but he speaks doubtfully. He would, I feel sure, have judged otherwise, had he not formed his theory about the relation of the Second Epiphanian Creed to the *Interpretatio* before he became acquainted with the Armenian Creed. He was also hampered by the common belief as to the origin and currency of the 'Constantinopolitan' Creed.

[3] A Greek original for the Armenian Creed has already been constructed by

reasonable doubt seems possible, and some others, being subjoined in the notes[1].

Πιστεύομεν εἰς ἕνα θεὸν πατέρα παντοκράτορα,
  ποιητὴν οὐρανοῦ καὶ γῆς[2],
    ὁρατῶν τε καὶ ἀοράτων.
Καὶ εἰς ἕνα κύριον Ἰησοῦν Χριστόν,
  τὸν υἱὸν τοῦ θεοῦ,
    γεννηθέντα ἐκ τοῦ πατρὸς μονογενῆ -
      τοῦτ' ἐστὶν ἐκ τῆς οὐσίας τοῦ πατρός[3] -
      θεὸν ἐκ θεοῦ,
      φῶς ἐκ φωτός,
      θεὸν ἀληθινὸν ἐκ θεοῦ ἀληθινοῦ,
    γεννηθέντα, οὐ ποιηθέντα,
    ὁμοούσιον τῷ πατρί,
  δι' οὗ τὰ πάντα ἐγένετο,
    τά τε ἐν τῷ οὐρανῷ καὶ τὰ ἐπὶ τῆς γῆς,
    ὁρατά τε καὶ ἀόρατα·
τὸν δι' ἡμᾶς τοὺς ἀνθρώπους καὶ διὰ τὴν ἡμετέραν σωτηρίαν
    κατελθόντα ἐκ τῶν οὐρανῶν[4],

Caspari (ii 31ff.); but it has needed much revision on account of erroneous theory as well as imperfect evidence.

[1] At the end of the volume the Cappadocian Creed is reprinted with the elements common to it with the Nicene Creed distinguished by uncial type.

[2] So Malan and Steck, assuredly rightly. The Greek forms (Interpr., Epiph.) omit οὐρανοῦ καὶ γῆς and insert πάντων, in both respects with Nicen.: the other Armenian forms (Neale, Mechit.) have both οὐρανοῦ καὶ γῆς and πάντων, with Jerus. and CP. (i.e. the 'Constantinopolitan' Creed). Thus the corruptions by assimilation to Nic. present themselves in the Greek forms, written in the fourth century; and assimilation to CP. belongs to the comparatively modern corruptions of the Armenian forms; just as we should expect.

[3] So Malan (distinctly in litt.), with Int. and Ep., and with Nic. Steck, Neale, and Mech. substitute πρὸ πάντων τῶν αἰώνων with CP., and the two last likewise throw back μονογενῆ to the preceding clause with Jer. and CP. The Vatican MS. of Int. has lost μονογενῆ τοῦτ' ἐστὶν ἐκ τῆς οὐσίας τοῦ πατρός by homœoteleuton owing to the preceding τοῦ πατρός: the missing words are retained in the Paris MS.

[4] Int. and Ep. omit ἐκ τῶν οὐρανῶν with Nic.

σαρκωθέντα, ἐνανθρωπήσαντα, γεννηθέντα τελείως[1] ἐκ Μαρίας
τῆς ἁγίας παρθένου[2] διὰ πνεύματος ἁγίου,
[ἐκ ταύτης[3]] σῶμα καὶ ψυχὴν[4] καὶ νοῦν καὶ πάντα ὅσα
ἐστὶν ἄνθρωπος(?)[5] ἀληθῶς καὶ οὐ δοκήσει
ἐσχηκότα,
παθόντα, σταυρωθέντα[6], ταφέντα,
ἀναστάντα τῇ τρίτῃ ἡμέρᾳ[7],
ἀνελθόντα εἰς [τοὺς][8] οὐρανοὺς ἐν αὐτῷ τῷ σώματι,
καθίσαντα ἐν δεξιᾷ τοῦ πατρός,
ἐρχόμενον ἐν αὐτῷ τῷ σώματι [καὶ][9] ἐν τῇ δόξῃ τοῦ πατρὸς[10] κρῖναι ζῶντας καὶ νεκρούς,

[1] So Malan. Steck omits γεννηθέντα: Neale omits ἐνανθρωπήσαντα. Int. inserts τοῦτ' ἐστίν between ἐνανθρωπήσαντα and γεννηθέντα: Ep. reads σαρκωθέντα τοῦτ' ἐστὶ γεννηθέντα τελείως ἐκ κ.τ.λ., deferring ἐνανθρωπήσαντα till after πνεύματος ἁγίου (where, with τοῦτ' ἐστίν added, it is prefixed to an altered amplification of the following explanatory clause): Mech. both defers ἐνανθρωπήσαντα and omits γεννηθέντα τελείως, thus following CP.

[2] So Malan (in litt.) and Steck, assuredly rightly. Int. has ἐκ Μ. τῆς ἀειπαρθένου, Ep. ἐκ τῆς ἁγίας Μ. τῆς ἀειπαρθένου: Neale and Mech. omit ἁγίας, with CP., and invert the positions of the Virgin and the Holy Spirit, likewise with CP.

[3] The presence of ἐκ ταύτης or some equivalent is attested by Malan and Steck ("from whom he") and Mech. ("and who took from her"), though omitted apparently by Neale ("assumed") as by Int. (ἐσχηκότα) and by Ep.: Ep. however likewise omits ἐσχηκότα, substituting τέλειον ἄνθρωπον λαβόντα before ψυχὴν καὶ σῶμα.

[4] So Int. and as to the order all the Armenian forms. Malan and Neale have "body", Steck and Neale "flesh", but apparently the Armenian is ambiguous: Ep. has ψυχὴν καὶ σῶμα.

[5] So Ep.: Malan, Neale, Mech., and apparently Steck have "in man": Int. (if rightly printed) has ἀνθρώποις. That ἄνθρωπος is at least not a clerical error is proved by various passages of Epiphanius cited by Caspari (i 11); it may have been substituted for ἀνθρώποις in the second Greek (Epiphanian) recension, but was more probably the original reading changed by scribes to an easier form. The Armenian rendering might stand for either reading: an original ἐν ἀνθρώπῳ would hardly have been altered.

[6] This and other participles have καί prefixed in various authorities. I have followed Malan and Steck.

[7] Ep. omits τῇ τρίτῃ ἡμέρᾳ: Malan (also in litt.) prefixes it to ἀναστάντα.

[8] So Ep. with Nic. and CP.. Int. omits τούς.

[9] So Malan (also in litt.) and Neale. Steck and Mech. apparently omit καί, as do Int. and Ep.: but see next note.

[10] So all the Armenian forms: cf. Mat. xvi 27; Mark viii 38. Int. and Ep. have only ἐν δόξῃ, but they add ἐνδόξως to the first ἐν αὐτῷ τῷ σώματι (see p. 117 n. 2). The probably Asiatic Creed of Irenæus (48: cf. 206) had ἐν τῇ δόξῃ τοῦ πατρός, as also the third formulary of Sirmium τῇ δόξῃ τῇ πατρικῇ, that of Nicé μετὰ δόξης

122   ON THE 'CONSTANTINOPOLITAN' CREED

οὗ τῆς βασιλείας οὐκ ἔσται τέλος.
Καὶ πιστεύομεν εἰς τὸ πνεῦμα τὸ ἅγιον τὸ ἄκτιστον τὸ τέλειον[1],
τὸ λαλῆσαν ἐν νόμῳ καὶ ἐν προφήταις καὶ ἐν εὐαγγελίοις,
καταβὰν ἐπὶ τὸν Ἰορδάνην,
κηρύξαν τὸν ἀπόστολον (or ἀποστόλοις)[2],
οἰκῆσαν (or οἰκοῦν)[3] ἐν ἁγίοις.

πατρικῆς, and its Constantinopolitan recension of 360 ἐν τῇ πατρικῇ δόξῃ.

[1] So all the Armenian forms, the Uniat adding the Latin CP. clause on the Procession. So also virtually Int. and Ep., but with various additions and transpositions, [τὸ] παράκλητον being the only added element common to both. The critical phrase of Int. is οὐκ ἀλλότριον...ἀλλ' ὁμοούσιον, in this place; of Ep. ἐκ τοῦ πατρὸς ἐκπορευόμενον καὶ ἐκ τοῦ υἱοῦ λάμβανον (so rightly Caspari, i 5 f., after John xvi 14 f., for λαμβανόμενον, the whole phrase, as he points out, being much used by Epiphanius), in a sentence added after ἁγίοις.

[2] Malan (also *in litt.*), Steck, Neale, and Mech. have κηρύξαν τὸν ἀπόστολον: Ep. has λαλοῦν ἐν ἀποστόλοις, having already inserted κηρύξαν before ἐν τοῖς προφήταις: Cod. Reg. of Int. (with the Armenian form given by Nerses of Lampron in the twelfth century, according to Mr Malan) has κηρύξαν ἀποστόλοις, Cod. Vat. κηρυξόμενον ἀποστόλοις. Τὸν ἀπόστολον, if right, must denote our Lord (Heb. iii 1: cf. Just. Mart. *Ap.* i 12 p. 60 A; 63 pp. 95 D, 96 AC; Orig. on Jo. xiii 20 p. 430 Ru.; Cyr. Al. *Expl. xii Capp.* p. 148 B=245 Pusey), with reference to the Baptism. The reading is difficult, especially through the absence of καί to connect this clause with the descent on the Jordan. Ὁ ἀπόστολος is also a singular term to be selected for absolute use; nor can it be explained by so remote and isolated a rendering of *Shiloh* in Gen. xlix 10 as Jerome's *qui mittendus est*. Yet it has in its favour the chief Armenian evidence, and it was far more likely to be altered than the other readings. It is moreover supported by the injunction in the Apostolic Constitutions (vii 22 1) for baptism in the threefold Name τοῦ ἀποστείλαντος πατρός, τοῦ ἐλθόντος χριστοῦ, τοῦ μαρτυρήσαντος παρακλήτου (cf. 26 1, ὁ ἀποστείλας ἐπὶ γῆς Ἰησοῦν τὸν χριστόν σου κ.τ.λ.); and Cyr. Hier. xvi 3 ἐν πνεῦμα ἅγιον, διὰ προφητῶν μὲν περὶ τοῦ χριστοῦ κηρύξαν, ἐλθόντος δὲ τοῦ χριστοῦ καταβὰν καὶ ἐπιδεῖξαν αὐτόν. For κηρύξαν cf. Clem. *Strom.* ii p. 449 παρέλκει ὁ διάκονος αὐτοῖς [Basilidians] καὶ τὸ κήρυγμα καὶ τὸ βάπτισμα, where the διάκονος, and therefore the κήρυγμα, is proved by *Exc. Theod.* 16 p. 972 to belong to the Baptism. Yet κηρύξαν ἀποστόλοις, which is not without Armenian as well as Greek authority, cannot well be neglected. It is at least less obvious than the somewhat feeble κηρύξαν ἐν ἀποστόλοις, and gives an intelligible sense as a compendious reference to John xvi 13 ff., where the truer but less pictorial word ἀναγγελεῖ is used three times.

[3] Οἰκῆσαν (Malan, Steck, and Mech.) is probably right (cf. Ap. Const. τὸ ἐνεργῆσαν ἐν πᾶσι τοῖς ἀπ' αἰώνος ἁγίοις), but may be due to assimilation: οἰκοῦν (Neale, Int., and Ep.) gives a more obvious sense.

Καὶ πιστεύομεν εἰς μίαν μόνην[1] καθολικὴν καὶ ἀποστολικὴν
    ἐκκλησίαν,
  εἰς ἓν βάπτισμα μετανοίας,
  εἰς ἱλασμὸν (?) καὶ ἄφεσιν[2] ἁμαρτιῶν,
  εἰς ἀνάστασιν νεκρῶν,
  εἰς κρίσιν αἰώνιον ψυχῶν τε καὶ σωμάτων[3],
  εἰς βασιλείαν οὐρανῶν,
  καὶ εἰς[4] ζωὴν αἰώνιον.

Τοὺς δὲ λέγοντας ὅτι Ἦν ποτε ὅτε οὐκ ἦν ὁ υἱός, ἢ Ἦν ποτε ὅτε οὐκ ἦν τὸ ἅγιον πνεῦμα, ἢ ὅτι Ἐξ οὐκ ὄντων ἐγένετο, ἢ ἐξ ἑτέρας ὑποστάσεως ἢ οὐσίας φάσκοντας εἶναι τὸν υἱὸν τοῦ θεοῦ ἢ τὸ πνεῦμα τὸ ἅγιον, τρεπτὸν ἢ ἀλλοιωτόν, τούτους ἀναθεματίζει ἡ[5] καθολικὴ καὶ ἀποστολικὴ ἐκκλησία[6].

The most marked feature of the Cappadocian Creed, as distinguished from the revised Creed of Jerusalem, is the clear and copious language by which Apollinarianism is precluded. The doctrine itself, as we have seen (p. 95), had certainly arisen before the Council of Alexandria in 362. On the other hand it is in 371 and the following years that we begin to hear it widely spoken of, and to find the name of Apollinaris attached to it. This one indication would point to 371—3, while on the other hand so late a date does not leave much time for the modifications introduced before the Creed was transcribed

---

[1] So Malan, Steck, and (with ταύτην added) Int.: Mech. and Ep. omit μόνην, Neale substitutes ἁγίαν, on which see Mr Malan's note.

[2] So apparently Malan, Steck, and Mech., the renderings of the first substantive being *expiation* and *Vergebung* (followed by *Nachlassung*). Neale has only εἰς ἄφεσιν ἁμ.; Int. καὶ ἀφέσεως ἁμ.; and Ep. omits all after μετανοίας. Notwithstanding Acts ii 38 it is best not to join this clause to the preceding, which the example of the early Jerusalem Creed shews to need no supplement, while the separate Western Remissionem peccatorum justifies a like separation here, and ἱλασμόν almost enforces it. The 'Constantinopolitan' analogy has little force on the other side, as μετανοίας is wanting there.

[3] Nerses omits ψυχῶν τε καὶ σωμάτων.

[4] So Malan, Steck, Mech., and Ep.: Int. omits εἰς, as also Neale, who however omits εἰς throughout this division.

[5] Malan inserts ἁγία.

[6] Nerses of Lampron (Malan) omits the whole Anathematism, substituting *Amen*.

by Epiphanius in 374. From the autumn of 370[1] Basil was bishop of Cæsarea, and thus at the head of the Cappadocian churches: but though the Creed is in harmony with his doctrine, no such repetitions of its phrases are perceptible in his writings as might have been anticipated if he were the compiler[2]: so that we are led to look back to the preceding years. Basil's immediate predecessor Eusebius, an unbaptized civil official raised to the episcopate by popular acclamation shortly after the accession of Julian, shewed some excellent qualities in trying times, but evidently had neither the inclination nor the capacity for such a work. Among known names that of Silvanus of Tarsus has the best claim to consideration. Next to Basil of Ancyra, Silvanus held the chief place among the Homœousian bishops of Asia Minor who suffered persecution under Constantius, welcomed Cyril in his exile[3], and gave Basil his early training. He formed one of the deputation from the East which sought communion with Liberius in 366 on the basis of the Nicene Creed[4]. Eustathius, whose name stands

---

[1] This is the date determined by Tillemont, Prud. Maranus, and Klose, in conjunction with Jan. 1 379 for the death of Basil, and the following autumn for the synod of Antioch. Pagi and Clinton place all three events a year later; but on untrustworthy authority.

[2] What is said here refers to Basil's writings generally, not merely to the Confession of Faith included in the piece *De Fide*, which seems to have been written comparatively early, whether it properly belongs to the preface to the *Ethica* or not (cf. Tillemont ix 28, 634 f.; Schröckh xiii 16). The leading terms on the Holy Spirit in the Confession (*Opp.* ii 227 D) are Καὶ ἐν μόνον πνεῦμα ἅγιον τὸ (or τὸν) παράκλητον..., τὸ πνεῦμα τῆς ἀληθείας..., τὸ πνεῦμα τῆς υἱοθεσίας κ.τ.λ.: two of them we shall meet in the Philadelphian Creed.

[3] Cyril had indeed closer relations with Silvanus than with the rest. On his expulsion by Acacius, it was at Tarsus that he sought and found refuge, and there he took part in the public services and teaching. Acacius remonstrated; but failed to overcome Silvanus's personal respect (αἰδούμενος) for Cyril and unwillingness to offend the people, who delighted in his sermons. Theodoret *H.E.* ii 22 (26).

[4] Tarsus itself was to have been the place of meeting for a great synod to be held in the spring of 367, for which the bishops chiefly concerned in this deputation sent forth invitations, its purpose being the confirmation of the Nicene faith with a view to reconciliation. Difficulties were created by some dissentient Homœousians in Caria; and it was finally forbidden by Valens under the influence of Eudoxius. Socr. iv 12 34 f.; Soz. vi 12 3 ff.

first as his colleague, an erratic and unstable person, is known to have receded afterwards from this position: but we hear no similar tidings of Silvanus, and Basil always speaks of him with unqualified reverence. Indeed as early as the end of 359 he had defended even the term ὁμοούσιος at Constantinople, in the presence of the indignant emperor[1], and it is morally certain that he would not hold aloof in later years. He died apparently in 369[2]. After an interval of some years, during which the Arians had the upper hand at Tarsus, he was succeeded by his own pupil[3] Diodorus, probably the greatest theologian, Gregory of Nyssa excepted, who took part in the Council of Constantinople in 381, the cherished teacher of Chrysostom and Theodore of Mopsuestia[4]. Supposing the revision of the Creed to have been made by an eminent bishop of Tarsus, it was likely to find ready acceptance in Cappadocia, with which Cilicia was closely connected. The ancient fame for learning was but one of the prerogatives of Tarsus; bewailing the condition of its church after the death of Silvanus, Basil described the city as "having such happy opportunities that it was itself a means of linking together Isaurians and Cilicians with Cappadocians and Syrians[5]". Two other geographical contiguities deserve mention. A sail of 120 miles across the Gulf

---

[1] 'Ἀλλὰ συλλογιστικῶς τε καὶ ἀληθῶς ὁ Σιλβανὸς πρός τε αὐτοὺς καὶ τὸν βασιλέα ἔφη Εἰ ἐξ οὐκ ὄντων οὐκ ἔστιν οὔτε κτίσμα οὔτε ἐξ ἑτέρας οὐσίας ὁ θεὸς λόγος, ὁμοούσιος ἄρα ἐστὶ τῷ γεγεννηκότι θεῷ ὡς θεὸς ἐκ θεοῦ καὶ φῶς ἐκ φωτός, καὶ τὴν αὐτὴν ἔχει τῷ γεννήτορι φύσιν. 'Ἀλλὰ ταῦτα μὲν καὶ δυνατῶς καὶ ἀληθῶς εἰρήκει· ἐπείθετο δὲ τῶν παρόντων οὐδείς, ἀλλὰ βοή τε πολλὴ τῶν περὶ Ἀκάκιον καὶ Εὐδόξιον ἐγίνετο, καὶ ὁ βασιλεὺς ἐχαλέπηνε καὶ τῶν ἐκκλησιῶν ἐξελάσειν ἠπείλησεν. Theodoret H.E. ii 23 (27).

[2] So Prud. Maranus Vita S. Bas. xii 6. Tillemont gives 373 (vi 592; ix 211). The evidence is not decisive.

[3] Basil writes in 376 (Ep. 244 p. 378 B): Διόδωρον δὲ ὡς θρέμμα τοῦ μακαρίου Σιλουανοῦ τὸ ἐξ ἀρχῆς ὑπεδεξάμεθα, νῦν δὲ καὶ ἀγαπῶμεν καὶ περιέπομεν διὰ τὴν προσοῦσαν αὐτῷ τοῦ λόγου χάριν, δι' ἧς πολλοὶ τῶν ἐντυγχανόντων βελτίους γίνονται.

[4] Two facts respecting Diodorus are worthy of note for our purpose, that he owed to Meletius his elevation to the see of Tarsus, and that he shewed especial zeal against Apollinaris.

[5] Ep. 34 p. 113 A. By 'Syrians' Basil probably means here the Syri of Cappadocia: but his language might be safely applied to the natives of Syria likewise, who had much intercourse with Cilicia.

of Issus would conduct from Laodicea, the home of Apollinaris, to Tarsus; and a sail of 150 miles, over almost the same waters, from Tarsus to Constantia, the see of Epiphanius. It would accordingly be no wonder if Apollinarian doctrine were known and dreaded at Tarsus before it spread to more distant churches: and as Epiphanius appears to have brought with him to Cyprus his shorter Creed from the neighbourhood of Jerusalem, in like manner his longer Creed could reach him in Cyprus from no nearer mainland capital than Tarsus, unless Antioch be excepted. According to the conjecture here hasarded, the probable date of the Creed would be 366—9: but neither time nor authorship admit of secure determination.

Next in order must be named the revised Antiochian Creed, which has unfortunately reached us imperfect. The first two divisions have been preserved in a Latin dress by Cassianus[1], as has been well known since the days of Ussher. Caspari has pointed out (i 73 ff.) that a few clauses of the same portion survive in Greek in a *Contestatio* comparing Nestorius to Paul of Samosata, dating from 429 or 430, which is said by Leontius (*Contra Nest. et Eutych.* iii, t. 86 p. 1389 Migne) to have been attributed to Eusebius afterwards bishop of Dorylæum[2]. Other clauses near the end have been recovered by Dr Heurtley and Caspari from Chrysostom's Homilies[3]. I have thought it worth while to try to restore the original of this Creed so far as the evidence goes (see p. 148): but some points must be left doubtful[4]. We do not possess any direct evidence as to the

[1] *De incarnatione Domini* vi 3 f., with some repetitions in the following chapters.

[2] Printed among Ephesine documents in Mansi *Conc.* iv 1109. An ancient Latin version is also extant (Theodoreti *Opp.* v 624 Schulze). The quotation extends from θεὸν ἀληθινόν to Πιλάτου: some earlier words are cited freely (see p. 64 n. 3).

[3] See pp. 75 n. 1; 80 n. 1.

[4] The *Credo* of Cassianus is possibly a reminiscence of the Latin singular. The same may be said of *Dominum nostrum*, which indeed loses *nostrum* in cc. 6, 7, 9: Eus.Dor. refers with apparent emphasis to ἕνα, which is moreover present in the Lucianic Creed. Not κατελθόντα of the Greek text of Eus.Dor. (so also Luc. and

Creed of Antioch in the early part of the fourth century, that is, in its condition intermediate between the Lucianic and the later forms[1]. It is thus impossible to say what changes, if any, were made at the final revision, beyond the insertion of

Nic.) but ἐλθόντα (*venit* Eus.Dor. *Latine* and Cass.) seems to be right: so Caspari 79. Again the printed text of the Greek Eus.Dor. has ἐκ Μαρίας τῆς ἁγίας τῆς ἀειπαρθένου, the Munich MS. and the Latin ἐκ Μ. τ. ἁγίας παρθένου, Cassianus *ex Maria Virgine;* Lucianus having had merely ἐκ παρθένου: doubtless ἐκ τῆς ἁγίας π. is right. Though distrusting the order in Cassianus, I have not ventured to write ἀναστάντα τῇ τρίτῃ ἡμέρᾳ or ἀνελθόντα εἰς τοὺς οὐρανούς. Speculation as to the missing clauses after νεκρούς must be precarious. The clauses on the Holy Spirit most likely to have been present are τὸν παράκλητον and τὸ πνεῦμα τῆς ἀληθείας, both found in various formularies of 341—360 in which Antiochene language would be gladly adopted, (among which that of Nicé has an identical beginning, the Third Sirmian almost the same, and also the characteristic δι' οὗ οἱ αἰῶνες κατηρτίσθησαν,) the former title occurs moreover in the early Creed of Jerusalem, in that of the Apostolic Constitutions, and in a Creed used by Lucifer (see next note); and both in the Philadelphian Creed, as also in Basil's Confession (*Opp.* ii 227 D). Yet further, τὸ πνεῦμα τῆς ἀληθείας stands in the daughter Creed of Mesopotamia, some of the other language of which on the Holy Spirit, and in the clauses following, may likewise be Antiochian.

[1] This is perhaps the best place to mention a form of Creed used by Lucifer in 358 (*Pro Ath.* ii p. 132 Coleti), which has apparently escaped the notice of editors. It exhibits a combination of Nicene with other Eastern language, but is unfortunately imperfect: "...qui catholicam damnaveris fidem, qui *Deum Patrem* negaveris *verum Patrem*, qui *unicum ejus Filium* dixeris non esse *verum Filium*, *Spiritum* quoque *Sanctum Paracletum* asseveraveris non esse *verum Dei Spiritum;* cum te contra et contra omnes Dei inimicos clamet sanctae ecclesiae fides *credere se in Deum verum Patrem innatum, et in unicum Filium ejus natum ex innato et vero Patre, hoc est, de substantia Patris, Deum de Deo, lumen de lumine, Deum verum de Deo vero, natum, non factum, unius substantiae cum Patre,* (quod Graeci dicunt omousion,) *per quem omnia facta sunt, et sine quo factum est nihil; et in Spiritum Paracletum, verum Dei Spiritum.*" The transcription of the Greek term, with an explanatory parenthesis added, is common in early Latin copies of the Nicene Creed. Elsewhere about 360 (*De non parc. in D. delinq.* p. 204) Lucifer gives the Nicene Creed pretty exactly, (omitting however μονογενῆ,) as the "belief of the Holy Church;" cf. *Mor. esse pro D. F.* p. 245: so that the combination quoted above may possibly have been unconscious and extemporaneous. But the peculiar phrases were certainly derived from some Creed, for that of the Apostolic Constitutions has εἰς ἕνα ἀγέννητον μόνον ἀληθινὸν θεόν, that of Alexandria according to Alexander has ἀγέννητον, and that of Antioch according to Cassianus *verum Deum Patrem omnipotentem:* the explanation subjoined to the Lucianic Creed likewise combines ἀληθῶς with each Person of the Trinity.

the three Nicene phrases, οὐ ποιηθέντα, θεὸν ἀληθινὸν ἐκ θεοῦ ἀληθινοῦ, ὁμοούσιον τῷ πατρί. Judging by internal evidence, we might suspect these to have been the only innovations. It has been suggested that the revision took place at the synod held at Antioch under Meletius late in 363 (see p. 96). A gathering however of scattered bishops, including men like Acacius, assembled to express acquiescence in the terms of communion arranged by Meletius, was hardly a body to which he would commit the revision of the Creed of Antioch, and there is no evidence or probability that the later Antiochian Creed was intended for any such purposes as the formularies of 341—360. To regard either this or any other of the five known revised Creeds as lowerings of the Nicene standard for the sake of dogmatic compromise is to mistake their whole nature: the process in each case consisted in the enrichment of a local Symbol for local use. That Meletius was responsible for the Antiochian revision, and that it took place in one of the early years of his episcopate, is likely enough.

We come next to a Creed which has for its base the revised Antiochian Creed, into which it introduces some fresh Nicene elements, with other additions of unknown origin. Our knowledge of it is again chiefly due to Caspari (i 113 ff.), who has for the first time published it entire in Syriac from a Munich MS.[1], accompanying it with some useful illustrations, in which he points out some of the Antiochian affinities. Dr Wright has been good enough to examine two MSS. in the Cambridge University Library, and two others in the British Museum; and has enabled me to introduce some corrections into Caspari's Greek rendering. This Creed is no other than the Creed in general use among the Nestorians. Some particles of it[2] were given

---

[1] Orient. 147: the extract was furnished to him by Schönfelder. Dr Wright observes that there is another MS. of this Creed in the National Library at Paris, Suppl. 56, No 24 in Zotenberg's catalogue.

[2] I find πρωτότοκον πάσης κτίσεως mentioned as in the "Nicene Creed"

by Renaudot (*L. O.* i 219) from a tract by Severus of Ashmonin against the Nestorian metropolitan of Damascus, and the clauses on the Holy Spirit by Dr Badger (*The Nestorians and their Rituals* ii. 78 f.: cf. 92): but it has not been printed as a whole till 1866, and then only at Christiania. As might be expected, it has nothing to do with distinctive Nestorian doctrine, but is simply a monument of the days before 431, preserved by the independence of the Nestorian Communion from being superseded by the 'Constantinopolitan' Creed, just as the Cappadocian Creed was preserved by the Armenian independence. Its home was doubtless Mesopotamia and the neighbouring countries, the great inland region where the Syriac language was supreme, and the decrees of emperors and Greek councils were not readily accepted. Over this region no Greek capital exercised such influence as Antioch; and it is natural that we find the Mesopotamian Creed to be a careful enlargement of the revised Creed of Antioch[1]. The analogies with the revised Creed of Jerusalem only illustrate the mutual independence of the two documents. There is enough of verbal coincidence to establish a limited community of materials: but it is incredible that the Mesopotamian compiler should have had the other composition in his hands without making larger use of it[2]. There is little variation of text

on which the Nestorian Elijah of Nisibis wrote a commentary in the eleventh century (Assemani *B. O.* iii 271 f.); and this and other distinctive phrases are similarly recorded as given in another anonymous commentary (ib. 280).

[1] A few Antiochian words are dropped in the process. They are καὶ μόνον ἀληθινόν, κτισμάτων, and ἁγίας.

[2] The Mesopotamian phrases neither Antiochian nor Nicene in the first two divisions (neglecting ἐκτίσθη and particles) are ἐκ [τῶν] οὐρανῶν, ἐκ πνεύματος ἁγίου after σαρκωθέντα, ἄνθρωπον γενόμενον (sic) for ἐνανθρωπή-σαντα, καὶ συλληφθέντα, and καὶ καθίσαντα ἐξ δεξιῶν τοῦ πατρὸς [αὐτοῦ]. In the first, second, and fifth there is a coincidence with 'CP.' language, and the absence of Μαρίας τῆς παρθένου in the second might be due only to its presence in a later Antiochian clause. But καθίσαντα is the form which preceded the 'CP.' καθεζόμενον; ἄνθρωπον γενόμενον is probably ancient, certainly not 'Constantinopolitan'; and συλληφθέντα, comparatively late (replacing σαρκωθέντα) in Latin Creeds (first at Ariminum in 359 [Hier. *Dial. in Lucif.* 17, cited by Caspari ii 203 f.], this part of the Creed being apparently

in the MSS.[1] except as to the presence or absence of the *Filioque*[2].

Conjectures as to authorship are even more hasardous here than in the case of the Cappadocian Creed[3]. If however, as

Western, though what precedes follows the formulary of Nicé), seems to be unique in Greek Creeds. From Καὶ εἰς ἓν ἅγιον πνεῦμα to ἓν βάπτισμα the Antiochian text is not extant for comparison. The three 'CP.' phrases τὸ ἐκ τοῦ πατρὸς ἐκπορευόμενον, τὸ ζωοποιόν, and ὁμολογοῦμεν ἓν βάπτισμα [εἰς ἄφεσιν ἁμαρτιῶν] cannot have come together by accident. But the collocations of the two former are altogether different in the two Creeds; and the 'CP.' sentence would assuredly have been used to better purpose if used at all. An inversion of the process is conceivable: but it is far more likely that both compilers used a common document, now unknown, and that it provided them likewise with the additions in the first two divisions. Except the three Nicene phrases selected at Antioch, the Mesopotamian Creed does not contain a word which distinctly savours of the controversies of the fourth century.

[1] One London MS. has "the Spirit *our* Life-giver." The suffix translated by αὐτοῦ after πατρός in two places cannot be relied on, such pronominal supplements being congenial to Syriac usage. There is perhaps some confusion in the clause on the Church; but the MSS. give no help: Alexander's paraphrase of the Alexandrine Creed (μίαν καὶ μόνην καθολικὴν τὴν ἀποστολικήν) suggests that τὴν should possibly be inserted before καθολικήν.

[2] It is absent altogether from the elder London MS., and *prima manu* from the Munich MS. and the Cambridge MS. next mentioned: it is present in the two other MSS. Whether the phrase on the Procession of the Holy Spirit retained the relative and finite verb of St John or, as at Jerusalem, assumed a participial form, cannot be determined from the Syriac; the preposition seems to be ἐκ, not παρά: but in either case this phrase must certainly be taken with the preceding τὸ πνεῦμα τῆς ἀληθείας, as in St John (xv 26): the repetition of τὸ πνεῦμα before τὸ ζωοποιόν removes all possible doubt.

[3] Nothing, I fear, of importance as to the early history, much less the origin, of the Creed can be elicited from the title given in one of the Cambridge MSS., which came from Malabar, and was probably written in the fifteenth century. It runs "The orthodox Faith of the Church which was composed [or 'ordained'] by the 318 Fathers and Bishops who were assembled at the city of Nicæa: and it is to be said at the time of the mysteries: Joseph, who was dismissed from the patriarchate, ordained it to be said at the time of the mysteries." The Joseph intended is Joseph I, patriarch of the Nestorians in 552—5. His name, though just legible, has been erased, as often occurs, Dr Wright tells me, in Syriac MSS. with names of evil repute. He was a physician, made patriarch for curing the Persian king Chosru; but, breaking out after three years into acts of strange violence towards other bishops, was deposed by a synod. It is said that in the disturbed state of the Church he held a synod by request of the bishops to confirm the canons, when a confession of faith (certainly not our Creed, as

seems likely, the Creed of Mesopotamia attained its present form not many years before or after the beginning of the last third of the fourth century, it is at least easy to single out the greatest and most honoured name among the heads of sees to the East of Antioch throughout the period. Eusebius of Samosata first comes into view at the election of Meletius in 361, when the two parties, having united in a common vote, concurred in depositing the subscribed instrument in his hands. When the Arians, repenting of their choice, endeavoured with the support of Constantius to substitute Euzoius for Meletius, no threats of personal violence could induce Eusebius to surrender the deposit, and his courage, we are told, won even the emperor's admiration (Theodoret *H. E.* ii 27 f. [31 f.][1]). In 363 he took part in the synod at Antioch which subscribed the ὁμοούσιον with an explanation; and in the memorial to Jovian his name stands second, next to that of Meletius (Socr. iii 25 16). On the death of Eusebius of the Cappadocian Cæsarea in 370 he was invited by the elder Gregory of Nazianzus to assist him in providing a worthy bishop for so important a see, and by his efforts and influence Basil was placed in the vacant throne in the face of a vigorous political agitation (Greg. Naz. *Epp.* 42, 44; *Or.* 18 p. 356 f.: cf. 43 p. 799; Bas. *Ep.* 145). Basil's cor-

the description shews) was agreed to. This statement receives some illustration from the fact that his predecessor Aba, a convert from the Magians, a vigorous patriarch of much literary activity, author of "Synodical Epistles", "Canons", and "Constitutions" on Church matters, and co-translator of the Old Testament and of a "prolix Liturgy of Nestorius", suffered persecution at the king's hands for his faith, and died in prison. Joseph may thus have consented in the beginning of his episcopate to complete and consolidate Aba's work, interrupted and suspended by the persecution; and the introduction of the Creed into the Eucharistic service may have been one of the ordinances. The Liturgical history of the 'Constantinopolitan' Creed in the Greek Church seems to be hardly less obscure. The above particulars about Joseph and Aba come from Assemani *B.O.* ii 411 ff., 434; iii 36, 75 ff., 432 ff. The title of the Creed in the Munich and other MSS. merely describes it in elaborate language as the Creed of the 318 assembled at Nicæa.

[1] Theodoret seems to have been especially glad to collect particulars concerning Eusebius. Cyrrhus, his own episcopal seat, lay between Antioch and Samosata.

respondence throughout his episcopate shews Eusebius as his most intimate and trusted friend: the twenty-two extant letters addressed to him attest at once the sympathy which met all Basil's private cares, and the counsel and laborious help which Basil was accustomed to expect from him in public affairs, whether local or affecting the whole East. At one time of desolation he is said to have put on a military dress and tiara, and to have traversed Syria, Phœnicia, and Palestine, ordaining clergy, and otherwise providing for the wants of the churches (Theodoret *H. E.* iv 12 [13]). In 372 his name stands second, between those of Meletius and Basil, in a letter from the Eastern bishops asking the help of their brethren of Italy and Gaul (Bas. *Ep.* 92): and five years later Basil had the grief of learning that in a conference between Peter of Alexandria and Damasus of Rome Meletius and Eusebius had been reckoned among Arians (*Ep.* 266), in evident reference to their early associations, with which in spite of Athanasius's counsels of 362 the West and its allies were determined to brand them for life. In the persecution of Valens, memorable for Basil's successful resistance at Cæsarea, Meletius, Eusebius, and Pelagius of Laodicea were selected for banishment to different countries (Theodoret *H. E.* iv 12 [13]); and the story of Eusebius's departure for his exile in Thrace bears equal witness to the veneration with which he was regarded and to his own generous patience (ib. 13 f. [14 f.]). Being restored on the death of Valens in 378, he ordained bishops to several important sees, including Edessa; but perished by the fanaticism of an Arian woman who threw down a tile upon his head as he was entering a petty town to instal its bishop, and in his last moments he bound his attendant friends to exact no retribution for the murder (ib. v 4). As bishop of Samosata, Eusebius was well placed for exerting influence over Mesopotamia. Samosata was the capital of Commagene, situated at the bridge over the Euphrates on the road from Edessa into Cappadocia and the interior of Asia Minor, and apparently on the frontier of Greek and Syrian civilisation, about 25 miles from Edessa the Christian metropolis of Mesopotamia: it was thus favourably situated for introducing a formulary of Greek origin into the regions to the East of the Euphrates. Other sees in the same region had bishops of some distinction during at least the latter years of the reign of Valens, as Edessa itself, Batnæ, and Carrhæ; and the possibility of the Mesopotamian Creed having been framed in some one of them is not to be overlooked. But in the total absence of direct evidence the personal qualities, the associates, and the reputation of Eusebius of Samosata mark him out as a fitter provisional representative of the Creed than any of his contemporaries.

The fifth revised Creed is that known as the Creed of Charisius, and is preserved in the Acts of the Council of Ephesus (Mansi iv 1348). At the sixth session of the Council, when the Nicene Creed was being read and entered in the Acts, a certain Charisius, presbyter and *oeconomus* of Philadelphia in Lydia, came forward and made a statement, which he supported by a formal memorial and some other accompanying documents. It seems that a little knot of Quartodecimans and Novatians in Philadelphia and the neighbourhood had resolved to join the Church. They had been instructed and admitted by two men called presbyters, Antonius and Jacobus, and by their direction had subscribed an exposition of faith somewhat in the form of a Creed[1]. Antonius and Jacobus had commendatory letters to the bishops of Lydia from Anastasius and Photius, men likewise called presbyters, who were at that time consorting with Nestorius at Constantinople[2]; and the exposition, Charisius said, was full of heretical blasphemy. He prayed that the exposition might be read, and also the letters in which the orthodoxy of Jacobus was attested, and himself, Charisius, a man of pious

---

[1] Προσεκόμισαν ἔκθεσίν τινα δογμάτων ἀσεβῶν, ὡς ἐν τάξει συμβόλου τεθειμένην. The resemblance is slight enough, but in the first few lines it is perceptible.

[2] Nestorius began his episcopate with an onslaught on various heretics, among whom the Quartodecimans of Lydia and Caria and the Novatians are specially named (Socr. vii 29). Chrysostom had set the example (vi 19 7).

belief (εὐσεβῶς φρονοῦντα), was excluded from the communion and services of the Church as a heretic. The memorial is followed by the exposition, of which Theodore of Mopsuestia was the author[1], and by the subscriptions of the converts at full length[2]. When all had been read, the Council decreed that no one should present or write or compose any other faith than the Nicene Creed, specially forbade the inculcation of any such faith upon new converts, and anathematised those who believed or taught the contents of the exposition or the doctrines of Nestorius. The place where the Creed stands is at the end of the memorial, followed only by the formal signature of Charisius to the whole document (τοὺς λιβέλλους), after which came the exposition and the subscriptions. It is headed Ὁμολογία πίστεως Χαρισίου πρεσβυτέρου, and is not accompanied by a word of explanation[3]. None of the Constantinople letters are preserved in the Acts; and as they are said to have contained an

---

[1] Reprinted by Walch 203 ff., and Hahn 202 ff. Both editors neglect to detach the last two sentences, which must have been added at Philadelphia for the abjuring Novatians and Quartodecimans: πᾶς ὁ μὴ δεχόμενος τὴν σωτήριον μετάνοιαν ἀνάθεμα ἔστω· πᾶς ὁ μὴ ποιῶν τὴν ἁγίαν ἡμέραν τοῦ πάσχα κατὰ τὸν τῆς ἁγίας καὶ καθολικῆς ἐκκλησίας θεσμὸν ἀνάθεμα ἔστω. Indeed it is not improbable that the preceding anathema in general terms was added at the same time, though unlike the others it is found in Marius Mercator's version: αὕτη τῶν ἐκκλησιαστικῶν δογμάτων ἡ διδασκαλία, καὶ πᾶς ὁ ἐνάντια τούτοις φρονῶν ἀνάθεμα ἔστω. The exposition itself, an interesting monument of the Antiochian contest with Apollinarianism, apparently supplied the ultimate original of a familiar Latin formula: at least *perfectus homo ex anima rationali et humana carne subsistens* is nearer to ἄνθρωπον τέλειον τὴν φύσιν, ἐκ ψυχῆς τε νοερᾶς (rationali M. Merc.) καὶ σαρκὸς συνεστῶτα ἀνθρώπινης than to the τέλειον τὸν αὐτὸν ἐν ἀνθρωπότητι,…ἐκ ψυχῆς λογικῆς καὶ σώματος of Chalcedon, or the *plena inquam humanitas, quippe quae animam simul habeat et carnem, sed carnem veram, nostram, maternam, animam vero intellectu praeditam, mente ac ratione pollentem* of Vincentius (*Common.* 13). But the formula may have passed though several hands as well as changed its context.

[2] These subscriptions disclose (1) that nearly all the converts in abjuring their heresies had made application to (παρακαλέσας passim) Theophanes the holy bishop of Philadelphia, (2) that three of them had thus made application to Charisius himself along with Theophanes, and (3) that Jacobus, to whom two of these three, and these alone, had likewise made application, was *chorepiscopus*. Evidently the zealous *oeconomus* of Philadelphia did not choose to tell the whole story.

[3] Reprinted at p. 150; also by Walch, p. 215, and Hahn, p. 191.

imputation against Charisius's orthodoxy, the Creed may have been imbedded in some lost accompanying reply of his, which would have made known its purpose. That he composed it is on every ground improbable: analogy suggests that he recited it as the Creed in which he had been baptised, and which he still accepted as a true statement of his faith. It may then be reasonably taken as the Creed of Philadelphia about the beginning of the fifth century.

The general brevity of the somewhat numerous clauses of this Creed has been already noticed. The second clause has an Antiochian sound[1], as have also the first two on the Holy Spirit, τὸ πνεῦμα τῆς ἀληθείας τὸ παράκλητον (see p. 126 n. 4); but from such coincidences[2] it is impossible to infer immediate connexion: of the revised Antiochian Creed there is not the slightest vestige. On the other hand several phrases have been copied from the Nicene Creed. In two respects the article on the Holy Spirit is unique: it omits ἅγιον and inserts ὁμοούσιον[3].

---

[1] Printed κτίστην ἁπάντων ὁρατῶν τε καὶ ἀοράτων ποιητήν: but κτίστην in this arrangement is harsh, and probably a corruption of κτιστῶν or κτισμάτων, though κτίστην καὶ ποιητήν occurs in several formularies of 341—360. The Antiochian Creed in Cassianus has *Creatorem omnium visibilium et invisibilium creaturarum*.

[2] To which γεννηθέντα ἐκ τῆς ἁγίας παρθένου might be added, were it not so obvious: the omission of Mary's name is probably due to the studied brevity.

[3] The presence of this epithet in one of the interpolations made in the Cappadocian Creed by the *Interpretatio in Symbolum* is not a true exception. It had been used in the first instance by Athanasius (*Ep. ad Ser.* i 27 p. 676 c), οὐκ ἄδηλον ὅτι οὐκ ἔστι τῶν πολλῶν τὸ πνεῦμα, ἀλλ' οὐδὲ ἄγγελος, ἀλλ' ἐν 'ΟΝ. μᾶλλον δὲ τοῦ λόγου ἑνὸς ὄντος ἴδιον καὶ τοῦ θεοῦ ἑνὸς ὄντος ἴδιον καὶ ὁμο-

οὐσιόν ἐστιν: compare his alternative language on the part of the Council of Alexandria (*Tom. ad Ant.* 5 p. 773 D), καὶ υἱὸν μὲν ὁμοούσιον τῷ πατρί, ὡς εἶπον οἱ πατέρες, τὸ δὲ ἅγιον πνεῦμα οὐ κτίσμα οὐδὲ ξένον ἀλλ' ἴδιον καὶ ἀδιαίρετον τῆς οὐσίας τοῦ υἱοῦ καὶ τοῦ πατρός. The Nicene phrases and ὁμοούσιον πατρὶ καὶ υἱῷ are the only elements of the Philadelphian Creed apparently due to recent controversy. It is on the whole best to take the rest of the articles on the Holy Spirit as a single clause, καὶ εἰς τὸ πνεῦμα τῆς ἀληθείας τὸ παράκλητον, as John xv 26 might suggest the combination of its two members, and an adequate motive is thus found for the neuter τὸ παράκλητον, which sometimes occurs, but always I think with a distinctly adjectival force. The neuter may however be a corruption here, and in that case τὸν παράκλητον might stand separately,

Hardly any historical associations exist, which it is possible to attach, however doubtfully, to the Creed of Philadelphia. We know little of the affairs of Western Asia Minor during the time when the revisions appear to have taken place. At Smyrna, the nearest maritime city, was held one of the synods by which the often mentioned deputation to Liberius was sent in 366 (Socr. vi 12 8, 10, 17); and Heortasius bishop of Sardis, the immediate metropolis, was one of those to whom Liberius's answer was addressed (ib. 20). He was previously acting in conjunction with Silvanus of Tarsus, and like him and Cyril of Jerusalem was deposed by the Acacians at Constantinople in 360[1], ostensibly on grounds of discipline, but undoubtedly from doctrinal motives (Hil. *Op. Hist. Fr.* 10 p. 693 C; Soz. iv 24 3, 11, 13; 25 1). It is thus certain that Lydia had a share in the Homœousian adoption of the Nicene faith in the period with which we are concerned: but this is all that can be said.

No exact determination of authorship or locality is needed for ascertaining the more essential facts respecting the origin and purpose of the later Eastern Creeds. The obvious uncertainty as to details cannot lessen the interest of the particulars brought together in the last few pages, in so far as they illustrate the distinctive features of the time which gave birth to these formularies, and the temper and policy of its representative bishops in Syria and Asia Minor. A simple scrutiny of the language which distinguishes the Revised Creed of Jerusalem from its predecessor affords some insight into the counsels of those from whom it proceeded. When however it is set side by side with the contemporary Creeds of somewhat similar composition, its true intention becomes yet clearer. The tradi-

---

as in the earlier Creed of Jerusalem. The Eunomian formula cited before (p. 91 n. 4), Πιστεύομεν εἰς τὸν παράκλητον τὸ πνεῦμα τῆς ἀληθείας, (in which the absence of ἅγιον is proved by various passages of Eunomius, *Apol.* 5, 26 ff., to have had no doctrinal intention,) was probably derived from some Creed allied to the Philadelphian.

[1] In the preceding autumn Theodosius bishop of Philadelphia itself had been deposed at Seleucia as an Acacian (Socr. ii 40 43).

AND OTHER EASTERN CREEDS 137

tion which invested it with associations borrowed from Nicæa has already been independently negatived by historical evidence: but comparison with the revised Creeds of other churches clothes it afresh with new and better associations, belonging to peaceful life and growth renewed after tragical interruption. The short age of Cappadocian and Antiochian supremacy stands out in welcome contrast between the devastating strifes on either hand: and its opening years have left no more characteristic monument than the one Creed which unites East and West by the confession of a true faith as read by the light of the highest Greek theology.

The Creeds in the following pages are arranged with a view to shewing as far as possible their relation to each other. Coincidences with an earlier Creed assumed as the basis are marked by larger type where the order remains the same: coincident words which have changed their place retain the smaller type, but are spaced. In the Cappadocian, Antiochian, Mesopotamian, and Philadelphian Creeds uncial type designates coincidence with Nicene language. The threefold notation in pp. 144, 148 explains itself.

It must be remembered that the Creeds of Cappadocia, Antioch, and Mesopotamia owe the Greek form in which they are exhibited here to a critical reconstruction. The Earlier Creed of Jerusalem is put together from fragments scattered through Cyril's Lectures. The other Creeds are preserved in continuous Greek texts, which in the case of the Nicene Creed differ much in minor details. The Nicene text here given, in which some points are unavoidably left doubtful, has been constructed by a comparison of the primary ancient authorities.

THE CREED OF CÆSAREA

Πιστεύομεν εἰς ἕνα θεὸν πατέρα παντοκράτορα,
  τὸν τῶν ἁπάντων ὁρατῶν τε καὶ ἀοράτων ποιητήν.
Καὶ εἰς ἕνα κύριον Ἰησοῦν Χριστόν,
  τὸν τοῦ θεοῦ λόγον,
  θεὸν ἐκ θεοῦ,
  φῶς ἐκ φωτός,
  ζωὴν ἐκ ζωῆς,
  υἱὸν μονογενῆ,
  πρωτότοκον πάσης κτίσεως,
  πρὸ πάντων τῶν αἰώνων ἐκ τοῦ πατρὸς γεγεννημένον,
  δι' οὗ καὶ ἐγένετο τὰ πάντα·
τὸν διὰ τὴν ἡμετέραν σωτηρίαν σαρκωθέντα,
  καὶ ἐν ἀνθρώποις πολιτευσάμενον,
  καὶ παθόντα,
  καὶ ἀναστάντα τῇ τρίτῃ ἡμέρᾳ,
  καὶ ἀνελθόντα πρὸς τὸν πατέρα,
  καὶ ἥξοντα πάλιν ἐν δόξῃ κρῖναι ζῶντας καὶ νεκρούς.
[Πιστεύομεν δὲ] καὶ εἰς ἓν πνεῦμα ἅγιον.
  * * * * *
  * * * * *
  * * * * *
  * * * * *

THE NICENE CREED,

exhibited with the Creed of Cæsarea as its base

Πιστεύομεν εἰς ἕνα θεὸν πατέρα παντοκράτορα,
πάντων ὁρατῶν τε καὶ ἀοράτων ποιητήν.
Καὶ εἰς ἕνα κύριον Ἰησοῦν Χριστόν,
 τὸν υἱὸν τοῦ θεοῦ,
  γεννηθέντα ἐκ τοῦ πατρὸς μονογενῆ-
  τοῦτ' ἐστὶν ἐκ τῆς οὐσίας τοῦ πατρός-
 θεὸν ἐκ θεοῦ,
 φῶς ἐκ φωτός,
  θεὸν ἀληθινὸν ἐκ θεοῦ ἀληθινοῦ,
 γεννηθέντα, οὐ ποιηθέντα,
  ὁμοούσιον τῷ πατρί,
δι' οὗ τὰ πάντα ἐγένετο‡,
 τά τε ἐν τῷ οὐρανῷ καὶ τὰ ἐν τῇ γῇ (or ἐπὶ τῆς γῆς)·
τὸν δι' ἡμᾶς τοὺς ἀνθρώπους καὶ διὰ τὴν ἡμετέραν σωτηρίαν κατελθόντα καὶ σαρκωθέντα,
ἐνανθρωπήσαντα, παθόντα, καὶ ἀναστάντα τῇ
  τρίτῃ ἡμέρᾳ,
ἀνελθόντα εἰς [τοὺς] οὐρανούς,
ἐρχόμενον κρῖναι ζῶντας καὶ νεκρούς.
Καὶ εἰς τὸ ἅγιον πνεῦμα.

 Τοὺς δὲ λέγοντας Ἦν ποτε ὅτε οὐκ ἦν καὶ πρὶν γεννηθῆναι οὐκ ἦν, καὶ ὅτι Ἐξ οὐκ ὄντων ἐγένετο, ἢ ἐξ ἑτέρας ὑποστάσεως ἢ οὐσίας φάσκοντας εἶναι [ἢ κτιστὸν] ἢ τρεπτὸν ἢ ἀλλοιωτὸν τὸν υἱὸν τοῦ θεοῦ, [τούτους] ἀναθεματίζει ἡ καθολικὴ [καὶ ἀποστολικὴ] ἐκκλησία.

---

‡ Denotes phrases having an unimportant deviation from the order of words in the Creed taken as the base.

THE NICENE CREED

Πιστεύομεν εἰς ἕνα θεὸν πατέρα παντοκράτορα,
πάντων ὁρατῶν τε καὶ ἀοράτων ποιητήν.
Καὶ εἰς ἕνα κύριον Ἰησοῦν Χριστόν,
  τὸν υἱὸν τοῦ θεοῦ,
    γεννηθέντα ἐκ τοῦ πατρὸς μονογενῆ -
      τοῦτ' ἐστὶν ἐκ τῆς οὐσίας τοῦ πατρός -
      θεὸν ἐκ θεοῦ,
      φῶς ἐκ φωτός,
      θεὸν ἀληθινὸν ἐκ θεοῦ ἀληθινοῦ,
    γεννηθέντα, οὐ ποιηθέντα,
    ὁμοούσιον τῷ πατρί,
  δι' οὗ τὰ πάντα ἐγένετο,
    τά τε ἐν τῷ οὐρανῷ καὶ τὰ ἐν τῇ γῇ (or ἐπὶ τῆς γῆς)·
  τὸν δι' ἡμᾶς τοὺς ἀνθρώπους καὶ διὰ τὴν ἡμετέραν σωτηρίαν
        κατελθόντα καὶ σαρκωθέντα,
  ἐνανθρωπήσαντα, παθόντα, καὶ ἀναστάντα τῇ τρίτῃ ἡμέρᾳ,
  ἀνελθόντα εἰς [τοὺς] οὐρανούς,
  ἐρχόμενον κρῖναι ζῶντας καὶ νεκρούς.
Καὶ εἰς τὸ ἅγιον πνεῦμα.
  Τοὺς δὲ λέγοντας Ἦν ποτε ὅτε οὐκ ἦν καὶ πρὶν γεννηθῆναι
οὐκ ἦν, καὶ ὅτι Ἐξ οὐκ ὄντων ἐγένετο, ἢ ἐξ ἑτέρας ὑποστάσεως
ἢ οὐσίας φάσκοντας εἶναι [ἢ κτιστὸν] ἢ τρεπτὸν ἢ ἀλλοιωτὸν
τὸν υἱὸν τοῦ θεοῦ, [τούτους] ἀναθεματίζει ἡ καθολικὴ [καὶ ἀποστολικὴ] ἐκκλησία.

Continued from the opposite page

[*The Anathematism added to the 'Constantinopolitan' Creed in the Epiphanian recension*]

Τοὺς δὲ λέγοντας Ἦν ποτε ὅτε οὐκ ἦν καὶ πρὶν γεννηθῆναι οὐκ ἦν, ἢ ὅτι Ἐξ οὐκ ὄντων ἐγένετο, ἢ ἐξ ἑτέρας ὑποστάσεως ἢ οὐσίας φάσκοντας εἶναι, ρευστὸν ἢ ἀλλοιωτόν, τὸν τοῦ θεοῦ υἱόν, τούτους ἀναθεματίζει ἡ καθολικὴ καὶ ἀποστολικὴ ἐκκλησία.

THE 'CONSTANTINOPOLITAN' CREED OR REVISED CREED OF JERUSALEM,

exhibited with the Nicene Creed as its assumed base

Πιστεύομεν εἰς ἕνα θεὸν πατέρα παντοκράτορα,
ποιητὴν οὐρανοῦ[1] καὶ γῆς,
ὁρατῶν τε πάντων καὶ ἀοράτων.
Καὶ εἰς ἕνα κύριον Ἰησοῦν Χριστόν,
τὸν υἱὸν τοῦ θεοῦ τὸν μονογενῆ,
τὸν ἐκ τοῦ πατρὸς γεννηθέντα πρὸ πάντων τῶν αἰώνων[2],
φῶς ἐκ φωτός,
θεὸν ἀληθινὸν ἐκ θεοῦ ἀληθινοῦ,
γεννηθέντα, οὐ ποιηθέντα,
ὁμοούσιον τῷ πατρί,
δι' οὗ τὰ πάντα ἐγένετο[3]·
τὸν δι' ἡμᾶς τοὺς ἀνθρώπους καὶ διὰ τὴν ἡμετέραν σωτηρίαν κατελθόντα ἐκ τῶν οὐρανῶν,
καὶ σαρκωθέντα ἐκ πνεύματος ἁγίου καὶ Μαρίας τῆς παρθένου,
καὶ ἐνανθρωπήσαντα,
σταυρωθέντα τε ὑπὲρ ἡμῶν ἐπὶ Ποντίου Πιλάτου, καὶ παθόντα, καὶ ταφέντα,
καὶ ἀναστάντα τῇ τρίτῃ ἡμέρᾳ κατὰ τὰς γραφάς,
καὶ ἀνελθόντα εἰς τοὺς οὐρανούς,
καὶ καθεζόμενον ἐκ δεξιῶν τοῦ πατρός,
καὶ πάλιν ἐρχόμενον μετὰ δόξης κρῖναι ζῶντας καὶ νεκρούς,
οὗ τῆς βασιλείας οὐκ ἔσται τέλος.
Καὶ εἰς τὸ πνεῦμα τὸ ἅγιον τὸ κύριον τὸ ζωοποιόν[4],
τὸ ἐκ τοῦ πατρὸς ἐκπορευόμενον,
τὸ σὺν πατρὶ καὶ υἱῷ συνπροσκυνούμενον καὶ συνδοξαζόμενον,
τὸ λαλῆσαν διὰ τῶν προφητῶν.
Εἰς μίαν ἁγίαν καθολικὴν καὶ ἀποστολικὴν ἐκκλησίαν·
ὁμολογοῦμεν ἓν βάπτισμα εἰς ἄφεσιν ἁμαρτιῶν·
προσδοκῶμεν ἀνάστασιν νεκρῶν,
καὶ ζωὴν τοῦ μέλλοντος αἰῶνος. Ἀμήν[5].

[1] Epiphanius inserts τε. [2] E. adds τοῦτ' ἐστὶν ἐκ τῆς οὐσίας τοῦ πατρός.
[3] E. adds τά τε ἐν τοῖς οὐρανοῖς καὶ τὰ ἐν τῇ γῇ. [4] E. [τὸ] κύριον καὶ ζωοποιόν.
[5] E. adds an Anathematism, for which see the opposite page.

THE EARLIER CREED OF JERUSALEM

Πιστεύομεν εἰς ἕνα θεὸν πατέρα παντοκράτορα,
   ποιητὴν οὐρανοῦ καὶ γῆς,
      ὁρατῶν τε πάντων καὶ ἀοράτων.
Καὶ εἰς ἕνα κύριον Ἰησοῦν Χριστόν,
   τὸν υἱὸν τοῦ θεοῦ τὸν μονογενῆ,
      τὸν ἐκ τοῦ πατρὸς γεννηθέντα θεὸν ἀληθινὸν πρὸ πάντων
                                                       τῶν αἰώνων,
     δι' οὗ τὰ πάντα ἐγένετο·
σαρκωθέντα καὶ ἐνανθρωπήσαντα,
   σταυρωθέντα καὶ ταφέντα,
   ἀναστάντα τῇ τρίτῃ ἡμέρᾳ,
   καὶ ἀνελθόντα εἰς τοὺς οὐρανούς,
   καὶ καθίσαντα ἐκ δεξιῶν τοῦ πατρός,
   καὶ ἐρχόμενον ἐν δόξῃ κρῖναι ζῶντας καὶ νεκρούς,
   οὗ τῆς βασιλείας οὐκ ἔσται τέλος.
Καὶ εἰς ἓν ἅγιον πνεῦμα,
   τὸν παράκλητον,
   τὸ λαλῆσαν ἐν τοῖς προφήταις.
Καὶ εἰς ἓν βάπτισμα μετανοίας εἰς ἄφεσιν ἁμαρτιῶν,
   καὶ εἰς μίαν ἁγίαν καθολικὴν ἐκκλησίαν,
   καὶ εἰς σαρκὸς ἀνάστασιν,
   καὶ εἰς ζωὴν αἰώνιον.

THE 'CONSTANTINOPOLITAN' CREED
OR REVISED CREED OF JERUSALEM,
exhibited with the earlier Creed of Jerusalem as its base

Πιστεύομεν εἰς ἕνα θεὸν πατέρα παντοκράτορα,
ποιητὴν οὐρανοῦ¹ καὶ γῆς,
ὁρατῶν τε πάντων καὶ ἀοράτων.
Καὶ εἰς ἕνα κύριον Ἰησοῦν Χριστόν,
τὸν υἱὸν τοῦ θεοῦ τὸν μονογενῆ,
τὸν ἐκ τοῦ πατρὸς γεννηθέντα πρὸ πάντων
τῶν αἰώνων²,
    φῶς ἐκ φωτός,
    θεὸν ἀληθινὸν ἐκ θεοῦ ἀληθινοῦ,
    γεννηθέντα, οὐ ποιηθέντα,
    ὁμοούσιον τῷ πατρί,
δι' οὗ τὰ πάντα ἐγένετο³·
τὸν δι' ἡμᾶς τοὺς ἀνθρώπους καὶ διὰ τὴν ἡμετέραν σωτηρίαν
κατελθόντα ἐκ τῶν οὐρανῶν,
καὶ σαρκωθέντα ἐκ πνεύματος ἁγίου καὶ Μαρίας τῆς
παρθένου,
καὶ ἐνανθρωπήσαντα,
σταυρωθέντα τε ὑπὲρ ἡμῶν ἐπὶ Ποντίου Πιλάτου, καὶ
παθόντα, καὶ ταφέντα,
καὶ ἀναστάντα τῇ τρίτῃ ἡμέρᾳ κατὰ τὰς γραφάς,
καὶ ἀνελθόντα εἰς τοὺς οὐρανούς,
καὶ καθεζόμενον ἐκ δεξιῶν τοῦ πατρός,
καὶ πάλιν ἐρχόμενον μετὰ δόξης κρῖναι ζῶντας
καὶ νεκρούς,
οὗ τῆς βασιλείας οὐκ ἔσται τέλος.
Καὶ εἰς τὸ πνεῦμα τὸ ἅγιον τὸ κύριον τὸ ζωοποιόν⁴,
τὸ ἐκ τοῦ πατρὸς ἐκπορευόμενον,
τὸ σὺν πατρὶ καὶ υἱῷ συνπροσκυνούμενον καὶ συνδοξαζόμενον,
τὸ λαλῆσαν διὰ τῶν προφητῶν.
Εἰς μίαν ἁγίαν καθολικὴν καὶ ἀποστολικὴν ἐκκλησίαν·
ὁμολογοῦμεν ἓν βάπτισμα εἰς ἄφεσιν ἁμαρτιῶν·
προσδοκῶμεν ἀνάστασιν νεκρῶν,
καὶ ζωὴν τοῦ μέλλοντος αἰῶνος. Ἀμήν⁵.

[1] Epiphanius inserts τε.   [2] E. adds τοῦτ' ἐστὶν ἐκ τῆς οὐσίας τοῦ πατρός.
[3] E. adds τά τε ἐν τοῖς οὐρανοῖς καὶ τὰ ἐν τῇ γῇ.   [4] E. [τὸ] κύριον καὶ ζωοποιόν.
[5] E. adds an Anathematism, for which see p. 140.

THE 'CONSTANTINOPOLITAN' CREED
OR REVISED CREED OF JERUSALEM,

exhibited with the earlier Creed of Jerusalem as its base, and with the Nicene insertion distinguished from the other alterations

Πιστεύομεν εἰς ἕνα θεὸν πατέρα παντοκράτορα,
ποιητὴν οὐρανοῦ καὶ γῆς,
 ὁρατῶν τε πάντων καὶ ἀοράτων.
Καὶ εἰς ἕνα κύριον Ἰησοῦν Χριστόν,
 τὸν υἱὸν τοῦ θεοῦ τὸν μονογενῆ,
 τὸν ἐκ τοῦ πατρὸς γεννηθέντα πρὸ πάντων
         τῶν αἰώνων,
  ϕῶϲ ἐκ ϕωτόϲ,
  θεὸν ἀληθινὸν ἐκ θεοῦ ἀληθινοῦ,
  ΓεΝΝΗθέΝΤΑ, ΟΥ ΠΟΙΗθέΝΤΑ,
  ὁμοούϲιον τῷ πατρί,
  Δι' ΟΥ ΤΑ ΠΑΝΤΑ ἐΓέΝεΤΟ·
ΤὸΝ Δι' ἡΜᾶϲ ΤΟΥϲ ἀΝθρώΠΟΥϲ καὶ Διὰ ΤΗΝ ἡΜεΤέΡΑΝ ϲωΤΗΡίΑΝ
        ΚΑΤελθόΝΤΑ ἐκ τῶν οὐρανῶν,
καὶ σαρκωθέντα ἐκ πνεύματος ἁγίου καὶ Μαρίας τῆς
           παρθένου,
καὶ ἐνανθρωπήσαντα,
σταυρωθέντα τε ὑπὲρ ἡμῶν ἐπὶ Ποντίου Πιλάτου, καὶ
      παθόντα, καὶ ταφέντα,
καὶ ἀναστάντα τῇ τρίτῃ ἡμέρᾳ κατὰ τὰς γραφάς,
καὶ ἀνελθόντα εἰς τοὺς οὐρανούς,
καὶ καθεζόμενον ἐκ δεξιῶν τοῦ πατρός,
καὶ πάλιν ἐρχόμενον μετὰ δόξης κρῖναι ζῶντας
          καὶ νεκρούς,
 οὗ τῆς βασιλείας οὐκ ἔσται τέλος.
Καὶ εἰς τὸ πνεῦμα τὸ ἅγιον τὸ κύριον τὸ ζωοποιόν
 τὸ ἐκ τοῦ πατρὸς ἐκπορευόμενον,
 τὸ σὺν πατρὶ καὶ υἱῷ συνπροσκυνούμενον καὶ συνδοξαζό-
             μενον,
τὸ λαλῆσαν διὰ τῶν προφητῶν.
Εἰς μίαν ἁγίαν καθολικὴν καὶ ἀποστολικὴν ἐκκλησίαν·
 ὁμολογοῦμεν ἓν βάπτισμα εἰς ἄφεσιν ἁμαρτιῶν·
 προσδοκῶμεν ἀνάστασιν νεκρῶν,
 καὶ ζωὴν τοῦ μέλλοντος αἰῶνος. Ἀμήν.

THE INTERPOLATED NICENE CREED
AS RECITED IN THE DEFINITION OF CHALCEDON,

exhibited with the interpolations distinguished from the original Creed

Πιστεύομεν εἰς ἕνα θεὸν πατέρα παντοκράτορα,
πάντων ὁρατῶν τε καὶ ἀοράτων ποιητήν.
Καὶ εἰς ἕνα κύριον Ἰησοῦν Χριστόν,
 τὸν υἱὸν τοῦ θεοῦ,
  τὸν γεννηθέντα ἐκ τοῦ πατρὸς μονογενῆ –
   τοῦτ' ἐστὶν ἐκ τῆς οὐσίας τοῦ πατρός –
  θεὸν ἐκ θεοῦ,
  φῶς ἐκ φωτός,
  θεὸν ἀληθινὸν ἐκ θεοῦ ἀληθινοῦ,
 γεννηθέντα, οὐ ποιηθέντα,
 ὁμοούσιον τῷ πατρί,
δι' οὗ τὰ πάντα ἐγένετο·
τὸν δι' ἡμᾶς τοὺς ἀνθρώπους καὶ διὰ τὴν ἡμετέραν σωτηρίαν κατελθόντα ἐκ τῶν οὐρανῶν,
καὶ σαρκωθέντα ἐκ πνεύματος ἁγίου καὶ Μαρίας τῆς
       παρθένου,
καὶ ἐνανθρωπήσαντα,
σταυρωθέντα τε ὑπὲρ ἡμῶν ἐπὶ Ποντίου Πιλάτου, καὶ
    παθόντα, καὶ ταφέντα,
καὶ ἀναστάντα τῇ τρίτῃ ἡμέρᾳ κατὰ τὰς γραφάς,
καὶ ἀνελθόντα εἰς τοὺς οὐρανούς,
καὶ καθεζόμενον ἐν δεξιᾷ τοῦ πατρός,
καὶ πάλιν ἐρχόμενον μετὰ δόξης κρῖναι ζῶντας καὶ
       νεκρούς,
οὗ τῆς βασιλείας οὐκ ἔσται τέλος.
Καὶ εἰς τὸ πνεῦμα τὸ ἅγιον τὸ κύριον τὸ ζωοποιόν.
 Τοὺς δὲ λέγοντας Ἦν ποτε ὅτε οὐκ ἦν καὶ πρὶν γεννηθῆναι οὐκ ἦν, καὶ ὅτι Ἐξ οὐκ ὄντων ἐγένετο, ἢ ἐξ ἑτέρας ὑποστάσεως ἢ οὐσίας φάσκοντας εἶναι ἢ τρεπτὸν ἢ ἀλλοίωτον τὸν υἱὸν τοῦ θεοῦ, τούτους ἀναθεματίζει ἡ καθολικὴ καὶ ἀποστολικὴ ἐκκλησία.

THE CREED OF CAPPADOCIA
NOW USED BY THE ARMENIAN CHURCHES,

exhibited with the Nicene Creed as its base

Πιστεύομεν εἰс ἕνα θεὸν πατέρα παντοκράτορα,
ποιητὴν οὐρανοῦ καὶ γῆς,
ὁρατῶν τε καὶ ἀοράτων.
Καὶ εἰс ἕνα κύριον Ἰηсοῦν Χριстόν,
τὸν γἰὸν τοῦ θεοῦ,
γεννηθέντα ἐκ τοῦ πατρὸс μονογενῆ —
τοῦτ' ἐстὶν ἐκ τῆс οὐсίαс τοῦ πατρόс —
θεὸν ἐκ θεοῦ,
φῶс ἐκ φωτόс,
θεὸν ἀληθινὸν ἐκ θεοῦ ἀληθινοῦ,
γεννηθέντα, οὐ ποιηθέντα,
ὁμοούсιον τῷ πατρί,
δι' οὗ τὰ πάντα ἐγένετο,
τά τε ἐν τῷ οὐρανῷ καὶ τα ἐν τῇ γῇ (or ἐπὶ τῆс γῆс),
ὁρατά τε καὶ ἀόρατα·
τὸν δι' ἡμᾶс τοὺс ἀνθρώπουс καὶ διὰ τὴν ἡμετέραν сωτηρίαν
κατελθόντα *ἐκ τῶν οὐρανῶν*,
саρκωθέντα, ἐνανθρωπήсαντα, *γεννηθέντα τελείως ἐκ Μαρίας τῆς ἁγίας παρθένου διὰ πνεύματος ἁγίου*,
[*ἐκ ταύτης*] *σῶμα καὶ ψυχὴν καὶ νοῦν καὶ πάντα ὅσα ἐ-
στὶν ἄνθρωπος*(?) *ἀληθῶς καὶ οὐ δοκήσει ἐσχηκότα*,
παθόντα, сταυρωθέντα, ταφέντα,
ἀναстάντα τῇ τρίτῃ ἡμέρᾳ,
ἀνελθόντα εἰс [τοὺс] οὐρανοὺс *ἐν αὐτῷ τῷ σώματι*,
καθίσαντα ἐν δεξίᾳ τοῦ πατρός,
ἐρχόμενον *ἐν αὐτῷ τῷ σώματι* [*καὶ*] *ἐν τῇ δόξῃ τοῦ πατρὸς*
κρῖναι ζῶντας καὶ νεκρούс,
οὗ τῆς βασιλείας οὐκ ἔσται τέλος.

Καὶ πιστεύομεν εἰc τὸ πνεῦμα τὸ ἅγιον τὸ ἄκτιστον τὸ τέλειον,
τὸ λαλῆσαν ἐν νόμῳ καὶ ἐν προφήταις καὶ ἐν εὐαγγελίοις,
καταβὰν ἐπὶ τὸν Ἰορδάνην,
κηρύξαν τὸν ἀπόστολον (or ἀποστόλοις),
οἰκῆσαν (or οἰκοῦν) ἐν ἁγίοις.
Καὶ πιστεύομεν εἰς μίαν μόνην καθολικὴν καὶ ἀποστολικὴν
ἐκκλησίαν,
εἰς ἓν βάπτισμα μετανοίας,
εἰς ἱλασμὸν (?) καὶ ἄφεσιν ἁμαρτιῶν,
εἰς ἀνάστασιν νεκρῶν,
εἰς κρίσιν αἰώνιον ψυχῶν τε καὶ σωμάτων,
εἰς βασιλείαν οὐρανῶν,
καὶ εἰς ζωὴν αἰώνιον.
Τοὺc δὲ λέγοντας ὅτι Ἦν ποτε ὅτε οὐκ ἦν ὁ γἱόc, ἢ Ἦν
ποτε ὅτε οὐκ ἦν τὸ ἅγιον πνεῦμα, ἢ ὅτι Ἐξ οὐκ ὄντων ἐγένετο,
ἢ ἐξ ἑτέρας ὑποcτάcεως ἢ οὐcίας φάcκοντας εἶναι τὸν γἱὸν τοῦ
θεοῦ ἢ τὸ πνεῦμα τὸ ἅγιον, τρεπτὸν ἢ ἀλλοιωτόν, τούτους ἀναθεματίζει ἡ καθολικὴ καὶ ἀποστολικὴ ἐκκληcία.

THE REVISED CREED OF ANTIOCH,

exhibited with the Nicene elements distinguished from the rest, and the three phrases of certain Nicene origin specially marked

Πιϲτεύω (? Πιϲτεύομεν) εἰc ἕνα καὶ μόνον ἀληθινὸν θεὸν πατέρα παντοκράτορα,
    κτιστὴν πάντων ὁρατῶν τε‡ καὶ ἀοράτων κτισμάτων.
Καὶ εἰc τὸν κύριον ἡμῶν (?εἰc ἕνα κύριον) Ἰηcοῦν Χριcτόν,
    τὸν υἱὸν *αὐτοῦ τὸν μονογενῆ*,
    καὶ τὸν πρωτότοκον πάσης κτίσεως,
      ἐξ αὐτοῦ ΓΕΝΝΗΘΈΝΤΑ πρὸ πάντων τῶν αἰώνων,
    καὶ ΟΥ ΠΟΙΗΘΕΝΤΑ,
        ΘΕΟΝ ΑΛΗΘΙΝΟΝ ΕΚ ΘΕΟΥ ΑΛΗΘΙΝΟΥ,
        ΟΜΟΟΥΣΙΟΝ ΤΩ ΠΑΤΡΙ,
    δι' οὗ καὶ οἱ αἰῶνες κατηρτίσθησαν καὶ τὰ πάντα ἐγένετο·
τὸν δι' ἡμᾶς ἐλθόντα (or κατελθόντα),
    καὶ γεννηθέντα ἐκ Μαρίας τῆς ἁγίας παρθένου,
    καὶ σταυρωθέντα ἐπὶ Ποντίου Πιλάτου,
    καὶ ταφέντα,
    καὶ τῇ τρίτῃ ἡμέρᾳ ἀναϲτάντα‡ κατὰ τὰς γραφάς,
    καὶ εἰc τοὺc οὐρανοὺc ἀνελθόντα‡,
    καὶ πάλιν ἐρχόμενον κρῖναι ζῶντας καὶ νεκρούϲ.

*   *   *   *   *   *   *
  *   *   *   *   *   *
  *   *   *   *   *   *
*   *   *   *   *   *   *

    [καὶ] [εἰς] ἁμαρτιῶν ἄφεσιν,
    [καὶ] [εἰς] νεκρῶν ἀνάστασιν,
    [καὶ] [εἰς] ζωὴν αἰώνιον.

THE CREED OF MESOPOTAMIA,
NOW USED BY THE NESTORIAN CHURCHES,

exhibited with the Revised Creed of Antioch as its base, and the additional elements of Nicene origin distinguished from the rest

Πιστεύομεν* εἰς ἕνα θεὸν πατέρα παντοκράτορα,
κτιστὴν πάντων ὁρατῶν τε καὶ ἀοράτων.
Καὶ εἰς ἕνα* κύριον Ἰησοῦν Χριστόν,
  τὸν υἱὸν τοῦ θεοῦ τὸν μονογενῆ,
  [τὸν] πρωτότοκον πάσης κτίσεως,
    [τὸν] ἐκ τοῦ πατρὸς [αὐτοῦ] γεννηθέντα πρὸ πάν-
                                   των τῶν αἰώνων,
    καὶ οὐ ποιηθέντα,
    θεὸν ἀληθινὸν ἐκ θεοῦ ἀληθινοῦ,
    ὁμοούσιον τῷ πατρί,
  δι' οὗ [καὶ] κατηρτίσθησαν οἱ αἰῶνες‡ καὶ ἐκτίσθη
                                   τὰ πάντα‡·
τὸν δι' ἡμᾶς τοὺς ἀνθρώπους καὶ διὰ τὴν ἡμετέραν σωτηρίαν
                         κατελθόντα ἐκ [τῶν] οὐρανῶν,
  καὶ σαρκωθέντα ἐκ πνεύματος ἁγίου,
  καὶ ἄνθρωπον γενόμενον,
  καὶ συλληφθέντα καὶ γεννηθέντα ἐκ Μαρίας τῆς
                                   παρθένου,
  καὶ παθόντα καὶ σταυρωθέντα ἐπὶ Ποντίου Πιλάτου
                                   καὶ ταφέντα,
  καὶ ἀναστάντα τῇ τρίτῃ ἡμέρᾳ‡ κατὰ τὰς γρα-
                                   φάς,
  καὶ ἀνελθόντα εἰς τοὺς οὐρανούς,
  καὶ καθίσαντα ἐκ δεξιῶν τοῦ πατρὸς [αὐτοῦ],
  καὶ πάλιν ἐρχόμενον (or ἥξοντα) κρῖναι νεκροὺς καὶ
                                   ζῶντας‡.
Καὶ εἰς ἓν ἅγιον πνεῦμα,
  τὸ πνεῦμα τῆς ἀληθείας τὸ (or ὃ) ἐκ τοῦ πατρὸς ἐκπο-
                         ρευόμενον (or -ρεύεται),
  τὸ πνεῦμα τὸ ζωοποιόν.
Καὶ εἰς μίαν ἐκκλησίαν ἁγίαν καὶ ἀποστολικὴν [τὴν] καθολικήν·
  ὁμολογοῦμεν ἓν βάπτισμα εἰς* ἄφεσιν ἁμαρτιῶν‡,
  καὶ* ἀνάστασιν νεκρῶν‡,
  καὶ* ζωὴν αἰώνιον.

  * Denotes words which may possibly be Antiochian, the reading in the Revised Creed of Antioch being doubtful.

THE CREED OF PHILADELPHIA,

AS RECITED BY CHARISIUS AT EPHESUS,

exhibited with the Nicene elements distinguished from the rest

Πιστεγω εἰς ἕνα θεὸν πατέρα παντοκράτορα,
    κτίστην (? κτιστῶν) ἁπάντων ὁρατῶν τε καὶ ἀοράτων ποιη-
                                                            τήν.
Καὶ εἰς ἕνα κγριον Ἰηcογν Χριcτόν,
    τὸν γἱὸν *αὐτοῦ τὸν μονογενῆ,*
    θεὸν ἐκ θεογ,
    φῶc ἐκ φωτόc,
    θεὸν ἀληθινὸν ἐκ θεογ ἀληθινογ,
    ὁμοογcιον τῷ πατρί·
τὸν Δἰ ἡμᾶc καὶ τὴν ἡμετέραν cωτηρίαν κατελθόντα *ἐκ τῶν*
                                                    οὐρανῶν,
    cαρκωθέντα,
    γεννηθέντα ἐκ τῆς ἁγίας παρθένου,
    ἐναΝθρωπήcαντα,
    σταυρωθέντα ὑπὲρ ἡμῶν,
    ἀποθανόντα,
    ἀναcτάντα τῇ τρίτῃ ἡμέρᾳ,
    ἀνελθόντα εἰc τογc οὐρανογc,
    καὶ πάλιν ἐρχόμενον κρῖναι ζῶντας καὶ νεκρογc.
Καὶ εἰς τὸ πνεγμα *τῆς ἀληθείας τὸ παράκλητον,*
    ὁμοούσιον πατρὶ καὶ υἱῷ.
Καὶ εἰς ἁγίαν καθολικὴν ἐκκλησίαν,
    εἰς ἀνάστασιν νεκρῶν,
    εἰς ζωὴν αἰώνιον.